THE HISPANIC LABYRINTH

THE HISPANIC LABYRINTH

Tradition and Modernity in the Colonization of the Americas

Xavier Rubert deVentós

Translated by

Mary Ann Newman

Transaction Publishers

New Brunswick (U.S.A.) and London (U.K.)

Copyright © 1991 by Transaction Publishers
New Brunswick, New Jersey 08903

Library of Congress Catalogue Number: 89-35256
ISBN: 0-88738-301-7
Printed in the United States of America

Library of Congress Cataloging-in-Publication Data

Rubert de Ventós, Xavier.
    [Laberinto de la Hispanidad. English]
    The Hispanic Labyrinth: Tradition and Modernity in the Colonization
    of the Americas
Xavier Rubert de Ventós; translated by Mary Ann Newman.
        p.   cm.
    Includes bibliographical references.
    ISBN 0-88738-301-7
    1. Latin America–History–To 1830. 2. Spain–Colonies–America–
Administration. 3. Colonization–Religious aspects. 4. Church and state–
Latin America–History. I. Title
F1412.R8613 1989
980' .01–dc20

                                                        89-35256
                                                        CIP

Contents

Introduction

This book develops a somewhat traditional and clericalist view of the colonization of the Americas. I took this stand for two reasons: both to adapt to the public I was addressing and, in contrast, to be critical with my own convictions. These attitudes, indeed, are the ideological core of this book. For the sake of clarity, let me begin by explaining how the book occurred to me.

In November of 1984, as director of the *Càtedra Barcelona-Nova York* * and member of the Spanish Congress, I was invited to give a lecture at the Wilson Center in Washington, D.C. In the course of the lecture, I made certain observations on the current political decisions being made in Spain that contrasted with the perception that the U.S. administration had of them. At McKinney Russell's invitation, a few representatives of the State Department and the Pentagon attended, later asking me to their respective departments to continue our discussion. Among my hosts were James Dobbins, Deputy Secretary of State for European Affairs, George Bader, Director of European Policy for the Defense Department, and Lucas Fisher, of the Bureau of Strategic Defense (see Appendix I). Throughout these conversations, I tried to make clear to them the cultural context and the historical memory that lay behind the conditions – very tough, to their minds – set by Spain for final entrance into NATO. Their ignorance regarding these issues – real or feigned, I could not tell – seemed surprising, but just as surprising was their often-repeated wish to understand our position better. As a result, I finally proposed that a meeting be organized to give the Spanish position higher "visibility" in Washington. Politicians and academics from both countries would participate in this meeting, which would serve as the framework for a personal encounter between Presidents Reagan and González. The director of the Wilson Center, James Billington, offered me his generous assistance, and together we outlined the project that I presented to the president of the Spanish government on my return to Madrid. He liked the idea and asked me to arrange the meeting.

From November 1984 to September 1985, I spent a great deal of time coordinating the event. Setting dates, outlining discussion topics, selecting

---

* An exchange program between the University of Barcelona and New York University (1983-1986).

participants and moderators, making last-minute changes – all in all, a very trying business. Further complicating the whole thing, I had thought to invite Monsignor Rivera y Damas, the Archbishop of San Salvador, to be the Latin American representative at this meeting. My reason was simple: he was trying to negotiate with the very guerrilla forces that the North American advisers and air support were trying to suppress. His participation in the meeting would thus mark a clear difference in position and sensibility between Spain and the United States. To allay any North American reticence or Salvadoran concerns, I asked the Reverend James Hickey, Archbishop of Washington, to receive and introduce Monsignor Rivera personally. I then flew to San Salvador where, with the help of Luis de Sebastián and Ignacio Ellacuría, the monsignor accepted my invitation. Washington then offered no objections to his participation in the program.

When everything was settled, I returned to Madrid, as my absences from Congress were beginning to seem too frequent. And just one week before the conference I realized that I had not yet written the paper I was to read. Carlos Andrés Pérez, Francisco Fernández Ordóñez and I were to be Monsignor Rivera's respondants. But I had not received the text of his speech, and there was no longer time to send for it. So I gathered up the books I had at hand – Bernardino de Sahagún, Liévano Aguirre (who is responsible for both the general direction of the book and for many specific references), Todorov, Parry, a collection of the Laws of the Indies (*Leyes de Indias*) and an anthology of Jesuit texts – and wrote the lecture that forms the nucleus of this book during a stopover in New York, on my way to Washington. This nucleus was later developed in successive stopovers, in my weekly travels to the European Parliament, often using second-rate editions, secondhand sources, and without the precision allowed by a more continuous and less spasmodic way of working.

Yet, I must make it clear that my talk was not, nor did it mean to be, naive. I knew in advance what line of thought I would be following in my response to the archbishop. In fact, I wanted only to stress how Monsignor Rivera himself symbolized a tradition that had come to harmonize with the very same American reality that the U.S. administration – with its alternately narcissistic or paranoid, cruel or simplistic attitude – often seems not yet to have grasped. What I did not know was that this line of reasoning would begin taking shape before my eyes as a traditionalist view of Spain's role in America – a view that often came into conflict with my own prejudices. For the time being, though, that was all it amounted to, so I put the notes and pages that correspond to the first three chapters of this book into that drawer where we finally bury the projects we think we ought to get back to "some day."

Against all expectations, that day soon came around. A trip to China and Japan, during which I read texts by Father Ricci and other Jesuits in Japan, India, or Canada, reawakened my interest in and admiration for the evangelical mission. So, I went back to my notes and decided to go on with this text, now using the Jesuits as a case study. The result, as you will see, is not the work of a historian, and I can only hope that if any outrageous errors have crept in, historians will not find them any more glaring than the inevitable clichés they no doubt will detect in other parts of the text. In any case, I trust that the comments and criticisms of J. L. Aranguren, Father M. Batllori, J. L. Martín Ramos, C. Martínez Shaw, A. Regalado, and M. Rius have averted the worst.

I could not end this introduction without noting that my challenge in the writing of these notes was Monsignor Rivera's speech at the Wilson Center. In fact, the whole book is in some way a gloss on the very contrast he drew between the Conquest and the Evangelization, or between the Discovery and the Development of the continent. It argues that the medieval and religious tradition that led to the conquest and establishment in America of centers of power (and not just *economic* centers like plantations and factories) is seamlessly linked with a "superstructural" modernization (administrative: the Catholic Kings; cultural: Cisneros; linguistic: Nebrija), and with an "infrastructural" colonization that was egalitarian and ethnically permeable. In contrast with Anglo-Saxon colonization, more entrenched in the economic spirit and more impermeable to cultural diversity, Spanish colonization is characterized by both its political superficiality and its ethnic and cultural depth. It is these two factors that, taken together, hindered the modernization and development to which Monsignor Rivera alluded.

But this is not just one more of those Spanish "meditations upon one's being" or laments for the dismembering of *"las Españas"* so dear to Americo Castro and Ortega y Gasset. Nor is it a repetition of the modern tendency of so many Latin Americans to "blame it on the other guy," attributing all their ills to the new dependency on the gringos. The former emancipation and the latter dependency are not so much the product of an internal or external destiny (Spanish "character," North American "domination") as of a complex blend, of a Hispanic labyrinth whose Classical formalism underlies its chaos just as clearly as its Catholic porousness underlies its Baroque order. All that aside, this labyrinth, like the one Octavio Paz described, does not just represent the situation of a people or a country; it is also emblematic of the human condition – evoked in the chorus of Andromachus – whose capabilities are often the other side of its ineptitudes. The limitations of this labyrinthine project – obvious nowadays – still should not keep us from acknowledging the lessons and guidelines that lie hidden yet within it. North Americans in particular would do well to heed them if they want to orient their world relations in a less erratic way. This, in a nutshell, is the message I wished to send in Washington.

This, then, is the "environmental" reason behind the content and direction of my discourse. But there was also another, more "ideological," reason underlying it. This reason led me toward the hypothesis that both Spaniards and Anglo-Saxons, Latin Americans and North Americans could each take a page from the other's traditionalisms: we, the Hispanics, should learn from their vernacular and local political traditionalism; they, the Anglos, from our classical and clerical cultural traditionalism. The hypothesis seemed ideologically "apropos" to me as it allowed for a departure from the cliches of progressive historiography whose conceptual lumps could just as easily gum up the view of the past as the gossipy details of *la petite histoire* or the great feats of National History. I thought that a more traditionalistic interpretation of the facts could, if nothing more, be useful toward this end. If the Frankfurt School had used Freud and German idealism for this purpose, I could certainly have recourse to Suárez and the Spanish Baroque.[1]

I have pointed out the two circumstances that guided these pages. I must now add that they also respond to a deep conviction. This conviction reads as follows: to be truly liberal or progressive, to be a true child of the Enlightenment, you must confront above all your own prejudices, and not just the prejudices of others; you must avoid the mirages of the moment, and not just exorcize old worn-out phantasms. To be Enlightened is not to try to fabricate a past in keeping with our personal convictions, intellectual needs, or theoretical commitments, but, as Kierkegaard said, "to try to be objective with ourselves and subjective with others." It is to be capable of confronting not only Kant's "guilty ignorance" but also the no less guilty progressive hallucinations into which his idealist followers have plunged us. It is to recognize, in a word, the cost of all advances, the ambivalence of all progress, the disenchantment inherent in all rationalization, the relativity of all success. This, above all, is what it means to be enlightened. Anything else is just to be dazzled.

X. R. de V.
Sant Martí d'Empúries, August 25, 1986

1

Encountering and Inventing America

As Monsignor Arturo Rivera y Damas, archbishop of El Salvador, has stated, "Despite having discovered America, Spain neither encouraged the process of industrialization [sic], nor increased development in the conquered lands." True enough. But might it not be true precisely *because* of the "discovery" rather than *despite* it? It has indeed been claimed that the newly conquered territory allowed Castile to continue to rely upon tribute rather than rational exploitation, and on the conquest of territory rather than labor, amassing an outrageous foreign debt in the process. The Renaissance spirit that brought Spain to America, the modern legal principles by which it organized its administration, and the rationality with which it designed the new cities, served paradoxically to give new strength to a patrimonial state and a social project molded by the Reconquest and its Crusader ideal. Spain then reexported America's silver to finance its military operations against the Protestant countries and to import from them their manufactured goods. Thus Spain's prominence in the geographical revolution left it at the tail end of the coming commercial and industrial revolution: *Novus orbis victus vos vicit.*

Monsignor Rivera later goes on to establish a clear distinction between Evangelization and Conquest, although I do not believe that this distinction does justice to the indigenous peoples and civilizations. According to the monsignor, evangelization would apply to a relationship between analogous or symmetrical cultures (e.g., Jewish and Roman); conquest would obtain when the Christian culture confronts what Claudio Sánchez Albornoz describes as "those incipient cultures or cultures in gestation that history has kept in barbarism or its environs, and into which Christianity introduces the magical triptych formed by faith, freedom and civilization." And again according to Monsignor Rivera, "Christianity... can only take root when accompanied by the permanent action of a superior race... as occurred with the peoples dominated and subjugated by Spain."

1

It is useful to recall whom these texts describe. They refer not only to the Casanares, the Sioux, or the Hurons but also the Aztecs, the Incas, or the Mayas, who, without benefit of the wheel or beasts of burden, had developed sophisticated systems of social stratification, state bureaucracies, urban structures, monumental architectures, and a calendar more accurate than its European counterpart. Before 1492, these peoples had organized a sedentary agriculture, a network of communication, and a system of taxation capable of unifying a territory no smaller than that of modern Mexico, which invested its surplus in the construction of great cities and ceremonial centers. Their genius for the monumental was curiously allied with a sensitivity for the minimal and a skill for detail exemplified in the latticework of Palenque and Monte Alban, the vessels and clay figures of Colima, and the statues of Tenochtitlán, where, as Bernal Díaz states, "there are three Indians who would take their place alongside the famed Apelles and Michelangelo and Berruguete, had they lived in their times."

Bernal Díaz was a soldier. Clearly, then, one need not be a pious Indianist to recognize in those lands something more than barbarous peoples or incipient cultures. Indeed, what could be less "incipient" than the Mayan culture, which, having discovered the vault and the calendar, a numbering system including zero, and a partially phonetic writing system, was already in decline by the time of Charlemagne. Or what could be less "primitive" than the budding Nahuatl culture, which, upon the literary and architectural base of the Olmecs, Toltecs, and Teotihuacans, had built a political-military empire and elaborated a complex moral theogony that synthesized both Eastern and Western worldviews. The remnants of this theology, compiled by A. M. Garibay, offer us the vestiges of a cosmic vision as original as it is modern. When I decided to study it, in what I considered to be an "anthropological" exercise, I soon found myself personally challenged. The Eastern sense of cosmic belonging and interdependence – as symbolized in the quincunx – blends here with Western individualism and will as represented by Quetzalcoatl. It is he who, like Adam or Prometheus, breaks with natural order by his sin, going on like Christ to be immolated, and thus calling us to the sacrifice: a personal collaboration with the cosmos – the "new sun" – in the daily struggle against chaos and entropy.

But we need not climb upon the pedestal of astronomy or theology in order to arrive at an appreciation of this culture. Willem von Humboldt himself was amazed to find that the Nahuatl language constituted "a complete and perfect system" to express nuances that none of the many languages known to him could express: "Only the Mexican language exhausts all possible cases, achieving such fine nuances that, for example, on saying 'I learn a given body of knowledge,' a sole pronoun added on indicates whether I am learning it myself *(ni-no-ne-machtia)* or whether someone is teaching me *(ni-no-*

Some will say, however, that the final proof of European superiority still stands: the nation that disembarked in America was Spain and not the other way around. And it is true that this fact, simple and definitive, has made us think of Europe and its culture as the agent of the encounter between the two worlds.[2] Whence the term *discovery* itself: a manifestation and exposure of what had been hidden to reason – and perhaps to itself.

But at 500 years' distance, this conventional role casting no longer rings so true. Both sides – Europeans and Americans – appear to be the agents of an equally overwhelming destiny: pawns in a process that neither one side nor the other had actually molded, parties to a pure encounter – surely, unless there is life on the stars, the last radical encounter of history – whose traumatic character was beyond their control, as neither of them had developed the necessary physical or cultural antibodies to prepare for the combination. This is why the combination was necessarily tragic and why neither one party nor the other has been able to remember or celebrate it without first glazing it in myth. On the Spanish side, the myth of the Discovery of those who apparently did not even know themselves; of Civilization and Evangelization as opposed to what Guzmán called "the moral unconsciousness of the natives (manifest in their eating of human flesh, fleas, spiders and raw worms, their being more prone to sodomy than any generation known before them, their not having beards, their getting drunk on smoke and not using money...").[3] And on the American side, the myth of a wondrous native culture that was brutally curtailed and to whose eyes "the father turns into the rapist, the founder into the usurper, the conqueror into the assassin": the antimyth of Cortés which, according to Octavio Paz, still impedes "the reconciliation of Mexico with its other half."

In fact, to our present-day eyes, both sides look more like the officiants or bit players of their own cultures than like subjects capable of having behaved any differently. Even the sole unquestionable advantage of the Spaniards, their technical and strategic superiority, is nothing more than the imprint left upon them – and through them – of certain factors they rarely recognized and never controlled. To paraphrase Quintana's famous statement, "These were crimes of history, not of Spain," the emphasis could be changed to read "These were the heroic deeds of history, not of Spain."

Important as it is – and, indeed, overwhelming for the Indians – this technical superiority could not have been sufficient to surmount the crushing numerical superiority of the Indians, their knowledge of the territory, and their lighter arms and armor, which the Spaniards themselves, sinking into the swamps or eaten up by mosquitoes inside their armor, often ending up adopting. Of course, gunpowder often turned out to be decisive against the spear, the brig against the canoe, cavalry against infantry, metal, in short, against stone – and in this sense it is legitimate to speak of a confrontation not between two cultures but between two ages of humanity. But what definitively conquers and befuddles the empires of the sun is above all the "total warfare" waged by Cortés as opposed to the "ritual struggle" arranged by pact *(la guerra florida)* that Teotihuacans and Tlaxcaltecans waged in order to add periodically to their supply of prisoners for sacrifice. Thus, what triumphs is tactical massacre over liturgical sacrifice, the linear view over the cyclical interpretation of history, the European "system" over the American astral "order" will over destiny. A perfectly integrated and theocratic society succumbs to a more individualistic and secularized culture in the service of a jealous and exclusive God whose "psychology" the Aztecs did not comprehend. A dramatic conflict, at once geological and gnoseological, in which the Spaniards represent open (adaptive) experience and directed (instrumental) reason, as opposed to closed (traditional) experience and open (cosmic) reason as incarnated by the Aztecs.

And I say "represented" or "incarnated" because nowadays both winner and loser seem more like actors (not to say puppets) than authors or directors of a play that overwhelms them both. The superior Spanish efficacy is no more than the product of the ethnic and cultural multiplicity of the European melting pot (classical and Christian, Arabic and Jewish, Gothic and Celtic, and so on) habituated and obligated by its own history both to confront and to adapt to and understand diversity. This is what allows Cortés to understand the language, learn the customs, and manipulate the signs of the enemy, exploiting their internal dissensions and their ancestral beliefs: to use their faith in the Plumed Serpent to feather his own nest. And it is also what allows him, with surprising lucidity, to sense the anthropological basis of his own genius in judging that of his adversaries: "For, considering," he writes in his *Letters*, "that these people are barbarians so far removed from any communication with other rational nations, it is truly admirable to see how far they have come in every way." It is this exceptional "critical" consciousness that, coupled with his strategic genius, enables him to win the battle of Otumba without the slightest strategic advantage, and explains in effect how, in three years (1518-1521), 508 men with sixteen horses, ten cannon, and a few muskets and harquebuses are able to dominate an empire whose capital, Tenochtitlán, alone is no less than five times the size of Madrid. Pizarro's personal "qualities" being quite different, the result is much the same: with fewer than 200 men, he took an empire that ruled more than 9 million subjects. And what both Cortés and Pizarro realize immediately is that capturing the indigenous leaders will allow them to use to their advantage the very rigid and ceremonial organizations of Tenochtitlán or Tahuantinsuyo – "a vertical and totalitarian structure," as Vargas Llosa comments, "that surely was more detrimental to its own survival than the firearms and iron of the Conquistadors." We need only remind those who seek time and again to attribute these events to the mere technical superiority of the Spaniards, of the disaster in Tenochtitlán when Cortés had to leave the city, called to account by the representatives of the crown in Veracruz, only to be forced to return again to recoup the losses incurred by the cowardly inventor of the pole vault. At this point this "squire, humble and exceedingly poor," "this captain of bandits," as Heine called him, is in effect revealed as the only state-of-the-art hero.

There are hypotheses galore to explain the material basis for this peculiar European technological and ideological development. Europe is the beneficiary of the convergence of Asian technology (gunpowder, paper, the crank, the stirrup), the Arabic sciences, the Roman legal structure, hydraulic dispersion, and a peculiar grass-eating livestock of considerable size. The geography of America, powerful and hostile, does not permit the surplus energy that is the basis of European "individual initiative"; what is called for, on the contrary, is social collectivism and a more geographical than historical mythology. "In Latin America, in contrast with Europe," says Ravines, "the pure excessiveness of nature turns it into an abstraction and human existence appears to be the simple function of an implacable and blind environment... in a constant struggle with the nihilism of its immensity." Be that as it may, the fact is that only in Europe did there emerge cities and autonomous bourgeoisies capable of rationalizing production and developing commerce on the basis of an individual initiative that just as clearly represents the cornerstone of its early geographical expansion as it does of the later industrial revolution.[4]

Now, to go on calling all of this "the discovery" requires that we retain the idealistic criteria of Hegel's 1820 analysis, all the while ignoring his most lucid observations on the issue. Thus, we cling to the Hegelian prejudice that prior to, or outside, the European State there were only peoples who, like termites or bees, had neither history nor self-awareness – who were "prehistory" or "geographical history," and who must be "discovered and saved from their own inertia and ineptitude" by the "bearers of the Spiritual torch."[5] But then we ignore the Hegelian realization that the conditions of American life made these peoples so vulnerable to mere contact with the outside that such contact was transformed into genocide. Their culture, says Hegel, "was to perish as soon as the Spirit approached it, disappearing in one gust of European activity." And it is again Hegel who points out some of the causes ("edible animals are not so nutritive there as they are in the Old World," and so on) that have later been adduced to explain the physiological and cultural vulnerability of the indigenous peoples. What Hegel could not imagine was that in many cases the issue was one of the express intention of a race that opted deliberately for its own extinction rather than accept a life of servitude. As Father Gumilla witnessed, "The men do not go near their women so as not to engender slaves." As for the women, "So as not to give birth to servants and handmaidens for the newcomers, they resolved to sterilize themselves with herbs and brews that they took for this purpose."

* * *

The "discovery" of America began to be celebrated in 1892, when Spain's head was still spinning from the loss of the colonies. So, in fact, what was really being celebrated was the discovery of having lost America. I believe that in 100 years we have been able to work out that trauma and leave "the discovery" – and its complement, "genocide" – behind, in order to begin to see one another as the artifexes of the last, dramatic acknowledgment between cultures that finally closed up the world as we know it. And this *recognition* involved both quite a bit of Heisenberg's *distortion* of the new continent (destined from then on to be "something thought about and imagined by others" – Leopoldo Zea) as well as the production or *invention* of a new reality (for just as America did not exist in 1492, neither did Spain, and only as a result of this encounter did both come to be what they are).

Would it be better if that encounter had never taken place? Perhaps. But just as in the proverbial operation that "was a success, except that the patient died," the failure of the Columbine enterprise might also have been a stroke of luck, except that neither America nor Spain would have existed. Something else would be there in their places.

2

Evangelization: Genocide and Recognition

But if it would appear difficult for either America or Spain to see itself as the subject of their encounter, it is nonetheless not so difficult to recognize Spanish responsibility, for better and for worse, in the resulting development whose high points are surely the *evangelization* and the *emancipation* of America. These two stages must be defined, not for the purpose of defending, as has been customary, the enlightened character of the Emancipation as opposed to the obscurantism of the Evangelization but, rather, to see them as two contrary and complementary facets – like the systole and diastole of one same process.

Let us begin with the Evangelization. The complicity and even collaboration of the priests in an R-rated story cannot be denied. It is nothing less than a process of exploitation, destruction, and, for the more evil-minded, even of bacteriological warfare (smallpox, measles, typhus, and malaria brought by the newcomers), though there are no attempts on record to inoculate the redskins with smallpox by selling them blankets infected with pus, as Jeffrey Amherst proposed in the North. According to W. Borah's calculations, later revised by Nicolás Sánchez Albornoz, by the early seventeenth century, the Indian population had reached one-tenth of its size at the time of the conquest; of the 25 million inhabitants present in New Spain at the time of Cortés's arrival, only 1 million remained. But a comparison with the other colony makes even these numbers pale: in eighty years of Franciscan presence (1770-1850), the Indians of California were reduced from 200,000 to 130,000; in thirty years (1850-1880), the Yankees reduce these 130,000 to 20,000. The examples of the Church's complicity are also numerous and well documented: from its direct collaboration in the legal fraud of the *requerimientos* (an unintelligible mixture of theological requisitions, legal warnings, and war declarations that was to precede all attacks)[6] to the political and theological sanctions supplied by Sepúlveda or Oviedo for the spoliation and exploitation of the natives. And it is likely that even the counterexamples we shall shortly see of unselfish protection of, and love for, the Indians would in fact work as an alibi analogous to that which Russell

9

attributed to the piety of Hildebrand, Saint Bernard, or St. Francis of Assisi: to impede the moral discrediting of the Church and thus legitimate its misdeeds. Having said this, however, we must recognize that, no matter how many similar examples are adduced, they can never obscure the positive and progressive influence of the Christian spirit that permeated the colonization and the conquest.

In contrast to the *superiority* of all classical conquests and the pure *instrumentality* of modern ones, the Hispanic evangelization is predicated on the assumption of the liberty and equality of the subjugated peoples. The "raw material" of evangelization is not serfs but souls. Todorov decries the danger of cultural genocide that follows from the recognition by the Dominicans and the Franciscans of an "already Christian nature" at the heart of indigenous psychology and religion, but he fails to see that in the code of the sixteenth century, this recognition presupposes the acknowledgment of the "human nature" of the Indians, from which follows, in the terms of Father Vitoria, the right not to be converted by force and, finally, in Fray Servando Teresa de Mier's words, their "right to independence." The evangelization of the conquered is, along with intermarriage, the clearest sign that they are held to be subjects and not objects, equals and not barbarians. That all Indians can and must come to be Christians means that they have the same rights as their conquerors to what the latter consider the knowledge of truth and personal salvation. "The Spaniard," as Nicol puts it, "does not erect cathedrals *for himself* alongside pyramids meant *for the Indians.*" In contrast with classical or Anglo colonizations, Catholic evangelists begin by considering conquered individuals to be their equals before God. And the juridical consequences of this are evident. "The Roman conquest," as Americo Castro observed, "takes two centuries to concede citizenship to its Peninsular subjects; the Spanish conquest gives conquistadores and conquered juridical equality from the first day, converting the latter into subjects with rights equal to those of their victors, and transplanting to this side of the sea its panoply of institutions, not always just and generous, to be sure, as indeed they were not in Castile itself."

* * *

The explicit confrontation between these two ways of interpreting the Evangelization dates from the 1550 controversy between Sepúlveda and Las Casas. According to the Aristotelian and racist idea espoused by Sepúlveda, the Indians, like the barbarians, "only partake of reason to the extent that it is implied in sensation" (Aristotle, *Politics*, 1254). Hence they are naturally destined to be the slaves of their lords (of the *gentes humanitiores),* just as matter is slave to form. According to the Christian idea as set forth by Las

Casas, there is no difference in the call to salvation of all men, be they sages or savages, for the grace of God can right all wrongs. But the most amazing thing is how the very logic of Las Casas defuses the fanatical or messianic spirit toward which Christian universalism is so easily swayed, opening the door not only to tolerance but even to the cultural relativism that textbooks ascribe to the Enlightenment. And it is precisely in contrast to the classics that Las Casas develops his argument:

> According to Strabo, Book XIV, the main reason that the Greeks called other peoples barbarians was that they did not pronounce the Greek language correctly. But from this point of view, no man or race can be anything but barbarian in relation to another man or another race.... Thus, in the same way that we consider the people of the Indies to be barbarians, they judge us to be so because they do not understand us.

From this standpoint not only Las Casas but Sahagún and Motolinía as well begin to place the generic religiosity of the Indians, and even the specific forms it takes, on a par with their own religion (later the Jesuits will go so far as to maintain that *God is the protagonist of polytheism*). Parallel to the "hesitant epic" of some of the conquistadores (Fuentes), we witness here a "hesitant evangelization" that is not sure whether to qualify Indian idols as gods or devils (Todorov), or their officiants as priests or sorcerers.[7] At one extreme of this surprising cultural relativism, Las Casas even goes so far as to defend human sacrifice and cannibalism (the great "evidence" offered to the Crown by Sepúlveda and Oviedo to demonstrate the inferiority and bestiality of the Indians). Here his reasoning is as radical as it is implacable:

> The highest manner of adoring God is to offer Him sacrifice.... But nature also teaches us that it is just to offer God, whose debtors we are for so many reasons, all things beautiful and excellent, because of the excellence of his Majesty. So, then, according to human judgment and to truth, there is nothing in nature greater or more precious than the life of a man or man himself. This is why nature herself teaches those who have not faith, grace or doctrine, those who love under the direction only of natural light, that, despite any positive law opposing it, they must sacrifice human victims to the true God or to those false gods they hold to be true, in such manner that in offering Him this supremely precious thing they may manifest to Him their gratitude for the multiple favors they have received.[8]

As we will see in greater detail, this cultural relativism and adaptation finds its most dramatic expression with the Franciscans and Jesuits among the tribes of Hurons or Casanares. After bearing witness to the skinning and eating of parts of Father Brebeuf's living body, Father Paul Lejeune writes to his superior general: "Do not be scandalized by these acts of barbarism. Before the faith was received in Germany, Spain or England, our nations were not more civilized than these.[9] The Savages are not lacking in intelligence, but rather in education and learning....

This cultural and educational relativism also impregnates Vitoria's writings: "Our finding them so simple and dullwitted stems from their bad and barbarous education, for among us, too, many country folk show very little difference from brute animals" *(Relectio de Indis,* par. II, n. 16). Here it attains its best juridical formulation. Vitoria rejects the baptism of Indian children against the will of their parents (for it would violate their parental authority); conversion by force of arms (for it would foster the sacrilege of feigned conversion – an argument taken up again by Suárez in *De Fide* [XVIII, n. 1538]); and even, like Las Casas, the appeal to cannibalism and other "abominations" as a means of justifying the conquest ("For Christians, too, offend God daily with blasphemies and homicides and such a principle would lead to a permanent war between Christian princes on the basis of supposed failings that only God can judge"). Vitoria then offers a juridical justification for the Carib perception that in taking over and disposing of their lands, "the Pope must be drunk and the King of Spain insane." The king has no right to invade lands occupied by the natives (who are therefore not *res nullius)* or to impose Christ's doctrine by blood and gunfire; the only justification for violence is the refusal to hear (not to accept) the Gospel or the need to defend the evangelizers physically – but never the spreading of the Christian word in itself. As for the pope, "he is not the temporal sovereign of the planet," just as Christ, whom he represents, was not. Thus, "the pagans are in no way subject to him and for this reason he cannot give the princes an authority he does not hold himself." This is the position later summarized by Suárez in *Defensio Fidei* (III, V, 307, 313) and in *De Fide* (d. XVIII, n. 1559):

> Just as a private man cannot legally obligate or castigate another private man, nor a Christian king another Christian king, nor an infidel king another pagan king, neither can the republic of infidels, which is sovereign in its command, be punished by the Church for its crimes, even if they offend natural reason.... Therefore, they cannot be obligated to abandon idolatry and other similar rites. And it matters not that these sins offend God. God did not make men judges to avenge the injuries done to him in any respect.

Vitoria's tract *Lessons and Relations* also negates the *two* sources of legitimation that the Crown uses for the Conquest: the cause of a just war – *de bellorum iustitia et honestetate* – based by Sepúlveda on both the conversion of the infidel and the 1493 papal bull *Inter Caetera,* whereby the Pope conceded to Spain "the islands and continents... to the West and South, with all rights, jurisdictions and belongings."[10] Indeed, Father Vitoria's denial that the papal bulls justify Spanish rights stands precisely in opposition to the callings of the lay jurists, Palacios Rubios and Sepúlveda, regarding America. The paradox could not be more radical: the jurists base their case on the papal concessions; the Dominican priest bases his argument solely on the natural right of all men to travel and trade. In a recent discussion, Rafael Sánchez Ferlosio pointed out to me that Vitoria was thereby formulating what would turn out to be the *ratio* and justification of the future economic imperialism of the northern countries. I could only respond that it seemed all the more admirable to me that this historical and ideological innovation should be the result of a bold critique of the imperialism of its own time.

Vitoria opposes the temporal interests of both his religion and his country much sooner and more radically than the Enlightenment. Later we shall take a look at the Jesuit attempt to put it into practice. Suffice it to say for now that it is expressed in a political and juridical theory of sovereignty that "is as different from the narrow monarchy of the Middle Ages as it is from the unlimited absolutism later described by Hobbes" (J. H. Parry). And it is custom or natural law (from which Vitoria derives the *ius gentium)* that serves Mariana, Suárez, and Vitoria himself to defend liberties and the right of insurrection against both old and new fetishes; against the monarchs of divine designation, certainly, but also against the new civil State and the new positive Law, both of which were to serve as the foundation of the new "contractual" absolutism. Thus, the liberal, and even radical, dimension of late Spanish scholasticism lies precisely in its attempt to neutralize both the King and the Pope, both divine law and positive law, by pitting the one against the other (see, for example, in *Defensio Fidei,* chapters III, V, 290, and all of chapter VIII).

Clearly, this is an arena into which prudish Spanish traditionalism never dared to venture, as Ramiro de Maeztu's interpretation of the "obligation to disobey" set forth by Father Vitoria suggests. Vitoria's text literally states that "when a war is known to be unjust, it is not licit for the subjects to follow their King, even when they are called upon by him to do so, because evil must not be done, and it is better to obey God than the King." Maeztu's cautious commentary in *Defensa de la Hispanidad* follows:

> Regarding Father Vitoria, we must be mindful of the fact that he was the first master of moral theology of his time and that among his disciples were the confessors of the kings of Spain. In those days they were among the scarce subjects who knew enough of the reasons for each war to be able to resolve in good conscience upon their justice or injustice. In fact, there are two classes of men: the governors and the governed. The governors are under the obligation to see that their fatherland always be on the side of reason, humanity, culture, and of the greatest possible good. The governed do not ordinarily have the knowledge to be able to judge in good conscience as to whether a war is just or unjust.

Thus, in Maeztu's hands, Father Vitoria's bold challenge turns into a pious invocation to obedience. In much the same way, Quevedo's argument against tyranny, in the hands of Julià Andreu of the Falangists, is transformed into the following lesson:

> The doctrinal content of Quevedo's *Marco Bruto* – which is the message and mission of the Falange – warns us that all the great problems of life must be posed and resolved according to strictly Spanish, fanatically Spanish, criteria. The long centuries of decadence during which our magnificent racial characteristics were adulterated have finally come to an end. Those lovely liberal theories still in vogue among the neoliberal countries of our poor Europe have corrupted us for long enough.... We must reject the so-called "rationalization of power" or the "rule of law" and all the other homilies of the Jewish technicians.... The day of the propagators of Hispanic imperialism is come. In laying the foundations of Falangist policy, José Antonio Primo de Rivera brought together the entire doctrinal repository elaborated in perfect and definitive form by the men who lived, struggled, and wrote during our fatherland's centuries of greatness!

Fernando Morán – currently the Spanish ambassador to the United States – has been urging us for years to "take back the symbols that the right wing has wrested from us." It is time for us to pay him mind.

*   *   *

The defense of political independence and cultural diversity arises not in opposition to but indeed from the very core of an attitude toward evangelization that Las Casas himself contrasts – unjustly [11] – with that of the Arabs. It is a Mohammedan practice, he states, to use coercion in the work of the mission.[12] Indeed, I do not mean to deny the autos-da-fè and the destruction of books and artifacts to which so many of the clergy applied themselves with holy zeal. But I do mean to stress the following: the invasion of European technology and strategy did not quite manage to "volatilize" that civilization so vulnerable to all exogenous factors – a phenomenon Hegel attempted to explain before Lévi-Strauss. And this was only owing to an attitude inherent to the spirit of evangelization that was anthropological *avant la lettre*. For once, Anthropology was the natural disposition (and not merely the bad conscience) of European expansion. And this disposition had as little in common with the attitude of classical conquest as it did with modern Protestant or Enlightenment colonization, imbued as they were with the "aristocratic spirit" and the "pathos of distance" so passionately pondered by Nietzsche. Never, before or after the Spanish evangelization of the sixteenth century, "has a conquering culture imposed upon itself such an obligation to know, analyze and narrate the spiritual and cultural traditions of the conquered peoples." And this is not thanks to a few "modern spirits" who, decrying evangelization, decided to take a "scientific" interest in these cultures but, rather, to the approach of the evangelizers themselves. The alliance of this anthropological spirit with Christian universalism explains the paradox, pointed out but not understood by Todorov, that the very same Franciscan father, Diego Landa, should have participated in the burning of the Mayan books and yet saved their knowledge for posterity by writing his *Relación de las cosas del Yucatán* (Yucatan Before and After the Conquest) and then gone on to establish an "alphabet" to interpret the mixture of ideograms and phonetic signs on Pascal's sarcophagus. Or that the very zealous and scrupulous Diego Durán, the Dominican obsessed with extirpating the pagan remnants of indigenous daily life, should, in his *Historia de las Indias de la Nueva España,* show an outrageous degree of identification with the rites and beliefs he censures. And one last example that can no longer be denied: the greatest anthropological monument of all time is the *Historia general de las cosas de Nueva España,* by the noble and pious Fray Bernardino de Sahagún. For the first time in history, this Franciscan scholar takes on the systematic task of seeking out sources of information, comparing and contrasting them, translating the pictograms, establishing correlations between images, fables and parables, and so on. Field study and hermeneutical study all in one, this history saves for posterity what probably would have been lost by its own system of oral-pictographic transmission. Beyond Anthropology and the Encyclopedia, but comprehending them both, we see here, as A. M. Garibay has observed, a true History in the Greek sense of *Istoreo:* "to see and to speak of what is seen, to explore directly and recount what has been explored, to gather data and make them available to those who did not acquire them." Moreover, this is a history in which "scientific" objectivity is combined with a nostalgia for and even identification with the culture it describes: "This is to the letter," he writes, "what has happened to these Indians at the hands of the Spaniards, for they and all of their things were so trampled and destroyed that no semblance is left of what they were before. Thus they are held to be barbarians and people of the meanest assay when, in truth, in matters of policy, they are a step ahead of many other nations with great political pretensions."

"Cuauhtémoc would have been amazed," writes Paz, "to find allies and defenders among the heirs of Cortés... [but], after all, the ideas of the Encyclopedia and of liberalism belong to the same western tradition as the Catholicism of Cortés and his missionaries." What I have tried to suggest, to the contrary, is that this "alliance and defense" is born precisely *of*, and not *in opposition to*, this missionary Catholicism with (1) *a sense of liberty and equality*, which is absent in classical imperialism (that sense, as Don Quixote tells Sancho, that "no man is greater than the next man if he does not do more than the next man") and (2) *a liturgical and formal sensibility* – ultimately ethnological – which neither the instrumental reason of Enlightenment imperialism nor Anglo-Saxon economical pragmatism provide for.

King Juan Carlos I himself has in the end succinctly described the ins and outs of this process: "When Spain reached America, our people found a concrete and very diverse reality, which stunned them and caused them to fabulate, to dominate and to study, as well as to carry out the work of evangelization. Indeed, in that encounter, through the marriage of races, brotherhood emerged alongside violence, foundation alongside destruction. But the fact is that this portentous natural and cultural reality of pre-Columbian America is available to us today thanks precisely to the very noteworthy pleiad of Spanish Chroniclers, the meticulous notaries of everything they saw and heard."

3

Conversion to America

Shipwrecked off the coast of the Yucatán, Gonzalo Guerrero and some of his companions manage to reach Isla Mujeres, where they are taken prisoner and enslaved by the Indians. Aguilar, one of Guerrero's companions who returned to Cortés's caravels, will years later act as La Malinche's cointerpreter, having a decisive influence upon the course of the Conquest.[13] Not Guerrero. Guerrero lets his hair grow long, pierces his ears, and marries and fathers the first *mestizo* children, for whose sake he does not hesitate for a moment to change sides and die fighting in Chetumal against the Spanish troops under Montejo. "You go on," Bernal Díaz reports his responding some years before to a group of Spaniards who wished to rescue him, "My face is covered with tattoos and my ears are pierced. What would the Spanish say if they saw me this way? And just look how beautiful my children are." The first apostate; or the first convert. The story of America's seduction is under way.

The Conquest and Evangelization thus find their counterpoint from the very outset in what Lezama Lima has called the *counterconquest,* a process that soon begins to produce conversions in the opposite direction, of those who either allow themselves to be won over by their opponents or simply change sides. And I am not thinking only of Las Casas or Vasco de Quiroga; I also have in mind those who deserted from Pizarro's army to defend the fort of Vilcabamba from the Spanish under the orders of Manco the Indian, or the Spanish Dominicans who in 1537, against Spain's interests, got Paul III to promulgate the papal bulls *Veritas Ipsa* and *Sublimis Deus,* which hold the thesis on the irrationality of the Indians to be heretical and the use of slaves to be sinful. But one need not go so far to detect the symptoms of this new virus. It is in Bernal Díaz's own narration of the conquest that Carlos Fuentes detects the first historical example of a fissure in the epic spirit, the sign of a *hesitant epic* in which it is no longer solely the role of the chorus to apply corrective measures to the hero's impassioned judgment; it is the hero himself who describes the situation with distance, magnanimity, and piety.

Still, this is not the most remarkable thing. Even more surprising is the fact that the Spanish monarchy should so often reject and even prohibit the publication of books like *Democrates alter,* which proclaim its just claims to conquest; or that it should allow itself to be carried away by the converts or Illuminati who advise the creation of "short-term" protectorates (for a term of six to eighteen years, after which time the Crown was to withdraw) or, simply, of an ideal independent state: a kingdom of God on earth. Sepúlveda must make a very strong case for the souls to be lost in order to change Charles V's mind after Las Casas convinced him to cede Peru to the Incas "in order to liberate the Indians from the diabolical (i.e., Spanish) power to which they are subject, return them to their original freedom and reestablish all their natural kings and lords." But Las Casas's failure, his series of failures, are never for naught, and they weigh from the very beginning upon a territorial division that takes into respectful account the idiosyncrasies of the land and its peoples. Soon an ordinance appears requiring that the *encomiendas* (trusteeships) correspond to traditional tribes and clans. A short time later, a royal warrant is issued whereby Charles V prohibits massive transplants of the indigenous population. And finally, a new decree drastically limits the uprooting of individuals: "Said natives need not leave their clime or natural habitat, wherefore those who are born and bred in hot lands shall not go nor shall they be taken to cold, nor those from cold lands to hot ... hence they are not to be taken obligatorily, in any circumstance, from their boundaries, settlements and native habitats."

From the very start, the Crown is consistent, though not always foresightful and intelligent, in its fight against the enslavement, spoliation, or exploitation of the indigenous population on the part of "civil society," made up first of the conquistadores and then of the lords and *encomenderos* (trustees). As early as September 1498, the Catholic Kings reject Columbus's suggestion when he writes them to the effect that "...in the name of the Holiest Trinity, as many slaves as might be needed could be sent on from here." Those the admiral actually dares to send are automatically freed by the decree of June 29, 1500, and escorted back to America by Franciscan friars. And even when the incipient industrial revolution begins to demonstrate the economical advantages of pure labor over whole men, the king and queen will continue to opt for free subjects over a mere cheap source of labor. Is it not indeed a symbol and harbinger that Admiral Columbus himself should return to Spain in shackles for having dared to practice allotment of Indians in Hispaniola, or that one of the Pizarros should die beheaded and another languish in prison for the last twenty years of his life?

Naturally, the struggle of the Crown with *repartimientos* and *encomenderos* (allotments and trusteeships) also works as a defense of the Crown's central administration against the tendency of trustees to set themselves up as absolute feudal lords. But from the time that Montesino's right to deny confession to those who mistreat the Indians is officially recognized in 1510, legislation and an administration devoted to the defense of the Indians are beginning to develop that so transcend the Crown's interests as often to be inimical to them. Not inappropriately, Spain has been considered the only colonial power to undergo a grave crisis of conscience and to raise the conceptual, juridical, and theological problems posed by the conquest. "This is a unique case," as L. Hanke and I. L. Aguirre put it, "of a great colonial power's investing a great portion of the intellectual efforts of its men not to resolving the problem of how more efficiently to exploit the natives, but rather of how to defend [from its own subjects] the inhabitants of the conquered territory." And so, Charles V even goes so far as to suspend the conquest (in his decree of April 16, 1550) and to prohibit new expeditions until such time as the moral and theoretical question of their legitimacy had been resolved.

*   *   *

The dark and brutal history of the encomiendas is exemplary in this sense. It all begins when the Crown declares slavery to be illegal and the conquistadores must find ways to justify their exploitation. To this end, they seek inspiration in the commission, or *comenda,* of medieval times, to wit: the Crown would "entrust" the Indians to the Spanish lords with authorization to require of them the gratuitous lending of "personal services" in exchange for which the holders of this privilege take upon themselves the task of their subjects' evangelization. However, what started out as authorizations of eight months to three years quickly turned into a right to the Indians' indentured labor "for a lifetime," with a further right to their succession "for one lifetime more."[14] This license was abolished by the laws of 1523 with three significant exceptions: the encomiendas of Cortés and of Moctezuma's two daughters.

But it is Cortés himself, scandalized by the excesses of the *encomiendas de servicios* (trusteeships of services) in Cuba, who proposes to Charles V that they be replaced in Mexico, following Aztec tradition, by the *encomienda de tributos* (tributary trusteeships). The emperor thus receives the tribute of the Indians directly and passes it on to the trustees to provide for their maintenance and education; a formula meant to prevent the direct dependency of the Indians upon the encomenderos, which would literally turn the latter into feudal lords. Cortés's proposal catches on quickly in the court of Charles V but not, of course, among the conquistadores, who were thus prevented from reaping the direct benefits of the exploitation of indentured labor and so fought the measure for almost two centuries.

By now not only has Cortés conquered Mexico; he has also been inspired and seduced by it. We must not forget that it was just at this point, with the incorporation of the organized masses of the Aztec and Inca empires, that the encomiendas de servicios he criticized began to bear their choicest fruits for the conquistadores. "They were no longer dealing with fishing and fruit-gathering tribes," writes Liévano Aguirre,

> but rather with political societies which had achieved a certain degree of maturity and enjoyed a hierarchical stratification, thus enabling the trustees to organize, with no great trauma, the intensive exploitation of native labor. Thus, the conquistadores and their lawyers in Spain placed all kinds of obstacles in the path of the encomiendas de tributos, for these had the effect of denying them control of native labor at a time when the most densely peopled and disciplined populations of the American empires were capitulating before the onslaught of the Conquest.

Not long before, Montesinos, the Dominican friar, had begun accusing the Spanish of being in mortal sin "for the cruelty and tyranny you inflict upon these innocent people" (Easter sermon, 1511), only to end up contesting Hernando de Mesa's arguments regarding "the natural inferiority and indolence of the indigenous people" in the 1512 sessions of the Junta de Burgos.[15] But neither this first step taken by the junta toward recognition of the freedom of the natives nor the recommendations of the Crown regarding their protection go into effect juridically until Charles V, on Cortes's advisement, promulgates *Ordenanza X* (the Tenth Decree of 1528) in Valladolid. This ordenanza organized the trusteeships as the simple paying of tribute to the titleholders, both prohibiting "personal services" and controlling the form of payment of said tribute: "For which purpose you shall inquire as to what they formerly were wont to pay their Indian lords... and you shall leave them what they need to get by and to provide for and feed their children, with repair and reserve to cure their illnesses, in such a manner that they shall be paying less than they did to their caciques in their condition as infidels."

But the Crown does not stop at prohibiting indentured labor. It tries to do away as well with the conditions that make such labor possible, replacing those colonial officials who show a tendency to be "in cahoots with" the encomenderos, protecting the hubs of the indigenous subsistence economies as an alternative to wage labor in the haciendas or the mines (royal warrants of February 22, 1549 and December 25, 1551) and regulating the working conditions of those who "of their own free will and being paid a just price, may go to farm and to work in the gold, silver and mercury mines." From the almost feudal sixteenth century encomiendas of the conquistadores, we will go on, in the seventeenth century, to the debt servitude *(peonaje de deudas)* of the great *haciendas*. This will be followed in the eighteenth century, after the liberalization of Campomanes, by the direct exploitation of the Grandes Compañías, which, inspired by British colonial policy, try to establish a system similar to that of the plantation (monoculture and indentured labor). At each of these stages, the communal reductions – to which we shall return shortly – served as a brake upon the pure and arrant transformation of the Indian population into an unprotected "labor market."

These laws naturally were not always complied with by a long shot, and some of them were later watered down, significantly from 1545 on. At that time, three years after the famous and radical *Leyes Nuevas* (New Laws), a combination of the insurrection of the trustees, the demographic crisis, and the first scarcity of colonists made it necessary once again temporarily to authorize tributary trusteeships and the lending of personal labor (new allotments of 1576) for public works and churches. But there was no lack of "converted" officials who had begun in the interim to take on the "viewpoint of the vanquished." * Núñez Vela, for example, the viceroy who in 1545 freed 300 Indians brought to him from Peru and restored their land to them, levied an embargo on a substantial load of silver from Potosí because it had been extracted by slave labor, and was finally beheaded by the marauding hosts of two trustees, Carvajal and Gonzalo Pizarro. Or Juan de Montano, the first visiting judge who dared to execute a Spanish trustee for mistreatment of the Indians, and who also paid for it with his life. Or Juan del Valle, the bishop who in 1558 attacked the fraudulent accountings of tribute and asserted that the Spanish were jointly liable to the Indians to offer reparations for prejudices suffered by them. Or Venero de Leyva, the president of the Audiencia, who, in Cartagena, imposed a penalty of 200 lashes or 1,000 pesos for the killing of an Indian.

* * *

A great deal has been said about using the crucifix to beat the Indians into Christianity or about using requerimientos to evangelize them. But it cannot be denied that each new legislative stage in the Indians' favor and against the interests of the colonizers (and later against the Crown itself) appears in the wake of a decisive act of pressure exercised by the men of the Church. Thus, to sum up:

1. In response to Ferdinand the Catholic's 1509 law accepting the regimen of trusteeships and the use of Indian indentured labor, we find the demands of the Dominican father Montesinos, from which result the

---

* This is a reference to *La visión de los vencidos,* by Miguel León Portilla.

1512 Laws of Burgos, wherein the right of establishing trusteeships is reserved to the Crown and the absolute autonomy of those who have already been "capacitated and Christianized" is recognized.

2. Las Casas then unleashes his fierce attacks upon the Laws of Burgos, which the Council of the Indies picks up on from 1523 to 1529, not restricting itself to criticizing the "abuses" of the trusteeships but even questioning their very legitimacy, justifying them only as a "temporary" resort.

3. This legislation of the Council of the Indies is in turn criticized from Mexico by Bishop Zumárraga, who is able to catch the ear of the Royal Council, which in 1530 decrees in Barcelona that all Indians ought "from this point on" to be under the juridical and administrative protection of a representative of the Crown.

4. The spirit and the letter of this decree is then decried by Father Vitoria in his Salamanca lectures and by the above-mentioned Dominicans, who, betraying the interests of their own country, obtain from Paul III the bulls that expressly deny any legitimation of the use of Indian indentured labor.

5. On the basis of these criticisms the New Laws of 1542 will be drawn up to place a drastic limit upon the rights not only of the trustees but of all the colonizers, whose insurrections take place immediately thereafter in reaction to these rulings.*

We stated at the close of a previous chapter that Castile has earned the honor not so much of the discovery of America as of its recognition. Similarly, I want to close this one by vindicating not so much its conversion *of* America as its conversion *to* America. A conversion whose symptoms we have seen crop up among the first cultural apostates and "hesitant" chroniclers, stretch all the way to the Crown and take on a more militant expression among the friars. But to see the ultimate examples of this "conversion," we must wait for the development of that "great split in the Hispanic family" known as the Emancipation of America.

---

* Schematically, and as a memory aid, the process could be written as follows: Ferdinand the Catholic's laws of 1509 + Montesino's critiques = 1512 laws of Burgos, + Las Casas' attacks = 1523 laws of Charles V, + Zumárraga's accusations = 1530 laws of Consejo de Barcelona, + Vitoria's lectures in Salamanca and Dominican pressure in Rome = New Laws of 1542.

4

Metabasis of the Amerindian Institutions: *Mita, Resguardo,* and *Mayordomía*

Idealism always borders on cynicism – and it would undoubtedly be an act of cynicism to assert that Spanish policy in America was directed by the ideas of its "converts." In fact, Spanish legislation inevitably responds to the tensions between the forces in the field: on the one hand, conquistadores, encomenderos, and settlers, and on the other, the Crown and the Church, "trying to reconcile opposing interests, including those of the Indians." F. Chevalier describes this situation "as a more or less stable balance, varying from one country to the next, between Indian communities under ecclesiastical and royal protection on the one hand, and great Spanish and criollo haciendas or small mixed-blood communities, on the other." This balance of interests is reflected in the laws that from the last third of the sixteenth century seek to make both the interests of the Crown and the freedom of the Indians compatible with the growing need for a labor force to carry out agrarian exploitation and public works, and to work the mines recently discovered in Potosí and Zacatecas. This labor force had vanished from the market as a result of the demographic crisis and the "success" of the *resguardos* protected by the Crown.

As J. H. Parry has pointed out, forced labor, which was a common practice in Europe at the time, in America took on an "added value" that was not only economic but also political, military, and cultural. It was *political*, because only the prospect of great benefits based on indentured labor could move people to confront the tremendous risks of the colonial adventure. It was also *military*, for the encomenderos and their gangs often went where the Crown could not – as in the case of the rebellion of the Indians of Nueva Galicia in 1540, put down by the trustees themselves not long before the New Laws cut off all their privileges. And finally it was *cultural*, because the colonizers considered the spirit of collaboration, continuity, and responsibility imposed by work to have a civilizing effect upon the indigenous tendency toward indolence, dispersion, and a subsistence economy.

As we have seen, Charles V's decrees of February 22, 1549, and December 25, 1551, still insisted that Indians should work only where and with whom they wished, for the time stipulated in a work contract and at a "just price" (i.e., higher than market price) to be established by the viceroy. But we have also seen that these decrees, which cost more than one viceroy and visiting judge their lives, were not successful in persuading the Indians to work for a daily wage. As a result of this resounding failure, the Crown agreed to organize a system of obligatory recruitment (the *Mita)* inspired by Inca tradition but contrary to the spirit of the New Laws of 1542.

Now, the *mita,* the *resguardo,* and *mayordomía* are all Indian institutions assimilated by the Spanish that have served as a basis for the argument that the Hispanic respect for native traditions is no more than a Machiavellian device for better exploiting the Indians. Let us briefly examine these institutions one by one.

*   *   *

Along with the mita or *turno* (1560-1630) the allotment of Indians reappears. Natives are no longer employed in the private service of a trustee but in *public service,* as regulated by the viceroys or courts of appeal. Each Indian hamlet or resguardo must provide a fixed quota of its male population by rotation – 15 percent for agriculture, 4 percent for the mines – to carry out tasks specifically authorized by the Crown. Specific jobs considered to be dangerous or unhealthy (work in the textile factories or sugar mills, pearl fishing, draining of wells, and the like) were expressly excluded from the rotation quota. According to Parry, public works – roads, bridges, public buildings – received preferential rights, along with churches, convents, and hospitals. From 1580 on, the labor force proceeding from the repartimientos is rarely used up in the construction of private buildings, or even the building of churches and convents, but is used almost exclusively for works such as the draining of Lake Texcoco or the canal of Huehuetoca.

The exploitation and abuses to which the mita gives rise are beyond all doubt. What remains to be seen is whether this abuse owed more to the brutality of the foremen or to the very accumulation of rules and controls that the Crown invoked to prevent such abuse. These controls tended to provoke either the overexploitation of a labor force that the owners were aware of having only temporary use of, or the conversion of the haciendas to a "submerged economy" contracting "black-market labor" that could work continuously, at any time, and do any type of work – mining or carrying, in sugar or textile mills – and that would soon generate that new form of servitude known as *peonaje por deudas.*

Another social structure that the Spanish try to preserve is the indigenous *resguardo,* including the system of *cargos* or mayordomías that oversaw them. As we have seen, the resguardo is an indigenous neighborhood or hamlet under self-rule, which the Crown recognizes and favors, first as a legal loophole in the face of the pure, bald parceling out of Indians in the encomiendas de servicios, later as an alternative to salaried work on the hacienda, and finally as their protection from the tendency to drift into a helpless peonaje por deudas. Based on the structure of the Indian *calpulli,* the resguardo was, according to Octavio Paz, "an economical, political, social and religious institution [that]... during the colonial period is able to live on alongside other forms of property thanks to the nature of the world founded by the Spanish: a natural order that admitted of diverse conceptions of property, just as it sheltered a plurality of races, castes and classes."

This is clearly not a strictly Marxist or functionalist interpretation of the issue, for which the permeability and capacity for assimilation of the Spanish culture would be nothing more than ruses. And this is why, against all evidence, a "materialist" anthropologist is able to maintain that the resguardos or *reducciones* and their system of cargos was an "entirely Hispano-Catholic [reality] of the sixteenth century... having no connection with aborigenous tradition and with no other purpose than to respond to the joint interests of the Crown, the Church and the hacenderos" (Marvin Harris, *Race and Work in America).* But Harris need only distinguish, within his own theoretical tradition, between "intention" and "function" to recognize that even when, as we have seen, this institution did respond to those interests, the simple overlapping and conflict between them constituted a de facto division of powers or balance of power of which the indigenous population was the "objective" beneficiary. What is more, it is not true, as he asserts, that the reducciones are a continuation of the earlier repartimientos of the Indians. Even during the time of the mita, they act as both a limit on and public control of "personal labor," and their function is exactly the opposite of that of the repartimientos. Indeed, they create autonomous congregations of the indigenous population. When the Indians were "reduced" (brought together and settled), their individual exploitation and control by the trustees and the breakdown of their cultural traditions were at very least held in check: The Crown was particularly concerned with the first point; the Church with the second. It should suffice to recall the series of reductions proposed by the friars, which aimed toward the self-determination of these communities and the continuance of their natural lords: the reductions of Las Casas with the Franciscans in Venezuela from 1515 to 1522 and again with the Dominicans (1561) in Vera Paz (Guatemala); the Franciscan reductions once again in the Orinoco and in Paraguay (1575), which foreshadow the work of the Jesuits in their defense of the Guaraní traditions and language.

Harris himself finally recognizes that royal protection of indigenous communal lands that could neither be sold nor mortgaged produces "one of the most fascinating counterpoints in the long colonial fugue: the holding in native hands until the nineteenth century of many fertile and well-irrigated lands long coveted by the hacenderos." And so it is not until the nineteenth century, in the name of liberal ideology, are the lands of the Church expropriated and Indian communal property dissolved, with the result that "practically every acre of high quality land in Mexico, Guatemala, Ecuador, Peru and Bolivia goes on to form part of the hacienda of a white or mixed-blood man." We need only recall as an example the effect of Melgarejo's 1867 laws of disentailment *(leyes desamortizadoras)* in Peru: in four years 680 landowners take possession of the lands from which 75,000 Indian or mestizo families had derived their livelihood. Half a century earlier, in 1803 – encomiendas and mitas notwithstanding – Humboldt had found the Indians "poor but free" and enjoying a "status preferable to that of the the peasants of a great portion of Northern Europe." But Harris must yet confront another flaw in his thesis. Alongside the Indians living on their communal lands, a mestizo community has also been emerging that by this time has achieved a level of political and economic power in Latin America that it would never reach in the United States. And once more Harris tries to water down the basic cultural explanation, now taking recourse to the jargon of structuralist anthropology: in Latin America *hyperlineage* is at work, whereby the lower – mestizo – segment is structurally associated with the upper segment; in the United States, what emerges is *hypolineage,* according to which "all those who have a demonstrable degree of indigenous or black kinship, be it visible or not, are considered to pertain to the subordinate class...." As far as I can see, this is nothing but a brilliant rationalization of the *apartheid* on which Anglo-American colonization is based; an academic explanation of why the only colonial art in North American territory is of Spanish origin, why neither the line of Tlatelolco storytellers nor Sahagún's informants prosper there, and why the seeds that will give rise to Sor Juana Inés de la Cruz, Garcilaso de la Vega, Morelos, or Cárdenas are not even planted.

*   *   *

But Spanish legislation does not protect the resguardos only in order to avoid obligatory *peonaje.* It also puts the native governing institutions – the *fiestas, cargos,* and *mayordomías* – to the task of preventing the emergence of indigenous caciquism. Once again, for Harris, this system merely plays into Spanish economic interests: "All the non-Indian sector has a powerful vested interest in the preservation of the system of the Fiesta: the system prevents the emergence of genuine native leaders, for it absorbs the Indians' excess wealth, cutting off any prospects of their accumulation of capital resources in the hamlet. The wealth thus absorbed is then employed for the maintenance of the Church hierarchy and to stimulate the entry of the Indians into the labor market outside the hamlet."

From this point on, Harris's inconsistency is manifest. How can he first maintain that the Spaniards "invent" these resguardos "with no connection to aborigenous tradition" only to affirm immediately thereafter that "they preserved the Fiesta system only "to prevent the emergence of native leaders"? In addition, if this is really their sole intention, why then did they reject the Incaic system of "biarchies," much more fitting to this end? Inca tradition, in effect, allowed for the dividing up of conquered tribes into approximately equal parts, and the placing of a chief at the head of each, *with a slight difference in rank between the two*. This was, according to Simmel, "the most perfect means of provoking a rivalry between the two leaders, thus preventing any joint action in the conquered territory."[16] And this was also a tactic used by the Crown with its own officials (equal division of authority between the viceroy and the appeals court, which as a result kept watch on each other) and with its noblemen (creating, as Olivares advised the King, ranks that provoked rivalry and made alliance among the aristocrats impossible), but never, oddly enough, with the natives.

But what, in fact, is the system of fiestas and what, besides the one pointed out by Harris, is its true function? In a previous book (*Ensayos sobre el desorden* – Essays on disorder), I compared it with Greek ostracism, and to reveal this structural kinship, we will have to make a brief detour into the classical world.

In the Turian constitution as described by Aristotle, the position of chief, once vacated, could not be occupied again for a period of five years. As a result, when those stricken with the "political vocation"[17] held too tight a grip on their power, thus endangering its free circulation, the ancients applied ostracism as a safety measure. Athens and the democratic cities of the Argos thus exiled for a given period "those who appeared too overbearing in power, either as a result of their wealth, their numerous contacts, or some other political influence," and in any case "saw to it that those who had accumulated too much power should be sent abroad for the period they were not in power." *(Politics,* V, 8).

Classical ostracism was therefore a device to forestall the consolidation of political power. The Amerindian fiesta and mayordomía was an analogous device by which to prevent the economic and administrative monopoly of power. Comparable to Plato, when he prohibited any citizen's holding property or wealth five times greater than the smallest holding, or to Marx, when he proposed collective ownership of the means of production, the Zapoteca or Zinacateca Indians did not consider the accumulation of wealth to be so much an injustice as an imbalance, an "exaggeration" that could quickly turn into a public peril. Thus, even to this day, when someone in the Indian populations of Oaxaca amasses excessive riches and tends naturally toward control of the means of production (tools, pulling animals, common lands), the people decree his ritual bankruptcy by naming him majordomo, or sponsor, of the patron saint's Fiesta, a sponsorship in whose execution the man so graced must spend his fortune if he does not wish to see himself "disgraced" and accused of impiety or black magic. In this way, the people guarded – and, to the extent that Spanish law protected the system, continue to guard – against hereditary accumulation and the emergence of classes by periodically redistributing the accumulated benefits. Once honored and impoverished by his responsibility as majordomo, the individual acquires a prestige and status whose benefits he reaps for the rest of his days. Not just his wealth but his very personality has been "socialized" and recovered for the community. In Chiapas I met one of these majordomos, whose hamlet had repaid him in prestige for the dispossession of his goods. He lived on charity and public veneration: "poor, but honorable," in a radical sense beyond our imagination.

This is the homeostatic function of the system of fiestas and mayordomías that the Austrian Crown sought to respect with its laws. Only in the nineteenth century did it take on the inverse – and perverse – function that Harris attributes to it from the outset. Indeed, Friar Toribio de Benavente (Motolinía) warned early on that in New Spain there were "some Indians who worked for two or three years, acquiring as much as possible with the intention of honoring the demon of the fiesta, a feast in which they not only spent everything they had, but even went into debt, having to work one or two more years to pay the difference." This accumulation of debt could then be manipulated in order to create a new peonaje de deudas. The Austrias tried to prevent this, limiting authorization of debt to 15 percent of salary, but from the time of the liberalization of Campomanes the system was relentless. Mendieta and Flannery tell us, for example, how one cacique, Marcial López, bought off the priests and corrupted the elders of the Valley of Oaxaca so that they would name people of scant means majordomo. He would then lend them money, using their fields as collateral, to pay the expenses of the fiesta that they were to provide. With the help of the outstanding mortgages, in a few short years Marcial López managed to acquire the lion's share of the community's lands and wealth.[18]

5

Imbroglio and Development

The Spanish did not plunge into the simple and linear "development" of America simply because they had succumbed to its charms. Surely, it would have been more efficient not to become involved in this identity crisis, seeing America and its inhabitants simply as the tabula rasa upon which to fulfill their interests and project their ideals, establish their fiefdoms and raise their families. And this is how things appear to be taking shape at the beginning, when upon the new virgin territory they flatly impose the medieval social structure of the comenda, the *nueva planta* (new grid) of Renaissance cities, the Iberian toponyms, and even their own myths and legends.[19] But the truth is that the Spanish soon begin not only to mix with the indigenous peoples, no longer casually but deliberately – the New Laws bestow full rights upon the mestizos and from 1503 on, under Ovando, miscegenation is directly promoted – but also to question the legitimacy of the conquest; to defend theologically the liberty and equality of the Indians; and to learn their languages and marvel at their cultural diversity.

This was not true of Anglo-Saxon colonization. "In South America and Mexico," Hegel wrote in 1820, "the inhabitants who show a feeling for independence are the criollos, born of the mixture of races with the Spanish and Portuguese.... This is why the English follow a policy in the Indies of hindering the production of a criollo mixture, a people with both Indian and European blood, who would feel a love for its own country." Here Hegel is attributing Anglo-Saxon behavior to tactical motives, as then and now conjunctural explanations are offered for Spanish behavior: (1) in contrast with the "founding fathers," the conquerors travel alone, which encourages their coupling with Indian women; and (2) in contrast with the Anglo-Saxons, who encounter nomad tribes considered by the natives themselves to be barbarous *(chichimecas)*, the Spanish face highly developed empires like the Aztecs and the Incas.

But neither one reason nor the other is sufficient to explain a much deeper and more complex cultural difference. Had the Anglo-Saxons by any chance stopped to see what was taking place with criollo nationalism in South

America before opting for the course of extinction or rounding up of the Indians on reservations? Did the Jesuits not defend the savage tribes of the Orinoco or the plainsmen of Casanare just as zealously as Las Casas defended the subjects of the Aztec Empire? And does all of this not have something to do with the paradoxical fact that the rational and systematic behavior that provides an explanation for a rapid and efficient conquest *is not* translated in the following centuries into a modernization of the Spanish colonies that would put them on a footing with their Anglo-Saxon counterparts?

Cortés's ability to manipulate the myths, exploit the dissensions, use the language, usurp the symbols, and take advantage of the superstitions of the Aztecs is one of the most spectacular examples of the "quick-witted astuteness and worldly science" (as defined by his enemy Las Casas) that characterizes modern European Renaissance style. In contrast with the still holistic and magical *Weltanschauung* of the Aztecs, this new attitude has a "disenchanted" concept of nature. It distinguishes clearly between facts and values, subject and object, natural law and social norms.   The world is a discrete, homogeneous ("extensive") reality where the point is not to participate in it, but to understand and control it. The "success" of this instrumental rationality when pitted against indigenous organization and mentality is as rapid as it is spectacular. "In fifty years," writes Uslar Pietri,

> the entire continent has been surveyed and subjugated, cities mapped out, jurisdictions established, law, religion and language imposed, schools founded, institutions organized, ports and roads opened, and a common and permanent lifestyle created.... In 1528 on the island of Cabruga, on the Venezuelan coast, a city with its own church and its own governor's palace had been erected, books by Boccaccio and Erasmus were arriving and municipal elections were being held. Another century was to transpire before New York was founded in 1629 and more than 200 years before Chicago would begin to rise on the shores of Lake Michigan.

And so we return to Monsignor Rivera's initial question: How and why did this initial advantage not translate later into the political and economic modernization of Latin America? I think this very speed is the main factor responsible for the later obstacles to development:

1. On the one hand, the very efficiency and precociousness of those modern legal and administrative structures will later curb the growth of the new liberal and mercantile structures. In the animal world this phenomenon is known as *neothenia* or premature growth. We will return to this point later on.

2. On the other hand, the rapid pace of the racial and cultural fusion does not allow for a unidirectional assimilation. Instead, the "modern"

culture is forevermore impregnated with the native values and reflexes that will continue to work on it from within. We have seen this in the language, and one need not be particularly clever to recognize in a great deal of the institutionalized corruption of the present-day Latin American administrations the echo of a heroic resistance to an impersonal bureaucracy imposed from without: the resistance of a culture that attempts to repersonalize it, even by means of institutionalized bribery *(la mordida)*.

3. Finally, the very ease and success of the conquest will reinforce the heroic spirit instead of the industrial, the seeking of booty or tribute in preference to rational exploitation, and the exaltation of honor over earnings; a verbal idealism always at hand to call for great principles (Justice, Liberty, and so on) instead of the cautious sense of industriousness that characterized the development of the Anglo-American countries. And we finally come full circle when, as Sergio de la Peña says, Latin America, which established the conditions for Spain's underdevelopment, ends up absorbing Spain's inclination toward underdevelopment.

The rapid Spanish conquest (in contrast to the slow Anglo-Saxon conquest) also had perverse effects on the development of the Iberian Peninsula itself, for which it turned out to be, as we shall see, a veritable "poisoned gift." Formally, this process is nothing new: the same capacities that make expansion or growth possible turn out to be lethal when they are not transformed so as to adapt to the new environment they have generated. Fichte similarly interpreted the crisis of the Hellenic city-state: Greek democracy conquers Persian despotism, but its own habits, more "city" than "state," lead it to found colonial cities in Asia that fight among themselves, weakening the metropolis, and thus leaving it vulnerable to takeover by the Romans. Analogously, Roman expansion and unification will in turn create the ideological basis and vehicle for expansion of the new Christian religion: first the Paulist Universal State (which still uses the structure of the Roman State to Christianize conquered peoples "from without"), and then the Germanic States, whose very identity and independence arise, according to Fichte, from Christianity itself.

In the case of Spain, as Max Weber put it,

colonial commerce did not stimulate work or technological development, for it rested on the principle of spoliation and not on a calculation of profitability based on the possibilities of the market.... Thus, the influx of precious metals in Spain supposes a parallel regression of the capitalist system in that country. The wave of precious metals passed through Spain without touching her, bearing fruit instead in countries which from the twelfth century on began the transformation of their work constituency, a circumstance that favored the genesis of capitalism.

Beyond and beneath this "boomerang effect," the fact remains that Spain repeatedly takes a stand against those "modernizing" cultural forces whose common denominator is the progressive independence of municipal civil society and the clear delimitation of temporal and spiritual orders. In the same year that Cortés takes Tenochtitlán, his liberal and individualistic spirit is defeated in Villalar (*see* pp. 90-91). The Castilians expel the *Jews* the year of Columbus's first voyage, try to prevent the participation of the *Catalans* [20] through Isabella I's will and testament, use American gold to fight against the *Protestants* and must then defend their independence against the children of the *Enlightenment*.[21] They oppose on all fronts the forces that are preparing modern development through the dis-enchantment of the world and the complementary distillation of pure Reason, Piety, Virtue and Self-interest. The Jesuit experience in America is, as we shall see, a heroic and frustrated attempt to conquer modernity without relinquishing the former spirit. But let us first take a look at this other process.[22]

*   *   *

The process of dis-enchantment of reality is to be carried out and secured in opposition to the Catholic Church. Lutheran Protestantism will see to "disaffecting" the secular world of religious loyalties and inertias, Calvinism will go on to place a now positive religious sanction on the affairs of this world, and finally, the Enlightenment will take care of replacing the old structures of legitimation with the new gods of Reason, Virtue or Progress. Meanwhile Spain, at odds politically with the whole lot, is incapable of using its political precociousness to get a head start on modern industrial society. (The first – and heroic – attempt to modernize economically while bypassing political or ideological modernization is undertaken by the Jesuits in Colombia, Paraguay, and Uruguay; the last – and pathetic, though not sterile – attempt is that of the Opus Dei in the 1960's, brilliantly represented in this encounter by Don Laureano López-Rodó.)[23]

Lutheranism thus collaborates in the process of removing God from the world and its affairs by locating Him inside the individual soul: this *intense piety* must roll back all worldly forms until they are reduced to a pure and pristine *res extensa* in which church bells are replaced by clocks, sermons by the personal reading of the Bible, and popes by princes. From there on in, the individual subject will be shouldering the tremendous responsibility and guilt before God ("you think you have escaped the cloister, but know that you shall be a monk your whole life long"), which until then had been sagely administered and exorcised with ejaculatories and indulgences, with homilies, devotions, and regular confessions. The elimination of confession means the destruction of the "fifth column" used by the Church to impose its criteria in the secular world, and the balance of power previously in effect between Church Morality and Reason of State is upset to the benefit of the latter. The lax and ambiguous dialectic between Sin and Repentance overseen by the Church gives way to a "clear and distinct" demarcation of spheres: internal piety and external political or economic laws, individual austerity and social pragmatism.

Lutheran Protestantism had thus acted as the "antithesis" that separated both spheres but it will be up to Calvinism to establish the new "synthesis" by predicating the preestablished harmony between worldly success and eternal salvation. Set apart by Luther, the lay virtues now step in to colonize the religious virtues and to restore a new bourgeois universalism: action takes the place of monastic contemplation; sobriety, that of ecclesiastic and courtly ostentation; predestination in the other world and the profit motive in this one, that of the traditional freedom and equality of man predicated by the Church. This reversal of roles will reach its peak when Erastianism goes so far as to demand that the dogma of the incarnation or the existence of purgatory be placed under the authority of parliament.

6

A Short Cut with No Reformation?

But was the mediation of this reformed ideology really indispensable for entry into economic and social modernity? Was the Baroque not an alternate route? Could Spain not have taken a short cut from the Renaissance directly into the Enlightenment and the industrial revolution without necessarily taking the ideological route? Yes, it could, and it did, but a certain toll was taken.

We have mentioned the Weberian explanation of Calvinism as an "organic" ideology of capitalism based on the three cardinal virtues of industry-asceticism-profit: a *work* whose products are not consumed *(asceticism)* but instead saved and invested *(profit)*. Calvinism censured pleasure and imbued the individual with a terrible anxiety regarding his salvation – his eschatological "status": predestined, not predestined? – but because it did not allow for a retreat from the world, it channeled this anguish into professional, lucrative activity, which came to be valued as a "sign" of predestination.

Work thus ceases to be a penance ("you will earn your bread") to become not an instrument or a means but, rather, the very purpose of life. Anything gracious, easy, or free becomes suspect for this cult of work. Only what is costly can be Great: *per aspera ad astra*. Only what is not gratifying can be Good: the *categorical imperative*. Beauty, like the edelweiss, can blossom only on the craggiest cliffs to award our ability and persistence. This lifetime of effort is a sign of both spiritual salvation and professional or commercial respectability. "Atheists do not trust one another in their affairs;[24] they come to us when they want to do business; piety is thus the surest road to achieving wealth." This is the model of the classical pre-Keynesian businessman: sober, farsighted, honorable, the jealous guardian of his reputation, who rejects luxury or pleasures with the feeling of having been faithful to his secular vocation. Franklin will synthesize this conception of the world in his *Advice to a Young Tradesman:* time is money; credit is money; money makes money; a punctual borrower reaps the benefits of credit;

the appearance of honesty increases credit; credit should be applied to productive investment; one must be vigilant and frugal in consumption.

It is this "of this world" asceticism that underlies the great accumulation of fixed capital in modern Europe. It is an accumulation that resulted from the efforts of men who, on principle – in the case of the businessmen – did not wish to, or – in the case of the workers or the colonies – were not free to consume in immediate gratification all the rewards of their toil. As Keynes wrote so graphically in 1918, "The Puritan repression and ethos prevented both rich and poor, bourgeois and proletarians respectively from eating the cake they were baking."[25] What was still missing, however, was a spiritual as well as theoretical justification of the profit motive and the tremendous differences in fortune that it generated. And this is precisely the function of the Calvinist theory of the businessmen or "visible saints" whose wealth ultimately redounds – thanks to what will later be called the "invisible hand" – to the benefit of the most needy.

Each and every one of the ingredients of this secularization of the world seems to be missing in Castile when it sets out to conquer and exploit American resources. Lacking are the Arabic ethic of artisanry and thrift, the sense of calculation, respect for one's trade or for business ("conscience in a merchant," Quevedo asserts, "is like virginity in a harlot, displayed for sale though there be no stock"),[26] the secular asceticism that brings in earnings (where Castilians continue to prefer "honor without ships to ships without honor"), the sense of a commonwealth or flexible community of interests (as opposed to the defense of the rigid unity of a "transnational Spain," which subsumes all other Iberian peoples). And these are precisely the ingredients that grow and develop, free of outside pressures, among the English of New England – and upon which they establish the foundations of the first modern and democratic country.

So the contrast between the Spanish and Anglo-Saxon colonizations should neither be attributed to the Enlightenment spirit nor to the lack of it. It is true that the Enlightenment applies the final stroke to the process of reformation and secularization that has been taking place up to this point, by setting up the cult to the new secular gods: Virtue and Reason, Progress and the Nation. But it is no less true that, by a curious paradox, the Enlightenment served above all as the ideology and religion of the new State, while it was the religious spirit of the Protestant Reformation that helped to constitute its socioeconomic basis. The very history of Spain is an *a contrario* demonstration of this. The Spaniards who conquer America are certainly Renaissance men, and the Bourbons, who organize its systematic exploitation and further the colonial insurrection, are by then men of the Enlightenment. What is missing in Spain is the professional Judaic substrate and the reformed ideology that in the interim ought to have nourished its modernization. What is all too present is the baroque addiction to the liturgies of bureaucracy and chivalry. And somewhere between the two falls what defines and embroils Spain: a "classical" respect for forms, an "Aristotelian" horror at pure profit or pure piety, a figurative sensibility, a rejection of impersonal and abstract relations – and also a deep-rooted Christian tradition of the freedom and equality of man. All the elements, in short, that prevent Spain's giving much credence to the new organic credo of modernity.

This credo, as suggested, entailed little more than a switch from the enchantment of the world to a new enchantment of the subject: gods are neither created nor destroyed; they are just transformed or replaced. It is true that in the meantime "things" began losing their magical weightiness, becoming transformed into pure matter or mere instruments of action. But it is now the individual subject who will inherit those virtualities and who, in turn, becomes magical: a being bewitched by his own *fatum*, predestined from all eternity to salvation or damnation, corroded by Pascal's "metaphysical shiver" and incapable of really intervening in the "business" of his salvation. The only province left to this Calvinist soul is the rational and technical control of the world. Efficiency now makes benevolence useless: "Compassion," writes Spinoza, "is bad in and of itself for the man who has Reason as his guide."

Catholicism still wants to avoid this schizophrenic credo by stubbornly defending both individual freedom and the value of the figures and images of this world. But was an authentic development really viable on the basis of this imbroglio? Was a rational exploitation that did not rule out compassion for people, attention to things, and moderation in one's actions even conceivable? Was it possible to embrace modernity without subscribing to its credo? Was a Catholic modernization – that is to say, both Christian and pagan – feasible? We opened the chapter with this question and we will be examining it in the next three.

7

Midway between Legalism and Benevolence

Over and over again the Laws of the Indies show concern for protecting the native people from inhuman treatment. "Converts" along the lines of Las Casas never tire of pondering the excellencies, even the superiority, of indigenous culture. This attitude has never ceased to provoke the irritation of those who, as J. Pijoan states, "from Fernández de Oviedo to myself, have lived in contact with the Indian population, and know that the Indians still show a deplorable physical and moral inferiority." For such observers, these laws smack of an almost mystical philanthropy. As Pijoan goes on to state: "According to them, one must not treat the Indian like a beast, like a slave, or even like a human being; he is a parcel of divinity which God has entrusted to the Spanish... and so, even as the pallid monarch (Philip II) is inflicting merciless death upon the Flemish Protestants, he is moved at the thought that his poor Indians could be suffering at the contact of blacks and gypsies."

Though his sarcasm may seem inappropriate, we must agree with Pijoan that these laws, like so many Marxist-Leninist predictions and dispositions, were "too much better" than the reality they reflected. We must not deceive ourselves, then, regarding their real observance nor, in spite of what we have seen, with respect to the efficacy of those do-gooding attitudes. Often both the defense of the oppressed and the idealization of the indigenous peoples are attitudes more gallant than they are practical, and more noble than operative. Some will try to protect indigenous society and others to preserve it, but neither the former nor the latter establishes any basis for its modernization and development. It is even clear that a paternalistic aristocracy – such as Sepúlveda, with his racist theories, had in mind – would often have been more effective in protecting the Indians than a distant Crown or a few benevolent friars who recognized their equality but could not guarantee respect for it.

Under Philip II, the *legal defense* of the Indians continued along the course charted by Isabella and Charles V. It continued to require exemption for the Indians and their encomiendas from payment of the *Alcabala* and even from the prohibition against charging day-workers (which nowadays would be called "reverse discrimination"), so that trade conditions would be more advantageous for the natives than for the criollos; and protection of Indian hamlets or reductions so that they can survive without being forced to sell their labor to the encomiendas or mines, and so on. Clearly, these laws are diametrically opposed to the famous Poor Law Reforms intended precisely to eliminate welfare alternatives of any kind in order to create a defenseless work force that must sell its labor in the marketplace. In contrast, Philip II's legislation continues to take its inspiration from the medieval principle, sanctioned by the Councils of Lyon (1274) and Vienna (1312), that "taking advantage of poverty" is a capital sin. Enlightenment thinkers will finally attack these "old-fashioned" devices, arguing that welfare protectionism or "political prices" for staples "merely favor," as neoliberals assert nowadays, "the indolence and natural backwardness of the poor."

The other route, the *theoretical idealization* of the native Americans, turned out to be no more practical or efficient than their legal defense. Ever since Columbus's and Vespucci's time we had been hearing tales of these "happier" American societies who "live closer to nature" and whom, according to Montaigne, "we surpass in every kind of barbarity." Later, Zumárraga and Vasco de Quiroga will prescribe "preserving, isolating and even imitating" this social order whose equality, humility, and joviality "seem to belong," as Vasco writes to Charles V, "to the Golden Age described in the *Saturnalia"* Some would consider these men, rather than Cortés and Pizarro, to be the "quixotic" Spaniards who cannot see the American forest for the books. What Zumárraga and Vasco see is often not reality but Lucian's or Thomas More's readings of reality. And Vasco will use this idyllic ideological view to organize his two ideal settlements (near Tenochtitlán and in the Patzcuaro lagoon), which were never to develop, for they represented from the outset the perfection of life in its natural "state": family clans, six hours of work with an equitable division of benefits and free services, and so on. An extreme case of that Spanish order "made more to last than to evolve" (O. Paz), which should not be taken lightly, when you consider that even today the Indians of the lagoon refer to "Don Vasco" with complete familiarity and trust.

*   *   *

The Jesuits of the time also adopted this ideological and philanthropic stance, but their further insistence upon the defense of blacks (whose importation was supported by Las Casas in order to protect "his" Indians) shows a more modern and rational, if no less heroic and selfless, sense of the equality of men. In the very heart of the slave market, Cartagena de Indias, Pedro Claver, a Catalan Jesuit, declares himself "slave of the blacks for life," devoting all his time to serving and comforting the dying slaves. On the first Friday of Lent in 1614, Cartagena is also the scene of the first sermon in support of blacks, which earns Father Luis Frías a trial by the Inquisition. The minutes of the trial, set down by Liévano Aguirre, are as follows:

> The said Father Frías stated that it was a greater sin to strike a black man than the Crucifix and, repeating this statement once again, he said and he said once more that it was a greater sin to strike a black man, as he was the creation and living image of God, than that Christ figure, gesturing with his hand toward the Crucifix to the right of the Main Altar, for to strike a black man is to strike the living image of God, whereas a Crucifix is a piece of stick or wood, a dead image which merely signifies what it is.

I cannot resist comparing this text with one written a century later by Montesquieu, with the Enlightenment in full swing:

> Sugar would be more expensive if slaves were not made to work on the plantations that produce it. The individuals in question are black from head to toe; and their noses are so flat that it is almost impossible to feel sorry for them. It is impossible to imagine that God, who is a wise being, has placed a soul, and above all a good soul, in an entirely black body.... One proof that blacks have no common sense is that they don't value gold. It is impossible to suppose that these people are men; this could bring us to doubt that we are Christians.

What most characterizes the Jesuits, though, is not their role in the idealization and defense of Indians or blacks but their awareness that in order to overcome the prostration of the natives, it would be necessary to "develop" their socioeconomic system. No more, and indeed no less than that. To say it in sociological jargon, this meant to aid in their development without supplanting their system with a foreign model; to "disenchant" their means without "hypnotizing" them with new ends; to initiate them into technological reason without perverting them with instrumental reason. This is a veritable handbook that warns us in advance of what the dreams of anthropologists and the perversions of colonizers have been and often continue to be.

Instead of legal paternalism and chivalric idealism, the Jesuits pose the problem in terms of *development*, not *charity – production*, not mere *protection*, of the Indians.[27] *But how could a modern project not sustained by the "organic ideology" of modernity be created?* This indeed is the impressive challenge the Jesuits pose to Spanish colonialism: to remain faithful to its original Renaissance and Christian spirit, which meant to cease *still* to be Medieval without *yet* becoming Protestant; to go beyond the ideology of the monk or the hidalgo but not replace it with that of the merchant or the bourgeois.

But has Marx not already explained to us that "you only surpass what you replace?" And have we not known from the time of Weber and Sombart on, from Heidegger and Habermas to the present, that technical development is impossible without a concomitant "spiritual" development, that capitalist modernization is not viable without its accessory ideological motor and legitimation? Viable or not, the Jesuit attempt not to tip the scales between the two styles of colonization – autocratic and populistic, rational and communal – is the only serious Spanish alternative to the Anglo-Saxon model, an alternative designed to achieve its political and economic success without paying the price of its theology of inequality of men.

Let us take a quick look at what this alternative consisted of. Pushed inland toward the unsettled jungle territory of the eastern plains by the encomenderos of Nueva Granada, in the mid-seventeenth century the Jesuits begin to spread from Popayán and Quito to the Amazon, and along the Orinoco to the Atlantic. Later, those who had settled down in the River Plate pushed into the Guaraní territories that nowadays form part of Paraguay and Argentina. In 1649 they convince Philip IV to take the Indians of the Paraná under his direct control, freeing them from the patronage of the encomenderos, payment of the mita, and the lending of personal services.[28]

Within a very few years the Jesuits achieve a spectacular development of these Indians whom they begin to *attract* through music and the "mechanical arts" ("The most effective way to establish a new village and secure the presence of savage families," according to Father Gumilla, "is to find a blacksmith and set up a forge, for the Indians take a great interest in this trade, and the use they make of the tools that were previously unknown to them is a great boon to them."); to *settle* by organizing warehouses and common crops; and finally to *instruct* and give them the mental training required for mechanical civilization in clock- and jewelry-making workshops. (The same weapons, by the way, that the Jesuits will use in China to take power "from above" and that they use here "from below" to organize a primitive society in which tailors and turners, carpenters and printers will proliferate within a short time.)

Land is divided into estates for work and the common benefit (God's land) and lots for personal use (Man's land). The "instruments of production" – principally oxen and plows – are also common property. Not, of course, out of "communist" principles, an idea that first was cause for criticism and later for praise, but out of a thoughtful combination of anthropological and pragmatic considerations. On the one hand, these seminomadic hunting tribes had no sense of individual ownership of land – or of women, for that matter – along the lines of the model of "prehistoric communities" described by

Morgan and Maine.[29] On the other hand, the lots of private land were not sufficient for the sustenance of the village, for as Father Cardiel puts it, "in order to get them to work the land it is necessary to force them and punish them, even when the fruits do not go to the community but rather to those who produce them: they do not measure their fields, they let the horses die of hunger before taking them to pasture, they eat the cows to save themselves the task of milking them, and above all else they prefer artisanry, which they can exchange immediately, to agricultural work for whose fruits they must wait several months."

A portion of the common earnings is set aside for feasts or allotted for spending, and another part is reserved for investment. Even in the primitive plains and jungle colonies a specialization or intertribal division of labor emerges – the Sálivas mostly produce cacao; the Tunebos, cinnamon; the Casanares, woven cloth; and so on – that within a short time favors the establishment of a series of mercantile communities along the Orinoco. To protect the reducciones from other savage tribes or from Dutch pirates (and later from the bands of Portuguese *mamelucos* who hunted for slaves, and from the Jupis, supported by the Order of St. Paul), they organized a cavalry that was victorious in the battle of Mborore (1641). A century later, in 1754, this same cavalry, under the command of Sepee, the caudillo, using the same rudimentary shotguns made of cane, manages to keep both the Spanish and Portuguese armies at bay on two separate fronts until the 1756 massacre at Caibale, as vividly depicted in the film *The Mission*. When this occurs, the town contains 100,000 inhabitants organized by thirty – yes, thirty – Jesuits.

No wonder, then, that the elitist and paternalistic style of the Jesuits should soon clash with the more straightforward and spontaneous spirit of the Franciscans, who had preceded them. In 1641 (the year of Mborore), the Franciscan bishop, Friar Bernardino de Cárdenas forms an alliance with criollo nationalists against the Jesuits. From 1719 on, a criollo and a Valencian, José Anguera and Fernando Mompox, respectively, will be pleading the nationalist cause against the Jesuit tendency to "be royalistic, cosmopolitan and to pander to foreign interests." A new class, the nucleus of the later emancipation, is taking shape in the cabildos and cities with more economic than political power. This class is just as likely to take issue with royal officials sent by Spain as with the exemptions stipulated by the Crown. As we know, the Jesuits had obtained a 1709 decree declaring the Indians on the reductions to be free from paying the tithe or working for the hacenderos. The complaints to the Crown about the resulting scarcity of available labor are incessant, soon joined by Mompox's accusations of contraband, illicit commerce and fraud in the rendering of accounts by the Jesuit reducciones to the cabildo.

Mompox's complaints are quite symptomatic. From the late seventeenth century on, the progress of the reducciones begins to attract investments, diverting them from the criollo encomiendas or latifundia. Within a few years, the colonial administration must draw up borders and maximum export quotas for the Guaraní missions in order to protect the inefficient system of production of the encomenderos and plantation owners. What an embarrassment for the delegates of the Crown to have to set up a protectionist system to defend themselves from an indigenous society whose rhythm of development was leaving them behind! It is certainly not strange that they should go about spreading the rumor that the borders were in fact decided by the others, that is, that the Jesuits were promoting an independent Indian empire. And to demonstrate this to the metropolis, the criollo landowners had only to describe the system of *ramadas* that surrounded the reducciones. "When the Reducciones saw themselves besieged by all kinds of purveyors and merchants," writes Bach,

> the so-called Tambos or Ramadas where foreign merchants had to stay were built outside of certain Indian villages like San Javier, San José and Santo Corazón, and furnished with all foreseeable needs. There they found good food, good drink, good beds and all the desirable comforts, and all for free; but they were watched over almost like prisoners of the State. Soon upon their arrival, all the entrances to the Ramada were covered by Indian guards, for whom it was categorically forbidden to speak a word with the visitors... The foreign merchant was permitted to spend three days in the Ramada.[30]

Who could doubt, after hearing this description, that something was afoot there? But what was, in fact, hidden behind the "Bamboo Curtain" (Liévano Aguirre's name for it) of the ramadas? What was being hidden and protected there was a development without money. Let us see what this could mean.

8

The Jesuit as Rousseau's Double

In Musil's *The Man without Qualities*, Paul Arnheim has this to say about money: "Money... is spiritualized force, a pliant, highly developed and creative form of force." And in his *Philosophy of Money*, Simmel describes the type of behavior that money tends to favor. The objectivity and impartiality with which it measures everything fosters the scientific and dispassionate consideration of reality. By setting the poles of potential satisfaction at a greater distance, it also fosters a more intellectual or "secondary" disposition that undermines the communal structure of traditional societies while generating the bases for tyranny. As Bertrand Russell recalls, after John Locke, "The first age of tyranny and private property is the one in which the monetary system was first used."

And the first age of "logic" as well. Pure business – *finance* – furthers and requires pure thought: *formal logic*. Even conflicts and enmities become less personal when "everything is negotiable" and "yesterday's enemy could be tomorrow's partner." Unlike constitutional kings, who *reign but do not govern,* money *governs without ruling* (M. Espinosa). Money, the symbol of universal "saleability," of "abstract selfishness" dis-organizes "natural" systems to replace them first with absolute monarchy and then with liberal individualism, and then to create parties or *partisans* in the sense in which Mirabeau spoke of them to the king: *"Vous compterez un défenseur nécessaire à vos mesures, un créancier interessé à vos succés."*

What the Jesuits are protecting is a technological and economic progress conquered *in opposition to* this "natural ideology" of modernization: against the profit motive, the theory of competition, and the eschatology of inequality founded on money that had received Calvinism's benediction. This is why I have used the Jesuit experience – and not the Franciscan, often so much more spontaneous and friendly – as an example of an alternative to Anglo-Saxon colonization. Just like the Yankees, the Jesuit project aims directly at economic and commercial development. But, in contrast, this development is inclusive and not exclusive. It is not organized without regard for the natives, like the Founding Fathers' version, but with and for them – often against the

Spanish. It represents a modern business spirit that nevertheless wants to preserve both the egalitarian root of Christianity (later interpreted in a socialist key by Abbé Lugon and by Cunningham Graham, the founder of Laborism) and the pluralism and classical respect for "form and measure" vindicated in 1793 by Josep Manuel Peramás, the former missionary, in his comparative study of the reducciones and Plato's *Republic* or *The Laws*. As A. Armani says, this study "did not so much set out to demonstrate the doctrine of the Jesuits as to show the universality of its good sense and *the possibility of adoption of diverse human experiences in the progress and development of social life."* Which means, if we are to believe this Catalan Jesuit, that democratic development and capitalist accumulation did not necessarily have to be such one-way propositions as Max Weber saw them to be through his rearview mirror. The Protestant communities stimulated a statutory and liberal modernity; the French revolutionaries gave it a more theoretical and Jacobinical touch; and the Spanish Catholics could have offered a point of equilibrium between the moral-autonomistic character of the first and the national-ideological character of the second by calling upon a tradition that offered Hispanic individualism, classicism, and moralism all in one. As we have seen, neither the new criollo landowners nor the Spanish kings were about to consider this alternative. Let us see if anyone is capable today of picking up the torch of this tradition in order to collaborate in the response to the "crisis of legitimation" of the democratic welfare state.

*   *   *

This challenge was, in any case, a tall order. So much so that some modern economists, instead of being so amazed as to reflect upon the enterprise, have instead tried to invert Max Weber's theory. To wit, H. M. Robertson, when, in *Aspects of the Rise of Economic Individualism*, he holds that "the idea that Calvinism relaxed the discipline of the Christians in their carrying out of commercial affairs is entirely false. It was Jesuitism more than any other religious movement which relaxed this discipline, paving the way for the most unbridled individualism in economic affairs and giving its blessing to any operation of the commercial spirit with their doctrine of Probabilism and Direction of Intent." The loose interpretation that the Jesuits had begun to exercise in Europe, according to which unbaptized infants could go to heaven, and ignorance or incapacity to fulfill one's obligations meant freedom from culpability (theses condemned by Jansen in the *Agustinus)* was bound to culminate in a *morale relâchée* "that accommodated the law of God to the perverse habits of the century" (Arnauld). Had Father Antonio de Escobar not gone so far as to justify the use of weighted scales by anyone who in good conscience considered the prices imposed by the prince to be unjust?

As we shall see shortly, it is true that the Jesuits appeal when necessary to the laws of the marketplace in order to oppose the absolute state and those of its rulings that hinder the needed industrial and commercial development. But no one is so radical as Laínez, Lugo or Escobar, all three Jesuits, in criticizing the "laws of the marketplace" when hunger raises prices and extreme need increases interest rates. As J. Bradrick has pointed out, the Jesuits are the toughest prosecutors of the *Contratus Germanicus,* the *Triple Contract,* and the other formulas by which usury is legitimized (*The Economic Morals of the Jesuits*). Their theologians persist in meticulously specifying the only conditions – *lucrum cesans, damnum emergens and periculum sortis* – that can justify the payment of a monetary interest rate higher than 5 percent. Their defense of development and production, "in order to alleviate poverty," thus runs parallel to their systematic rejection of such economic development when it appears to acquire a logic of its own, offending – in the name of the laws of the Marketplace or the needs of the State – the classical sense of limits, Christian charity, or Renaissance individualism. And so, by keeping the new economic laws in the service of traditional principles, the Jesuits established wherever they went a paternalistic liberalism that addressed with relative success what continue to be the three great items of unfinished business on modernity's agenda. Let us examine their solution under the auspices of Gracián's three bywords or "enterprises."

1. *God... was not satisfied that trees bear only fruit, but flowers as well: let utility be combined with pleasure* (Gracián).

In the first place, the Jesuits confront the problem of accelerated modernization of backward peoples, but without the dogmatism and inhumanity with which both modern capitalism and communism have dealt with it. That is to say,

a. Without the "economic" inhumanity of the series of Poor Law Reforms that turned the poverty of the many into the necessary condition of general progress, and turned work into the Puritan counterpart of pleasure. Thus, we see the missionaries equitably handing out the capitalist interest accumulated on the mills and farms, organizing the first welfare system for widows and orphans, trying to take advantage of the curiosity or interests of the indigenous people to "instruct by delighting," and even staging Indophilic theatrical productions (the rich Castilian Epulon and the poor Indian Lazarus) on the reductions.

b. But also without the "messianic" inhumanity of the established socialisms that sacrifice the standard of living of their citizens to a military economy or to the construction of a perfect system for future generations. In this sense we have seen how the Jesuits refuse to lower the Indians' standard of living for the benefit of development and investment – indeed, neither growth in itself nor socialist revolution are among the saints on their humanist altar. Montesquieu said that these missions "had shown, for the first time ever, how the union of religion and humanity is possible." He would have been closer to the mark if he had said "the union of economic development and humanity"; the former was nothing new, but the latter most certainly was.

2. *When you've see one lion, you've seen them all... but when you've seen a man, you've seen only one, and not very well at that* (Gracián).

The Jesuits also try to adopt and to adapt the customs of the place for which purpose they learn the local dialects, respect native hierarchies, and use them to elaborate conspicuous systems of insignia, ranks, or decorations, which they apply to eke out economic stimuli. But even more than in America, it is among the cultured peoples of Asia that they offer the best examples of this curiosity and flexibility that makes of them, like Newton, "inveterate apprentices," whose "chameleonism" adapts itself to exotic habits in order to lure souls to Christ. In India, to overcome the obstacles posed by the caste system, they worked on two parallel fronts: the famed "Jesuit-yogis" who walked in rags among the pariahs, and the others who dress in yellow linen tunics and recite the Vedas or the sutras to convert the higher caste. In China, they astutely translate *Deus* as "Heaven" *(T'ien)* so as not to run afoul of ritual Confucian impersonalism. They use their ability to predict eclipses with precision to set themselves up as the authorized interpreters of the naturalist doctrine of the Tao and win over the Chinese emperors who, as in Egypt or the Yucatán, hold the calendar to be the principal legitimation of their power. In Paraguay, the borderlines or *tambos* are drawn up not only against the penetration of the "capitalist spirit" but also against the "Castilianist spirit." Thus, political dissidence is added to economic dissidence. Too Indianist for the criollos, too cosmopolitan for the Spaniards, the Society of Jesus is seen by all as being insufficiently patriotic. For the Jesuits, the borders with Brazil are not unconditional. They fight to keep the Spanish from becoming *corregidores* in Indian territory. They defend the Guaraní language and the theses of the Franciscan Father Bolaños against the Crown policy of linguistic unification spelled out in its 1550 "instructions to the viceroys." The present-day existence of the only truly bilingual state in Latin America bears witness to their persistence. And perhaps it is not irrelevant to this persistence to point out that the three men who founded the first Jesuit mission in what is now Paraguay were Manuel Ortega, Thomas Fields, and Joan Saloni, Portuguese, Irish, and Catalan, respectively.

Sensitivity to the problems of home rule and native languages, still very much alive in those countries, probably served to slow down Castile's more centralizing tendencies.

Now, this deference to, respect for, and even adaptation to other races and cultures is what has systematically – and, as we shall see, symptomatically – been lacking in Anglo-Saxon and North American colonialism. The latter brand of colonialism has moved between the exploitation of natural resources and the projection of its cultural projects, never understanding the nuances of the sensibilities or liturgies of the conquered peoples, never losing its ideological, racial or linguistic virginity. Hegel was acutely aware that this lack of a sense of otherness was the only thing that was going to keep the United States from being a fully modern country. What he could never have imagined was that right down to the present day – in Vietnam, the Philippines, or Central America – it would go on ignoring what the missionaries learned in the sixteenth century and often continue to practice: from Archbishop Rivera of El Salvador to Emeterio Barceló, the Jesuit mediator in the negotiation of the Aquino government with the communist guerrilla forces of Mindanao and organizer of the collective farms for the reincorporation of the guerrilla fighters into society.

3. *To all, but to mine enemies, forgotten* (Gracián).

As we have seen, the model and catechism of the missionaries countered the Calvinist and capitalist axiom that in order for there to be progress, *economic power* must be concentrated in the hands of the few. To state it more bluntly, their experience was a practical refutation of the axiomatic character of this principle. Nor were they any less severe when it came to the concentration of *political power* in the hands of the few, a trend in which Spain had taken an early lead and which enlightened despotism reaffirmed. Though they are critics of economism, they do not as a result turn into the "ideological vanguard" – as has at times been suggested, though not in these terms – of Spanish despotism or imperialism. Like the Dominicans in 1537 (see p. 17), they do not hesitate to betray the "interests" of Spain and the "rights" of the Crown in the name of popular sovereignty.

It is not by chance that this circumspection towards the Jesuits begins to crop up under Charles V and Philip II, culminating in the confrontation and dissolution of the Jesuit Order by the Bourbons. At the Council of Trent, Charles V supports the "conciliatory" arguments of Domingo de Soto and Melchor Cano, both Dominicans, against the theology of the Jesuits who appeared to challenge the new absolute monarchy. The court advisers are right in sensing that despite its "theological perversions," Protestantism is the natural ideology of the new absolute state – as the Enlightenment will be of enlightened despotism – and this is why they refuse to turn a deaf ear to the charges of "Erasmianism" or of "Neo-Pelagian voluntarism" that the other orders bring against the Jesuits.

However, it was unlikely that an order that had refused to subject human will and freedom to divine predestination would now agree to collaborate in its subjugation to the prepotency of the monarch. So, the Jesuits' wariness under the Austrians soon becomes confrontation at all levels under the Bourbons. On the colonial level, the Jesuits, who had accused the *hidalgos* and criollos of inefficient colonization, are equally critical of colonialism, now – finally! – understood in its modern sense, that is, as the systematic economical exploitation by the new companies that take it from brutality to impersonality, or from the arbitrary to arbitrage. The confrontation finally escalates into armed struggle when in the 1750 Treaty of Madrid the Crown cedes to Portugal all the territory on which the Orinoco, Amazonian, and Uruguayan missions are located. The Jesuit-trained Guaraní "flying cavalry" defeats the allied Spanish and Portuguese troops when they try to implement the treaty, obliging them to sign the 1754 armistice, the original version of which, to add insult to injury, is written in Guaraní.

Humiliated by the Jesuits in America, the monarchs feel equally threatened by them in Spain, for, following the teachings of Suárez and Mariana, they are spreading a doctrine on the popular origin of sovereignty that was sure to "alarm all the absolutist monarchs of the time" (M. Batilori). Thus, they are forbidden to speak of this issue in public, whether in the classroom or from the pulpit. Though the Jesuits are enemies of Protestant Intimacy, they are no less opposed to the Absolute State: the two demonic, limitless forms that the internal and external world acquire from the end of the seventeenth century on. How not to see them as the natural allies of this dismembering (*"desarticulación"*) that Ortega would later interpret as "the continuation of the territorial breakdown suffered by Spain for three centuries" and "the clearest manifestation of the state of decomposition into which our people has been falling... ever since 1580"?

Really, now! Finally, the Esquilache uprising and an apparently forged letter (in which the director general of the Jesuits states that Charles II is the son of Cardinal Alberoni, not of Philip V) give Charles III the pretext he needs to expel the Jesuits and pressure Clement XIV into dissolving the order. The texts Liévano offers of Charles III's "exposition" to the Pope and of the brief by which the Pope dissolves the society, sum up in a way everything that has been said here. I will take the liberty of quoting at length, inserting two parenthetical statements and a few italics:

> The disorders caused by the so-called Society of Jesus in the Spanish dominions – says the exposition – and its repeated and by now long-established excesses against all legitimate authority, have obliged the

Catholic King, by virtue of the power he has received from God to punish and repress crimes, to destroy in his States such a *continual focus of unrest...* The corruption of the practical and speculative morality of these priests, diametrically opposed to the doctrines of Jesus Christ, can no longer be placed in doubt. Nor is there anyone yet unconvinced of the tumult and transgressions of which they are accused... for they have declared adhesion to a political and worldly system contrary to all the powers God has established on this earth, *which is the enemy of the persons who exercise sovereign authority*, bold in inventing and maintaining *sanguinary opinions* [this refers to the right of tyrannicide], acting as the persecutor of prelates and of virtuous men... Not even the Holy See has been exempt from the persecutions, calumnies, threats and disobediences of the Jesuits... As long as the Jesuits exist, therefore [as we know, this was the first point of conflict at Trent], it will be impossible to attract to the bosom of the Church the principal dissidents who, seeing how these priests *stir up the Catholic States*, insult the holy persons of the Kings, *incite the people and combat public authority,* their removal will prevent the dangers of such misfortunes. The Catholic King, moved by these very notorious reasons, and desiring to fulfill what is owed to religion, to the Holy Father, to himself and to his vassals, begs His Holiness with the greatest insistence that he extinguish absolutely and completely the so-called Company of Jesus, secularizing all of its individuals and not permitting them to form congregation or community, under any title of reform or new Institute.

Dominus ac Redemptor, the 1773 brief by which the Pope satisfies the King's desires and dissolves the society does not mince words:

Inspired by the Holy Spirit, in whom we trust, moved by the duty to reestablish concord within the Church... and moved as well by other reasons of prudence and government that we harbor in the depths of our soul, we abolish and extirpate the Company of Jesus, and its charges, houses and institutes.

We need only remember the attacks of Dominicans, Franciscans, and Augustinians to understand what he is referring to when he speaks of a "duty to reestablish concord within the Church," and we need no more than the italics I inserted in Charles III's exposition to guess at those other "reasons of prudence and respect" that Clement XIV harbored "in the depths of his soul." Acts and reasons that Willem von Humboldt deplored in 1804 out of pure scientific interest in knowing the indigenous languages and cultures: "How happy we would be if they had only allowed the Jesuits more freedom and provided them with other means to penetrate even farther into the land...; if by suppressing the Jesuit Order, the intrigue and divisiveness had not also destroyed with a vengeance their work in the most distant parts of the land – an enterprise which will still be the amazement of posterity, less partial and less ungrateful."

But what surprising and heteroclitic unanimity suddenly loomed up against them! The monarchies of France and Spain, the Dominicans and the

Augustinians, the Criollos and the Crown, the governments of Portugal and Flanders, the Papacy and the Protestant Princes.[31] Proof, if any is needed, that politics, and in particular a common enemy, makes strange bedfellows. How is it that no one has stressed the deep analogy with the no less suspect unanimity – which included the Jesuits themselves – that emerged against the "impious Rousseau"? Indeed, the philosopher from Geneva manages to unite against him not only the Paris Tribunal and the Council of Geneva, but also the papacy and Diderot, the Jesuits and Voltaire.

The analogy is by no means casual. In *De la modernidad,* and referring precisely to Rousseau, I said that only a reactionary like him could "refuse to be one more bit player in the provincial cult to progress or a mere tool of the dominant political and economic interests." Now I feel that I must add the Jesuits to this family of "reactionaries" who persist in saying what *no one* (that is to say, no one among those who have the voice and the power) wants to hear in his own time. And what both he and they are so stubborn about in the eighteenth century is very very similar – so much so that one must appeal to what Freud called "the narcissism of petty differences" to understand their mutual antagonism. It can be summed up in the three following statements:

- that commiseration, not fear or hunger, is the foundation of civil society;
- that a reversible pact, and not divine or positive right, is the basis for political society;
- that convention or convenience, and not natural right, is the basis for private property.[32]

These are the theses that, mixed in different quantities, generate the unanimous repulse of "all of Europe" – with Pascal at the head. Only Kant, who rejects all the *de jure* legitimations of power on the basis of a *de facto* situation (the very issue of servitude [Grotius], the "pact without return" [Hobbes]), will reclaim and give a definitive theoretical formulation to the tense Loyolan or Rousseauist "voluntarism," according to which "I always have the power of the will and not the strength of execution; I am a slave out of vice and a free man out of remorse." And that states above all that "whenever a people finds itself obligated by force to obey and it obeys, it is doing a good thing; but as soon as it can shed the yoke and does shed it, it is doing an even better thing."

This peculiar mix of liberal and traditional ideology, so different from the enlightened or utilitarian blends, seems to be the inspiration behind everything from the thinking of Suárez and Rousseau right down to the present part-autonomistic, part-voluntaristic, and part-socialistic development of Spanish democracy. A blend to which R. M. Morse thinks Latin America

– and not just Latin America – could look for inspiration today: "In ideal terms," Morse writes, "it is to be hoped that the mixture of Iberian political culture with Rousseauism would satisfy western humanistic aspirations more fully than the grafting of Marxism onto Russian national tradition or the Anglo-Atlantic mixture of liberalism and democracy."

9

From the "Pactum Translationis" to the "Contrat Social"

The Jesuit influence on the ideology of American independence is well-documented; it can be seen in everyone from Hidalgo and Morelos in Mexico to Nicolás Cuervo in Peru, Diego Villafañe in Argentina, Javier Clavijero in Mexico, and Ignacio Molina in Chile. Not to mention Father Juan Pablo Viscardo, the author of the paper that inspired General Miranda's first revolutionary proclamation: "Nature, Reason and Justice have prescribed this moment to emancipate us from a Spanish tutelage... so tyrannical that all our sense of duty obliges us to terminate it." The royal decree of December 3, 1769, ordering the confiscation of all the worldly goods of anyone who possesses a portrait of Saint Ignatius of Loyola alerts us to the Jesuits' role in the very gestation of this ideology.

Carlos Pereyra is convinced that this Jesuit influence *preceded* Rousseau's, whose *Contrat Social* was published the same year that Charles III released the above-mentioned royal decree. But, as C. Stoetzel has observed, above and beyond mere precedence in time, scholastic theology and, in particular, Suárez's theory of the "Pactum Translationis" were more suitable (and by the same token more subversive) tools for delegitimizing Spanish authority over the American peoples. For Suárez, sovereignty is a power that is retained *in habitu* by the people "in order, in determined cases, also to recover it *actu*," even when it has been transferred to the prince *(Defensio Fidei,* III, III, 2). So, when Napoleonic troops invaded the Iberian Peninsula, and the House of Bourbon abdicated in Bayonne (1808), civil authority automatically reverted to the hands of the people who had designated the king as their sovereign. The vacancy of the legitimate throne – and its usurpation by Joseph Bonaparte – paved the way for the application of the *Pactum Translationis* because, as the Venezuelan Declaration of Independence states, "the Bourbons... having neglected, been derelict in, and trampled upon the sacred duty they contracted with the Spaniards of both worlds who had used their blood and their treasures to place them on the throne..., are thus incompetent and incapable of governing a free people."

The doctrine of the social contract could never have legitimized this type of revolt in societies in which the third estate had not yet formed a civil society capable of establishing such a pact. In Rousseau's contract, once the individuals have transferred sovereignty to the prince, they lose *totally and definitively* their original freedom for the sake of acquiring another freedom – civil or political – for which the *Volonté Générale* is the sole, exclusive, and absolute source of all rights. It becomes a question of the "total and unreserved alienation unto the community of each associate with all his rights." And because "there are not nor can there be interests contrary to the sovereign (the General Will), he need offer no guarantees regarding his subjects, for it is impossible for the body to injure its members."

In contrast, the doctrines of Mariana and Suárez *can* actually limit power and legitimize personal revolt against it. (1) *Limit it on principle* because "the perfect civil community is free and is not subject to any man outside itself, rather retaining all its power within itself; its regime... is democratic... which precludes submission to another man by natural right, for God has conceded this power to no man, and if He had, it would only be by choice, that is, by pact" (Suárez, *Defensio Fidei*, III, II, 122-123).[33] (2) *Limit it on the basis of everything that constitutes "civil society"*: individual happiness, private life, religion, family, or simply "humanity insofar as it is not united in a single political body."[34] (3) *Legitimize even insubordination,* because "when royal power is legitimate it has its origin in the people... who can summon the King and, if he neglects the health and advice of the people, they can strip him of his crown, for when they transferred their rights to the Prince, they did not give away the Supreme Power.... Thus, when the governor has taken power unrightfully and without the consent of the citizenry, it is licit to take his life and strip him of the throne" *(sic,* and in this order, Mariana, *De Rege et regis institutione).* For Suárez, too, "the tyrant can be killed by any simple member of the State who suffers his tyranny for: (1) if it is licit to do so in defense of one's life, it is all the more so in defense of the common good; and (2) it is as if it were a case of a defensive war against an unjust aggressor, though it be the King himself" *(Defensio Fidei,* VI, V, 1647-1653). Though he does not hesitate to recommend certain prudence and parsimony in the use of this right:

"it is fitting *[sic]* that his death be necessary for freedom to be achieved in the kingdom, for if it were possible to be free of the tyrant by any other less cruel means, it would not be licit to kill him immediately without a greater authority and examination of the case" (ibid., 1659).

Now, to understand these texts, one cannot forget that, in direct opposition to Rousseau, for Mariana and Suárez sovereignty tends *naturally* (in the Aristotelian sense) to be transferred to the state – but never *totally*. Individuals and peoples always keep an inalienable quota of their original sovereignty, on which basis they can, at any time, by and of themselves, rescind the *social contract*. This is the "right of retraction" that the leaders of the American emancipation exercise immediately after the "betrayal of Bayonne," without the slightest need to wait for a substitute general will to be formed, which in any case would be the result, not the condition, of the popular rebellion. This is, as you see, the argument that Sartre developed theoretically in his *Critique of Dialectical Reason*, and which has recently been used by Father Lambino of the Jesuit Order to justify Marcos's ouster before a constituted "general will" had legitimized such an action.

Hence, my *a priori* hypothesis regarding the relative influence of Suárez and Rousseau in emancipation ideology: *it could be anticipated that the Rousseauist "contrat" would be invoked wherever criollo society had achieved a notable degree of development and dominion, while support would be sought from the Suárez "Pactum" wherever this American civil society was still incipient, and middle classes with a defined national and political consciousness did not yet exist.* A comparative study of this type would surely explain many of the ideological alternatives of the emancipation.

At issue are two conceptions of freedom that are more or less "right" for a revolutionary movement, depending upon the level of development achieved by the community. What Rousseau inaugurates is a new concept of liberty as the *Aufhebung*, through education and the state, of an original freedom lost completely in the "social contract." This is the new liberty, born of and by the State, ultimately mythified by Hegel. In contrast, the theories of Suárez or Vitoria do not require obedience to this new statutory liberty, but clearly and simply sanction individual disobedience of any law or sovereignty considered to be unjust.[35] No state can ever legislate and administer that residue of freedom that the individual has not transferred to the political pact or contract.[36] This is a freedom which cannot be *decreed* by the state, but must be *usurped* from it; it can be protected by the state, but never enacted by it. As you can see, we are dealing with a very medieval, but also very modern, mistrust of the State, of any state, as the incarnation of Truth and Liberty.[37] A mistrust that, as we will see presently, is also at the "localist" heart of the North American system: *It is error alone which needs the support of government; truth can stand by itself* (Jefferson).

Rousseau's *Volonté Générale* retains the structure of absolute monarchy, but turns it upside down: the tyranny of the monarch now becomes, as de Tocqueville pointed out, the tyranny of the majority. Parliament by universal suffrage is also, as Proudhon showed, identical in substance to the Monarch:

it is, like him, absolute, infallible, inviolable, irresponsible.... In both cases, power has moved from the personal to the collective, from the hereditary to the elective, but it continues to be a *total* power over individuals and, in any case, *superior* to them. Ortega was right to state, in another context, that it is absurd to guillotine the Prince only to replace him with the Principle.

Only the existential split or "unhappy consciousness" introduced by Christianity will allow for relativizing the very nature of this sovereign[38] to whom the Christian gives up only part of his liberty – a part whose extent and importance only he can determine (and not the sovereign, as in *Du Contrat Social* [I, IV]). Suárez's individual – in contrast to Rousseau's citizen or Aristotle's *zoon politikon* – cedes no more than a sector of his life, alienates no more than a portion of his liberty. Thus, as Grotius says after Suárez, the public *subjectio*, unlike the private, does not suppress the *sui iuris esse*, or call for an infallible, charismatic monarch, superior in all events to his subjects: the philosopher-king of the classics or the general will of the neoclassics, "which need offer no guarantees to its subjects." Popular Will, which is *identical* to Divine Will, according to Rousseau, now inherits the mythic and absolute character of the former, but – being only *analogous* to Divine Will, according to Suárez – it retains the dignity of the latter but not its absolute character. Popular Will dilutes it without taking its place.[39]

Liberty for Suárez is a thing to be saved and, if necessary, usurped from the public powers. In contrast, the corollary to the modern doctrine of the "general will"[40] is that citizens must be "educated for freedom and happiness." As Rousseau recognizes unhesitatingly:

> The legislator... must feel disposed to changing human nature, so to speak, to transforming each individual..., to altering the constitution of man in order to strengthen it. It is necessary, in a word, for him to take a man's own strengths away from him, in order to give him others that will be strange to him and which he can make no use of without the aid of others.... For the will of the people is a blind will which often does not know what it wants, for it rarely knows what is good for it.... It is necessary to make man see objects as they are and show him the good path he is searching for; it is necessary to free him from the seduction of individual interest and will.

This is why the perfection of this enlightened despotism comes about when the king (Frederick II) or the minister (Turgot) are themselves philosophers. General education emerges with them, of course, but a new and more powerful means of legitimizing social differences emerges along with it, for although one can rebel against the power of the noble "titles" that suppose no merit, it seems morally and legally obligatory to accept the inherent superiority of those who hold academic "titles" – new titles that seem to incarnate a Reason as objective as it is administrative.[41] As Simmel wrote:

> Accessibility... to theoretical knowledge often ends up having consequences which invert its practical results. Since circumstances transcending personal qualifications decide the actual use of this knowledge,... general access to it gives rise to an ever more inaccessible and untouchable aristocracy, as a distinction between high and low enters into play which, in contrast with an economic-social distinction, cannot be remedied by decree or revolution, or through the goodwill of those involved. Jesus could tell the rich youth, "Give everything you have to the poor"; but he couldn't say, "Give your education to the humble." There is no advantage... before which the disfavored feel internally so diminished and defenseless as education. This is the reason that efforts to seek practical equality usually disregard intellectual education, for diverse reasons: Buddha, the cynics, Christianity in some of its forms.... To which must be added that the determination of knowledge by means of language and writing gives rise to their accumulation and condensation, making the differences between superior and inferior greater and greater.

None of this casts the slightest shadow upon the undoubtable benefits of general education, which the Enlightenment struggled for, or upon the political efficacy of Nebrija's transformation of vernacular Castilian into an "artifice" of Spanish domination in 1492. But was it really liberty and equality that this educational fervor was all about? No; its political efficacy was of a very different nature. It aided above all in the socialization and nationalization of the people – in their technical or professional training, the bureaucratizing of their expectations, and the formation of a National Spirit. (Which explains the only apparently paradoxical fact that the European Community has been more wary of free cultural and university circulation than the free circulation of goods and capital.)

No wonder, then, that the Renaissance men who did not share this political project should exercise their pedagogical paternalism very differently. For the Jesuits, what had to be spread above all was the Catholic faith: *Societatis Iesus tota orbe diffusa implet profetiae Malichae.* From that vantage point, knowledge was the *côté aventure* that could be put either to the task of spiritual "seduction" (China), or to the task of the autonomous "development" of new communities (California or Paraguay, Canada or Brazil), whose customs the Jesuits themselves adopted without the slightest hesitation. No wonder either that they should be reluctant to leave in the hands of statesmen or educators the absolute power they had contended for with the Protestant God himself. That is why their critique of the Enlightenment is different from – in a sense diametrically opposed to – traditionalist critiques. For them, *it is not divine omnipotence that limits educational intervention and the creation of the "new man,"* but just the opposite: *it is the very restriction of this divine intervention that stands as a model of the threshold at which wise men and prophets, princes and educators alike must come to a halt. By no means were the critics of divine Predestination about to leave man in the hands of pedagogical Post-determination!*

The Jesuits clearly participate – at times too actively – in the modern tendency to reject "peripatetic subtleties" and "scholastic barbarism" in the name of a more useful and agreeable knowledge, one more suited to manipulating both things and persons, as befits a modern power that has moved on from the technique Bertrand Russell attributed to the *pig* (pure brute force), to that of the *donkey* (the carrot stick of propaganda), and of the *elephant* in the ring (direct training). It was also the Jesuits who introduced the new critical and scientific mentality into America from the early eighteenth century until their expulsion in 1767. Did Lord Bacon himself not write that the texts of the Jesuits were peerless and that they ought to be the model for all centers of higher education? The only thing the Jesuits refuse to do is to place this newly conquered liberty in the service of the new deterministic and worldly idealism. "The experimental method," Father Castel argues against Montesquieu, "allows itself an air of divinity that tyrannizes our convictions and imposes itself upon our reason. A man who reasons... offers me freedom of judgment. One who shouts, 'These are the facts,' considers me a slave." This is why they resist sacrificing the freedom wrested from the old "facts" (Miracles, Predestination of Substantial Forms) on the altar of the new "facts" (Nature, the State, the Marketplace, the Enlightenment, or Positive Science), which from then on will incarnate the attributes of divinity. Had this attitude prevailed, perhaps it could have prevented the pathetic continuity that links old and new mythologies: Catholic dogmatism with Enlightenment sanctimony, animism with reverential positivism, and messianic eschatology with Marxist scholasticism.[42]

But was it really so indispensable – the reader must be asking – for the Jesuits to cling to this last transcendent legitimation that they are so reluctant to let go of, despite the modernity and pragmatism of their plan? Is it not this very reference to the Absolute that places the ultimate obstacle in the path of a truly civil and liberal conception of power? I wonder myself, given my limited enthusiasm for those absolute orders or truths that come to legitimize politics. Not only do I wonder, but I am also fearful when I see how the right to unveil the Will of God, the Order of Nature or the Sense of History can then be left in the hands of a caste of specialists.

For me, the best attitude toward politics still follows from the classic – and minimalist – Ciceronian definition: "The Republic is a group of free men associated to live well." By the same token, I share with Glucksmann the ideal of "maintaining in society the competition of demands and opinions that do not constitute an ordered set." My hope is for a State that will not attempt to set itself up as a metaphysical and substantive *coincidentia oppositorum* à la Nicholas de Cusa, limiting itself to staying at ground level, on a par with, and at the service of, spontaneous agreements among citizens that always make of the State a relatively redundant entity. But I also know that this is a passion as legitimate as it is futile. Experience demonstrates that once the scale has grown from "democracy" to "republic," the *res publica* cannot be detached from transcendental legitimation without politics' inventing its own autonomy and discovering its own transcendence. We have seen how, from its beginnings in Hobbes and Rousseau, this autonomy led to an "energumenic" state. I describe in another book *(De la Modernidad,* pp. 179 ff.), the development of the following step, i.e., when this autonomous State is shown by Hegel to be a "concrete universal," and "the very incarnation of Law and Morality." And today finally we are attending to the last step, in which the new political fundamentalism – be it Islamic or liberal, communist or papal – no longer seems satisfied with this universality and tries to join together the bureaucratic apparatus born of the "concrete universal" with the ideological apparatus of the medieval "religious universal" in order to legitimize its monopoly on force and truth. The process, moreover, has a certain logic in itself: just as the autonomy of human Knowledge (Cartesianism), Belief (Reform) and Possession (Capitalism) is being demanded, we can logically expect the autonomy of a Power free of all transcendental sanctions or controls to emerge as well, thus breaking – in the jargon of Habermas – "the link between the cognoscitive, practical-moral, and expressive-aesthetic spheres... which leads to the social coercion and reification of each separate sphere."

It was on surveying this situation that I came to fantasize about the theory of late Spanish scholasticism and the experience of the Jesuits as a possible liberal "maximin": the late secularization of the principle of theological legitimacy as an alternative to the modern theologization of the principle of secular legitimacy, long ago criticized by Feuerbach and Marx. In the end, I think (see chapter 21) that the limitations of both principles of legitimization can be overcome only by a democracy seen and lived as tradition, convention, and tact.

In this chapter we have seen that perhaps the Jesuit appeal to a transcendent principle was not so unnecessary or dispensable. In the next we will see that perhaps its historical failure was not so inevitable either.

10

A Nonadaptive Mutation

The fact remains that the Jesuit project did not prosper. Or, to put it in Darwinian terms, it turned out to be a "nonadaptive mutation." History took care to shelve those who sought a process of modernization not founded upon either the nation-state ideology that was to articulate Europe, or the ideology of profit and competition that would soon underwrite the rise of the United States. This is a fact; can it be taken for a law? This is what happened; does this mean it is the way things *had* to happen? What did prosper was the absolutist state allied with the nationalist ideal and/or Protestant ideology, but is this sufficient reason for dismissing as frivolous any consideration of other possible courses?

Certainly, for believers in strict historical causality – be they efficient, like Enlightenment thinkers, or final, like idealists – no consideration of "what might have been," of alternatives that did not prosper or past blind alleys, has any legitimacy. For them, everything (apparently) anecdotic turns out to be logical, everything (apparently) contingent is at heart necessary. And it is a short step from there to the direct canonization of whatever has taken place throughout history.

"If a chance battle causes the downfall of a State," Montesquieu wrote, "this means that there was a general cause determining that this State should perish as a result of said battle." "The only fitting way to write," a present-day British historian insists, "is as if what happened must of necessity have happened in any case." Here we have two still liberal examples of that modern *positivist idealism* that began by prophesying the past, went on to canonize the present as the "logical" culmination of what had gone before, and ended up prescribing the future as its necessary "dialectical" outcome. Nowadays we see an overabundance of commentary upon the political barbarities propitiated by this modern idealism; I need not go over that ground again. Let me only stress:

1. For its critics, the impressive theoretical efficacy it actually had,[43] and

2. For its acolytes, the present-day half-narcotic, half-narcissistic effect of its effort to see all historical formations as larval forms of what, as Nietzsche stated ironically, "was meant to culminate in us, modern men": as a yet unconscious stage of Technology or Psychoanalysis, of the Market or the State.

In contrast to what is usually said, it is not only Hegel, Marx, and Comte who are responsible for this schema. Heidegger himself reproduces it when he sees in technology both the "culmination" of modern nihilism (the Christian reduction of being to value + rationalist criticism and the Nietzschean demythification of value itself) and the "realization" of Western metaphysics (of the humanist distinction between subject and object). And it is similarly reproduced by all the historians who discover in the rejection of the absolute State or of the Laws of the Marketplace the seal of the Jesuits' reactionary character and the sign of their inevitable historical failure.[44] Clearly, from this dogmatic and hallucinatory view of history, it was senseless for the Jesuits to attempt to oppose the "inevitable process" that was to lead to the State or the Market, to the Desert or the Revolution.[45]

Even so, if this profuse and still diffuse phenomenon known as postmodernity has any meaning at all, it lies precisely in its rejection not only of that vanguardist conception of the present (of the "latest" art, method, class, social formation, and so on, as the "culmination" of all that went before) but also of the simplistic teleological reconstruction that its rearview mirror reflected of all that had preceded it. In contrast to this "provincialism of the present" that I described in 1963,[46] the present appears before us as something much more tentative or aleatory. And we are beginning at last to reject the censorship that had been weighing upon those political and spiritual moments that seemed to tell a different story: Jesuits or Shakers, the Counter-Reformation or the Baroque.

Nowadays, philosophy and anthropology, theoretical physics and even history itself seem to have formed an alliance to end that censorship, urging us to peruse these "alternative histories" without fear; causality has ceded its prestige to chance; the image of progress has become complicated and enriched with the images of "dissipation" and the "fluctuations" offered by science.[47] Not even new theories can masquerade as the final and inevitable outcome or corollary of those that went before.[48] They package themselves instead as a dissipation of dogmas, a marginal experience, a dissolving of the lumps that have formed in the course of modern interpretation, an attempt to save their blind spots even at the expense of generating new ones...

*   *   *

The aim of this book is more modest. This is not an attempt to rewrite history but simply to thin out some of the conceptual lumps that have come to galvanize or gum up our view of the past. And one of these "lumps" is just right for the task.

It is generally agreed that Counter-Reformation Spain finally took precedence over the open-minded Spain that was beginning to bud under the Catholic kings and would not appear again until the eighteenth century. But the rigidity and intransigence that hold sway from the early 1700s are political rather than religious. The Inquisition, which annihilates those who defend liberties, whether they be of a traditional *(comuneros, Illuminati)* or a Renaissance (Jesuits) nature, is the brainchild of a regalist, *secular* branch. In one given year – 1526 – Isabel of the Cross is arrested and Ignatius of Loyola is forbidden to preach. In contrast, around that time the current ideology among high Church officials (Fonseca, archbishop of Toledo; Alonso Manrique, inquisitor general) becomes Erasmianism, to which they appeal to condemn popular superstitions and to propose the idea of a Universal Empire.

The story begins in 1478, when Ferdinand and Isabella drag the right of "presentation" of bishops out of Sixtus IV as a reward for their defense of the faith, and it continues with Charles V's open war on Paul IV (1555), right up to the tensions between Philip II and Pius VII. It is not the religious attitude of the clergy but the Crown's regalist mentality that fosters and organizes the Inquisition in *opposition* both to the Roman Church (right to judge priests, to censure papal bulls) and to general internal politico-religious dissent as exemplified in the investigation of converts and prosecution of *Illuminati;* the prohibition on studying abroad.[49]

It is not at all strange that the Jesuits should often find themselves up against *both* the Crown *and* the Inquisition, nor that the Counter-Reformation of the second half of the sixteenth century should turn out to be much more liberal and tolerant than the inquisitorial regalism of the first half of the century. As J. H. Elliott reminds us, the year 1577 – the Council of Trent and the appointment of Cardinal Quiroga – witnesses the reformation of the clergy, the institution of works of charity and welfare (the brothers of Saint John of God), the decidedly progressive turn taken by scholasticism in Spain, the freeing of Fray Luis de León by the Inquisition, the protection of scientists such as Arias Montano, and the recuperation of the *Illuminati* tradition at the heart of Spanish mysticism. This is the spirit, at once Renaissance and counterreformist, that sets sail for America and attenuates the rigidity of the Castilian administrative system. This rigidity meanwhile persists in Spain precisely because the "counterreformist" movement does not enjoy in the political realm at home the cultural and political success it achieves in America. Indeed, the comuneros are the clear representatives of this individualistic and traditionalist spirit in rebellion against a precocious unification and expeditious modernization that will strangle civil society instead of building upon it. In short, this spirit represents the defense of the Spanish medieval freedoms against the incursions of modern absolutism. And once again the "lumps" that stereotype our view of history crop up to cloud our understanding of this comunero movement, which Marx did not hesitate to call the only "serious revolution" in the history of Spain up to the nineteenth century – a revolution oddly combining the new Renaissance spirit with the old medieval longing for charters and privileges.

In reality, the unification and modernization of Spain under the Catholic kings is a *profoundly superficial* movement. This is neither a paradox nor a play on words. It is superficial because it does not unify the market but leaves the medieval monetary and customs systems intact. The aristocracy also retains its economic and social privileges. The empire is equally incapable of defending its market with a consistent mercantilist policy. What results from all of this is a still-patrimonial state onto which a layer of legal and religious unification has been grafted. But this layer is, in turn, very deep, for it soon controls the living social forces: agriculture (subordinated to the latifundial and exportation interests of the *Mesta);* the Cortes (which never attain legislative power or the power of convocation); the cities (to which the Crown sends *corregidores* in 1480 to watch over the mayors); and the guilds (under state sway long before they have had time to develop).[50]

But these forces resist disappearing and set up Charles V's final hurdle. The Valencian *germanías* (brotherhoods) bring together the petty bourgeoisie, artisans, and weavers who confront nobles and civil servants with their proposal for a commercial republic along the lines of Venice. The Castilian comuneros include farmers, the municipal militia, the low nobility, and the clergy. This coalition, similar to the one that will constitute the seed of parliamentary democracy in England under the Tudors, is unable to obtain the commitment of the high landowning aristocracy. (In contrast with the British gentry, in Spain this class would rather be bureaucrats than bourgeois.) The armed uprisings in cities as distant as Valladolid, Jaén, and Valencia clearly delineate the broad range and revolutionary character of the movement. Its liberal constitutionalist program is patent in all its demands: expulsion of the corregidores, defense of the independence of the Cortes, right of the cities to convene the Cortes, and so on. Why, then, is it said that the comuneros and germanías are purely xenophobic and obscurantist movements emblemizing the reaction of a closed-minded Spain to the fresh breezes of Europe? The confusion arises from the same progressive prejudice or "lump" that we have already been considering: the incapacity to understand that if the unitary state represented at that time a superior *form* of political organization, its liberal, pluralistic, and constitutional content was represented by traditional forces like the comuneros, who did not wish to bow before it.[51] This is a prejudice into which Marx did not fall when he recognized in the comunero revolt a movement that, had it won, would have permitted Spain, like England, "to trade local independence and medieval sovereignty for the general control of the middle classes and the common prevalence of civil society."

We have seen that the Baroque spirit and the Counter-Reformation were able to some extent to absorb and elevate cultural tradition inductively to the point of organizing it on the scale of the new national state. From a political standpoint, however, the survival of the traditional liberties was much more problematic and the state tended to organize itself deductively upon their rubble. The contrast between these two forms of modernization sums up the assets and liabilities of both Latin American colonialization and Spanish unification.

We shall return to all of this later on. For the moment, let us just register the fact that the defense of pluralism and liberties was no less the domain of the Counter-Reformation and Ignatius of Loyola than it was of Erasmus and the new absolutism. The Inquisition, in any case, was more useful to the purposes of the latter than the former.

11

"Ripresa e Coda"

What have we said up to this point?

1. For the purpose of establishing certain nuances in Monsignor Rivera's distinction between conquest and evangelization, I started out by recalling the development, sophistication, and self-awareness of pre-Columbian culture, which is by no means a "geographical culture" in need of the European spirit to become conscious – no more, in any case, than any culture is in need of another as a mirror in which to recognize itself.

2. We cannot thus see indigenous culture as a mere "object" of the conquest. And, by the same token, we cannot see Spanish culture as its "subject." In light of modern anthropology, the obvious technical and strategic superiority of the Spanish turns out to be nothing but the product of a different level of desacralization of the World. Two levels of desacralization which both sides incarnate and whose causes overwhelm them both.

3. Where, on the contrary, it does appear that the Spanish can legitimately consider themselves to be subjects – subjects different from and even superior to those of other conquests – is in their colonization-evangelization, which is as distinct from the racist character of classical conquests as it is from the instrumental attitude of the Anglo-Saxon ones. In fact, Spain should take pride in having "recognized" America, rather than in having "discovered" it. It is further evident that this text is written from the experience of the obvious superiority of the economic and political results of the colonization of the United States of North America as opposed to the "Disunited States" of the South: development, federalism, and democracy, where we have left a trail of underdevelopment, fragmentation, and caciques.

4. It is nonetheless possible that the poor results of the Spanish colonization are also the flip side of its virtues, the price paid for the

deed to which Latin America owes it existence. In this sense, the religious, linguistic, and genetic contribution of Spain constitutes no more and no less than the actual *invention* of America.

5. In effect, the mixture of bloods and cultures that produces a new race and a new culture (Bolívar, Vasconcelos) takes place from a deep-seated conviction about the equality of man. Some inhabitants of those latitudes may think that an Anglo-Saxon conquest would have done more for them – perhaps, but it would have done it for someone *else*, for they would simply not exist. This belief in the equality of all men also paves the way for the first *avant la lettre* anthropological concern – the interest in the other as other – that we see budding in a simple soldier like Bernal Díaz, overflowing in Las Casas, and producing the magnum opus of Sahagún.

6. Under the influence of this same spirit, the Leyes de Indias are set down to defend the freedom of the natives against the criollo oligarchy of the trustees. It is true that these laws were never quite carried out, but by the same token they symbolize better than anything else the *pathological* destiny of western civilization: the scientific and military subjection of the world and the chronic "bad conscience" that derives from it.

7. The economic "development" of the metropolis that could have resulted from the conquest is blocked in Spain by the very ease with which American wealth is secured and by the political booty associated with it: viceroyalties, captaincies, corregidores, public tribunals, cabildos, and "other treasure troves of bureaucratic favors," thanks to which, as Claudio Sánchez Albornoz puts it, "the Crown can continue to see the penniless cosmos of our aristocratic poverty and the stellar masses of our people spin about its orbit... by launching multitudes of active and settled Spaniards, who would otherwise have gone on with their economic labors in Spain, upon overseas exploits and into the bureaucracy of America." The flip side of this rapid imposition of legal and administrative patterns was the precociousness with which, as we have seen, cultures and races blended together. Martín Cortés, the son of Hernán Cortés and the Malinche, is a veritable symbol of how, from the very beginning, "even the children born of casual and temporary unions with the natives are recognized and economically cared for by their Spanish parents" (Parry).

Without this "imbroglio," development would doubtless have been easier, as the course of the Anglo-American colonies demonstrates. However, the character and religion of the Castilian conquest – and the sophistication of the native cultures – did not allow for an aseptic and economical exploitation of the new lands. What Spain lacks is the ideology that would serve as the basis for a linear, rational, and systematic exploitation based on the axiom of inequality among people and cultures. This is why the efforts of the Crown are directed more toward *protecting* the Indians than toward *developing* their communities.

8. The Spanish Jesuits tried to synthesize the modern imperatives of development with the Christian principles of equality and liberty: *to develop the economy without disenchanting reality*. They were trying to develop a model of modernization that would use neither the Calvinist impulse nor the Enlightenment legitimization on which the orthodox model was based – and this put a political and military end to their experiment. This failed attempt still and all continues to symbolize an alternative model for developing without paying the price – concentration of power, planned pauperization, cultural color blindness – that the former model exacted.

What's more, Jesuit probabilism is surely, together with Anglo-Saxon jurisprudence or customary law, the most elaborate attempt to replace traditional, dogmatic morality with a worldly and individualistic ethics adaptable to the chronic ambiguity and accelerated change of modern society, all the while confronting the latter's *new* dogmas: patrimonial and instrumental Reason, Statism, and Faithism *(Fideismo)*. "Charity is more demanding than religion," says Antonio Dunia, the theologian. No one sins by refusing to obey the promulgated law, continues Antonio Escobar. In any case, it is permissible to follow one's own opinion, even when confronted with the more probable opinion of the judge or the sovereign, if only because the former is of greater benefit to the freedom of the citizen than to the authority of the prince (Castro Palao, Tomás Sánchez). The "lax conscience" of probabilism has an analogous function here to that of common law tradition (see p. 89). Both introduce flexibility, relativism, and distance toward the accepted norm. In one case, via a *rationalized traditionalism;* in the other, as is appropriate to a "continental" philosophy, via a *socialized individualism*.

That brings us this far. From here on in, I will try to (1) analyze the "meditation upon the self" that began in Spain with the loss of its colonies and that took place in all of Europe following the success of the English colonies; (2) contrast systematically the categories into which both colonizations fall in order to call attention to the classical root of the Latin American version as opposed to the Gothic origin and character of the North American type; (3) give an account of the reasons, both structural and occasional, that underlie not only the efficacy of the Anglo-Saxon model but also the limits and stumbling blocks it confronts nowadays; (4) tell North Americans (for this discourse was originally meant for them; see the introduction) that inspiration in some of the facets of Spanish colonialism, even in some of its failures, could help them understand their own problems abroad; (5) suggest, finally, to Latin Americans that the Spanish democratic experience could perhaps guide them along the road to the synthesis being tested here between traditionalism and socialist voluntarism, between our Latin "conventions" and the Anglo-Saxon sense of politics as a "convention." Or stated in a different way, between traditional and contractual conventions. That will be our final word.

12

The "Meditation upon One's Being"

We have been examining the attempt to organize a system that would be productive without necessarily being competitive: to introduce the Spanish colony into modernity without exacting the price of the ideology of inequality, exploitation, and acculturation that goes along with it. Right next door to this (failed) *surmounting* of medieval, patrimonial colonialism, we could seek on the California coast an exception to it: the Franciscans' colonization of California, where Catalan mercantile sense, work ethic, and tolerance (celebrated from the *Dispute of Barcelona* with the Jews to the *Book of the Gentile and the Three Wise Men* by Raymond Lully) led them to set up their missions as both social and productive units. Still, the same attitude that inspired Spanish colonization must be recognized in the content, if not the style, of these "exceptions," which in California or Arizona stand in clear contrast to Anglo-Saxon colonization.

But does it make any sense to keep talking so emphatically about *Spanish* colonization, or even to go so far as to identify with it? The indignation of Fernando Savater regarding this point is to some extent understandable: "If it is already stretching it to say, for example: 'We Spaniards *are* one way or another,' it is even more intolerable to affirm: 'We Spaniards were or *did...*' when referring to the 16th century! In this way, it is implied that Hernán Cortés or Viriato form part of our personal past almost like the child or adolescent we once were...."

Nevertheless, I think that Savater's indignation would fade if he recalled that between Viriato and Cortés something occurred that, as Américo Castro often said, has a great deal to do with the consciousness and identification of that "us." "By the year 1000," Spengler has written, "the most important men everywhere feel like Germans, Italians, Spaniards or Frenchmen. Six generations before, their grandparents felt, in the depths of their souls, like Franks, Lombards or Visigoths." What's more, in Catalonia, we do not need to read Spengler to know that the "we" who conquered America often enough affirmed itself in opposition to *our* "us."

Savater's umbrage regarding the history we have been taught (similar to the feelings I expressed in the first chapter when I insisted that the conquistadores were just as much the "object" of the process as were the conquered) immediately vanishes if we reject a fetishist image of history and come to see it simply as "the study of the past which makes what occurred comprehensible and coherent by reducing events to a dramatic model and seeing them in a simple way" (Huizinga). Then we can start quibbling over the gamut of models by which our history has been written: Thucydides and Augustine, Machiavelli and Burckhardt, Spengler and Marx. And we can also, as I propose to do shortly, question the particular "dramatism" of the schema – imperative unity versus degenerative dispersion – with which, still hung over from the loss of the colonies, Spanish history has been understood from the Generation of '98 onward.

Whenever Spain has felt disconcerted and self-conscious, this dramatic "meditation upon itself" has cropped up, though it is rarely on target in its diagnosis of the country's problems. This is what late eighteenth century critics and apologists for the importance of Spanish culture are up to (Masson, Denina), when what is really at stake is the political revolution initiated in England or the United States and on the verge of breaking out in France. And it crops up again at the turn of the following century as the authors of the Generation of '98 bemoan the loss of the empire, when what is really being lost is the industrial revolution. Like the famous general who was always "poised to win... the previous battle," here, by all accounts, we are always poised to confront the previous revolution – *une révolution en moins*. Objective crises so quickly become "crises of conscience," or of confidence, that *reflection* seems to be completely absorbed or exhausted in the push for *justification* of "the present prostration" of Spain. And in both the eighteenth and nineteenth centuries, positions are divided between an *exacerbated nationalism,* on the one hand, which seeks out our glorious antecedents and which finds in our "peculiarities" justifications for our "apparent" or partial backwardness in "certain areas," and on the other, an *enlightened nationalism* that exalts this past while turning its back on it and proposing a transplant of European "culture" (Father Juan Andrés, J. Ortega y Gasset).

*   *   *

Given to associating prestige with magnitude, Castile experiences the loss of the colonies as a terrible defeat, "and as if it did not have many centuries of history behind it," E. Nicol goes on,

Spain begins to question itself as young nations do. Patriotism is fanned by self-contemplation; and if by chance this contemplation falls upon something that isn't good, even this is loved simply because it is part of our being.... If the fields were barren, then barrenness had a beauty that excited the soul and opened the horizons of adventure. Perhaps that was the very place where the deep motives of that spirit of enterprise embodied in discoverers and conquerors should be sought. It was of no avail to recall that at the time of the conquest those same fields were not so desolate, or to point out that their present-day desolation was not inspiring similar feats. What ought to have been the object of agricultural cultivation was transformed for the moment into the object of poetic cultivation.

As an illustration of this attitude, we need consider only the theses of Américo Castro and Ortega y Gasset. While Ganivet limits himself to cultural relativism – "the *most important* philosophy of each nation is its own, even if it be quite *inferior* to the imitation of foreign philosophies" – Americo Castro plunges ahead into pained self-affirmation: "Rather than continuing to complain about Charles V, the Iberians, and so many other *causes* of Spanish misfortune, we must look deeply into what our ancestors *preferred to do*... and thus understand their noble *(hidalga)* refusal to take advantage of the fabulous riches of the Indies." You ask why they preferred it this way. Américo Castro's theory, so often rehashed, goes more or less as follows. Throughout the reconquest, under the influence of Jewish and Arabic caste systems, a *castizo* Spanish character[52] is formed, giving rise to closed groups defined by their hierarchy and tradition of beliefs. Old Castilians form the most prestigious "caste," so that, in a burst of historical irony, the castizo spirit ends up segregating or expelling its own importers – and depriving Spain of their virtues and abilities. From this mixture the *hidalgo* ideology blossoms, for which any technical skill, accumulation of wealth, or even cultural information is seen as a suspect "sign" of a "noncaste" origin. (Note the telling common origin of *caste [casta]* as restricted, pure lineage and *chaste [casto]* meaning sexually or linguistically pure, virtuous.) The hidalgo may "be poor, but he holds no debts where blood is concerned" (Quevedo). The only recourse for the old Castilian, or anyone who wants to look like one, is to subject or "subdue." (As el Cid "subdues" the lion, so the conquistador subdues the people, and the matador subdues the bull[53]). Any less important or grandiose manner of "doing" could raise doubts upon the "being" of the hidalgo. Whence, according to Castro, the imperative character of the Castilian *"señor"* who cannot lower himself to the laborious technical control of things but rather requires the domination of people – other "consciences" to ratify and reflect his nobility – as in Hegel's chapter on "Domination and servitude" (B, IV, 4) in the *Phenomenology*.

Few things are more symptomatic of this character described by A. Castro than Ortega's own "meditation," still phrased in terms of "command" and "submission." But Ortega wants to secularize and modernize this traditional caste spirit:

> It is as absurd to ignore the existence of an essential constitution of each society according to which individuals are divided into diverse social categories on the basis of a genealogical principle, as it would be to try to deform the system of sidereal orbits, or to refuse to recognize that man has a head and two feet, the Earth North and South, and the pyramid an apex and a base. Once this magical principle of the regime of castes is removed, what will be left is a deeper conception of society than those that enjoy prestige today.

But we also know that, according to Ortega, a "perversion of affections" takes place in Spain whereby "it is common to hate all select and exemplary individuality simply because it is just that." Since "the revolt of the masses," Spain "is incapable of humility, enthusiasm and admiration for what is superior," and has lost "that original gravitation of ordinary but healthy souls toward egregious physiognomies," that docility in the presence of the exemplary which, according to Ortega, is "the psychic function that man adds to the animal and which blesses our species with productivity in contrast with the relative stability of other living beings." I believe quite the opposite. I think, rather, that it is a stroke of luck and an honor for Spain to have retained that "perverse" popular spirit: the radical and liberal heart of Juan Crespo that is less disposed to imposing his will than to "dying for his opinion," and that maintains the mulish skepticism or reticence that comes through in Rebolledo's words:

> Let someone else go kill the Moors
> they haven't done a thing to me.

Equally to Spain's credit is the introduction of ambiguity and doubt into the epic genre, which as a result ceases to be an epic to become a novel: both in the *Quixote*, where "Sancho is the mirror of concience that looks upon and takes the measure of the genial knight" (M. Zambrano), or in the *True Story*, in which Bernal Díaz "presents the drama in the form of a mutual ignorance on the part of both the defeated emperor and the triumphant conquistador of what was really happening to them" (C. Fuentes).

As Machado said, *"Todo necio confunde valor y precio"* (All fools confuse value and price). And we could add that all *imperative* Spaniards, as described by Americo Castro and Ortega, confuse value with command, and citizenship with submission. Or, on the national level, they confuse virtue with magnitude, greatness with domination, development with expansion, and identity with unity. Ortega is a perfect example of this monumental confusion. For him, the "nationalizing disposition" is neither a practical know-how nor even a democratic knowing-how-to-live-together but a lordly knowing-how-to-command, defined as follows: "To command is neither simply to convince nor simply to obligate but an exquisite mixture of the two: moral suggestion and moral imposition are intimately blended in any act of ruling." In accordance with this inverted Calvinism, "The industrial ethic... is morally and vitally inferior to this warrior ethic" for which "men's actions are integrally bound by honor and fidelity, two sublime norms."

Clearly the men Ortega is dreaming of are those specialists in "commanding, subduing, and subjecting" – a Castilian specimen that political and economic history had already seen to shelving and for which, once the colonies are lost, Ortega tries to find a new *internal* task: a "great inspirational enterprise," a "gigantic project," or a "suggestive plan for a common life." The only problem is that the necessary raw material of the imperative spirit is the underdog, so that this spirit cannot see in his rebellion – the rebellion of anyone who does not feel the inspiration or the suggestion of the project – anything but the symptom of an "emotional perversion of the nation, much broader and more grave than its political perversion, which for centuries has done nothing but undo, detach, crumble, and grind up the national structure." Whence the "suggestive task" that Ortega attributes to this imperative spirit, now bereft of its empire: to struggle so that the *disaggregation* of the colonies does not turn into the *decomposition* of this "integral Spain... created by Castile, and which, we have reasons to believe, only Castilian heads generally have organs fit to perceive."

This is Ortega's way of opening a "new frontier," a new crusade, for this imperative spirit that has been left without a function but that (appropriately enough) resists its "industrial recycling." Meanwhile, during this same period, María Zambrano is already warning Spaniards against "this pure and coherent will... that has been left idle but which, like don Quixote, doesn't learn from its failures."

According to Castro and Ortega's definition, the hidalgo spirit needs to control not only things but also peoples and countries. Ortega's own theoretical contribution to the argument is that this imperative spirit can be engaged in subduing the "sorry spectacle" of the "nationalisms and separatisms of the present that do nothing but carry on the progressive territorial dismembering that Spain has been undergoing for three centuries." And this is Ortega's most significant contribution: to assure or reinforce the continuity of the imperative spirit in the continuity of one identical enterprise, the struggle against this "disaggregation which has filled the last centuries of our history without interruption and which has become especially acute today, now that Spanish existence has been reduced to the peninsular arena, under the rubric of particularism and separatism."

Ortega's "meditation upon one's being" adds to Américo Castro's *castizo* nationalism two clear "projects" for channeling nostalgia: the *forced unification of Spain as a substitute* and *pious Europeanism as a compensation* for the lost colonies. Precisely in order to reactivate the "American dream," this peculiar fundamentalism must now turn its back on America to seek and preach two new assimilations: both the integration *of* Spain itself and its integration *into* Europe. Whereby the multinational reality of Spain is at one shot twice betrayed, for Spain is both more and less than a conventional state, because *it is what it does not include and it includes what it is not.* It *is,* also, Latin America; however, it merely *includes* Catalonia or the Basque country.[54] And so any integration like the one proposed by Ortega, in which this unconventional reality is forgotten – the reality of a country diffuse around the edges, open inside and out – would be a betrayal of Spain only in the sense in which it can be said that Bayonne or the expulsion of the Jews were.

This is not all. For that "project" to be carried out, the two great lessons, one theoretical and the other practical, that Spain could perhaps have derived from its American experience must be ignored. The theoretical lesson is that the tragedy was not the loss of the colonies but the fact that, as E. Nicol has so rightly pointed out, *"with the freedom of the so-called colonies, for Spain freedom and motherland began to look like adverse ideas."* The practical lesson is that the irrational fragmentation of Latin America was not the product of the weakness of the state, but of a rigid nationalism that lacked the flexibility to connect its parts. Instead, it multiplied in its image and likeness the petty caudillos or national despots anointed with the sacred task of uniting territories that soon only an army would be capable of holding together.

13

The "Meditation upon One's Doing"

We asked if it was legitimate to go on speaking of "Spanish" colonization and somehow identifying with it. And we have seen the emphatic nationalistic response that accompanied the Spanish "meditation on one's being" at the end of the nineteenth century: a caricaturesque reinforcement of those features of colonization that the Jesuits had already tried to overcome. Fortunately, by that time Spanish thinkers were no longer in a position to inflict anything but their books upon Latin America.

But it would not be fair to attribute this judgment across the board to all the thinkers who came after the generation of '98. From diverse and often opposing positions, both Unamuno and Eugeni d'Ors, María Zambrano and Joan Maragall, were able to engage in meditations that were not only less "resentful" but also less steeped in the very vices of Spanish colonization. In spite of his theoretical (and I think somewhat snobbish) nationalism, Unamuno takes a greater interest in the cultural production of Latin America, Catalonia, or Portugal than in their national reintegration; he is more concerned with their literary richness – Eça de Queiroz, Vaz Ferreira, Camões, Sarmiento, Maragall, Torras i Bages – than with the lost unity of *las Españas.* The unity predicated and practiced by Unamuno does not aspire to imperative integration but to decentralization and mutual cultural recognition: "For not only is Latin America little and poorly known in Spain... but I suspect that the Spanish American republics themselves, from Mexico to Argentina, have only a very superficial knowledge of one another."

Eugeni d'Ors as well seems to put something of a damper on the frenzy of these "meditations." In spite of his multiple, ridiculous, and varied dabblings in imperialism – the Catalano-Mediterranean empire (1906), the Catalan Lands (1908), the Catalano-Helvetic confederation (1919), the Pan-Hispanic Union (1922), the poetics of the European "Ecumenon" as against the colonial "Exoteron" (1933), the Falangist idea (1939) – Ors still and all never stops seeking an alternative to the tin-soldierly *ethos* of domination over people in the orderly control of and domination over things. He favors a poetics of the "job well done" *(obra ben feta),* midway between the ethics of work and the ethics of pleasure, between rigorousness and virtuosity, that would blend both technical control and aesthetic respect for what things look like. A more Mediterranean version, in a word, of that expansive and showy Hispanic disposition, civilized by Eugeni d'Ors's sense of limits and forms. A sense that María Zambrano also demands (or dreams of) for her country and her times: "a time in which even outbursts are charged with a longing for moderation, in which even extremism responds to the hunger for moderation." But we shall come back later on to this more "formal" than "imperial" version of what it means to be Spanish. For the moment, I need only point out the contrast between the reflections of the previous chapter and two "meditations" that do not long for the unity of Spain as a substitute or for "integration to Europe" as a compensation; I am referring to Angel Ganivet and Joan Maragall.

* * *

In clear contrast with the "imperative spirit" attributed to the Spanish by Américo Castro (and which he himself took such care to exercise at the University of Barcelona, seeing to it that there were never more classes scheduled in Catalan than in Spanish), Ganivet saw the history of Spain split from one end to the other by a "spirit of independence" anchored in the very structure of the peninsula, "an almost independent territory which seeks to be fully independent." The insular spirit is aggressive: the English people "have been struggling for seven centuries against foreign enemies everywhere except in England," and even when it defends itself – against the invincible Armada or during the Second World War – its success is based on preventing disembarkation. In contrast, "continental nations which have frequent and unavoidable relationships rely on a spirit of *resistance.*" This is why "France's wars, whether defensive or offensive, were always border wars, cast in the traditional mold." What about the Napoleonic empire? Ganivet does not hesitate to declare it foreign to the spirit of "a people not cut out to colonize, which cannot go beyond political domination, the protectorate, for its nature recoils at abandonment of the native soil."[55]

Neither island nor continent, the people of the Iberian peninsula are "more isolated than those on the continent, though not free from attack or invasion. And since they only need a defensive organization in the event of danger, they trust their everyday preservation to the *spirit of independence.*" Thus, their wars are either civil or insurgent, and their men are better warriors or guerrillas than military officials. How, then, to explain the conquest of America?

"The Spanish," Ganivet points out, "conquer out of necessity, spontaneously, out of a natural impulse toward independence, with no other aim than to demonstrate the greatness hidden within the apparent pettiness." What they set out to find in America is their own independence: "personal independence, represented by 'gold'; not the gold earned in industry and commerce, but pure gold, in nuggets"; a wealth, we might add, as blinding as it is fragile, "which the sun engenders in Indian soil to be consumed by the sea" (Calderón).

What will, then, be an Ideal for the Enlightenment and Rationalism, the State and the Individual alone and on their own, without "intermediary structures" to act as middlemen in their relationship, is to Ganivet's mind a point of departure in Spain. State structure and individual adventure, A. Castro's imperative spirit and Ganivet's individualistic spirit, are the two sides of one same coin that has no edge; that is, the minimum thickness of a civil society that would know not only how to accumulate or spend but also how to keep wealth rolling along, resolving differences by pact and engaging in transactions. But it is not a point of departure in Catalonia, where, to use the words of Ganivet, the very "territorial spirit" of Europe – for which the Catalans always serve as the buffer zone (the *Marca Hispanica)* – impels the Catalans to follow the principle of *resistance.* And their maritime expansion, directed toward "civilized" countries, had to be at least as commercial as it was expansive, as diplomatic as it was imperative.

No wonder, then, that in the Catalan context the "meditation upon one's being" should take on a peculiar cast, and in a certain sense an exemplary one. One the one hand, Maragall certainly shares in the *pathos* we have been recording. But this very analogy of *pathos* allows us to contrast more clearly the difference in both the *mythos* and the *ethos,* in the imagery and ideology to which Maragall appeals:

> When we Catalans say *Visca Espanya* [Long live Spain, in Catalan] we mean indeed for Spain to live – do you see? – for its peoples to rise up and move, and speak, and do for themselves, and govern themselves and run the government.... Spain is all these things which are now rising up, speaking, and standing up to those who have until now lived off its apparent death.... Are we Spaniards? Yes, much more than all of you. *Viva España* [Long live Spain, in Spanish], yes, long live Spain. But, how should Spain live?

At a far remove from the "chains of centralist uniformity" and the "provincial back streets of the caciques," Maragall believes that "Spain must live with her face to the four winds of the seas that surround her, basking in the freedom of her diverse peoples, each one of which will bring its own soul and its own government to reshape together the living Spain." On this basis, Maragall can call for "Spanish solidarity against the falsification of Spain." And today his grandson, the mayor of Barcelona, picks up on this theme and urges us to participate in the construction of the unfinished Spanish reality. As Pasqual Maragall writes:

> It has often been said that Spain is an unfinished reality and Catalonia a tortured reality. If this is so, Catalonia is more of a reality, more real as a nation than Spain.... The minute the ghost of an oppressive and totalitarian Spain disappears, it is possible and necessary to think about Catalonian participation in the Spanish construction of this unfinished reality. Naturally, the first step is for Spain to admit that it is under construction, that the scaffolding is up.

Grandfather Maragall's distance from the previous "meditations" becomes even more patent when he opposes not only Ortega's "substitutive" unity of Spain but also its counterpart, his "compensatory" Europeanism. This Spanish "Europhoria" emerged, and now reappears, when no broader (i.e., colonial) unity was at hand, yet the desire to be saved in the Great Cause of a "higher unity" continues to be felt. In contrast, Maragall's Europeanism is, like Jefferson's Americanism, more local than national. "We must now seek all the virtues of brotherhood and Europeanism in considering ourselves Catalans...." Nor is Maragall moved by the proclamation of any ideal unity, not even European unity. "We needn't think that merely by virtue of proclaiming ourselves Europeans, we are going to play any important role in the great arenas." The poet goes even further: for him, too much *wishing ourselves* Europeans involves two contradictions. In the first place, if our desire were fully granted, "What would we then have to offer Europe?" And in the second place, the very way of "being European" to which we aspire does not exist, because Europe is by definition – or at least by any nonfascist definition – a plural, open, and indeterminate reality which suffers, and enjoys, a chronic "lack of being."

"To be European, in itself, doesn't mean a thing," not even artistically, "for European art is a convergence of French art, German art, Italian and Russian art..."; or politically, either, for "the weightiest of European peoples, the English, are the most characteristic national type... and they have never tried to be world-class, instead making world-class be what they are." And in clear contrast with Ortega, who exalts the compensatory Europeanism of the Castilians, Maragall closes with an ironic comment on the very same tendency among Catalans: "If all you want to be is a spiritual province of, say, France, then it's not worth your while to raise such a hue and cry and disturb Spain's slumber with all your nonsense."

*   *   *

The differences between the meditations of the previous chapter and those of this one are considerable. For Vicens Vives there are two ways of reacting to the U.S. defeat of Spain in 1898. One is "pessimistic, aristocratic and abstract"; the other, "constructivist, bourgeois and historicist." The Catalan proposal to finish up the job of a Spain "still under construction" comes up against the Castilian fear that such a project would question the very being of Spain. What ought to come together is put asunder. Why?

We are attending the last act of Castile's "disencounter" – as systematic as it is tragic – with its own federal tradition, analogous to the one we have already seen (p. 50) with its communal and religious tradition. If Menéndez Pidal and Ortega were right in thinking that "Spain was only strong when her center was strong, and weak when the periphery was strong,"[56] then it would be easy to conclude that

a. the centrifugal forces of the periphery were the cause of Spain's decadence, and
b. the historic and now renewed mission of Castile was precisely to keep these forces in line.[57]

This syllogism is based on a double error: first, understanding the balance of power between center and periphery as a "zero-sum" game in which whatever one side gains must be lost by the other; and second, seeing the progress of its periphery as the cause of "Spanish" – *i.e., Castilian* – decadence. This is a syllogism, or mirage, that Castilians and Catalonians tend to share, though they place a different value upon it.

The first error is to mistake for the cause of the phenomenon what is only the cause of its perception. We have seen how the "discovery" of America is actually discovered when the colonies are, in fact, being lost. And analogously, the "imperative and unitary spirit" is discovered just as, in the Count-Duke of Olivares's day, its effectiveness begins to fade. Thus, just as Minerva's owl opens its wings only at dusk, so does the "spirit" of the conquest speak only as its deeds are fading away. A spirit, moreover, that, as we shall see, not only turns out to be the by-product of its own weakness but even accentuates it.

The "imperative spirit" was not the solution but part of the problem itself. But neither was the Catalan spirit of mercantilism and compromise a solution. In fact, both attitudes merely reflect ways of life that, having dug in their heels after some initial success, become incapable of adapting to new situations. On the one hand, we see the early Castilian political consolidation that later does not know how to make its superstructure take root. On the other, the Catalan merchants whose civil society, petty and backbiting, does not know how to adapt to the new age and provide itself a modern political superstructure. Instead of merging, these two attitudes tend to become polarized in a process that maintains a systematic disunity between the State and the dynamic forces it contains. We have seen how both Charles V and Philip II rejected instead of integrating the spirit of the municipal communities, and how the religious spirit of the Counter-Reformation was able to hold sway only in opposition to the regalist and inquisitorial vagaries of the Crown. We have also seen how Charles III's modernization was carried out not by recovering but by expelling the enlightened, individualistic Jesuit ferment that formed a part of Spain's own tradition. And, even earlier, with Ferdinand the Catholic's death, the unity of Spain was not achieved by integrating the impetus of Catalan civil society but by opposing it. Ideological progressivism on the one hand is countered by pragmatic traditionalism on the other in a process of caricaturization or "schizmogenesis" of both – each giving in to its own inertia and incapable of taking its destiny in its own hands. So, federal ideas do not blossom in Spain out of determination but impotence: the mirage of a Spain that is weak when and because its center is weak is writ in stone.[58] The state that made the voyage to America was the same one that domesticated the living forces of the country: the possibility of a more practical than doctrinal – more "Anglo-Saxon" – colonial development was thwarted.

It is only fair to say that the vices of this "Anglo-Saxon" colonialism were also thwarted. Still, this is not due to the perfection of the Spanish state, but rather, thank God, to its precarious nature. Indeed, Spain exported to America both the openness of the "classical" Counter-Reformation spirit of her friars and the federal idea of her viceroys. This allowed, until Philip II, for respect to be accorded both the courts and constitutions of the Iberian states and the customs and traditions of the Latin American states. Perhaps this explains why only in Latin America are some of us able once and for all to feel Spanish: because this spirit was more able to prosper there than in the peninsula itself.

14

On the Difficulty of Thinking North America

I started out by suggesting that the discovery of America was Spain's *lot,* and its conquest the mere *logical product* of the confrontation of two cultural models: a European world "view" as against an Amerindian cosmic "order." In contrast, colonization or evangelization appeared to me to be an unequivocally Spanish *project;* here Spain was no longer only an actor in the play but actually the hard-core director of it. And I have ended by finally rejecting the idea of "Spanishness" coined by Spanish thinkers still nostalgic for, or resentful about, the loss of the colonies.

This is not to say that such a meditation can be carried out coldly and dispassionately. By no means. But its *pathos* must change. Nationalistic pride or nostalgia must be palliated, at least, by the embarrassment of contrasting the practical results of the Spanish and Anglo-Saxon colonizations. Any pride that might be derived from the "invention" of a culture or a race cannot allow us to forget its precarious output and the state in which this continent nowadays confronts its northern neighbor: underdevelopment, the military-cacique mold, chronic administrative corruption, fragmentation, and dependency – all of this in contrast to the economic development, federal unity and stability, political democracy, and real independence of Anglo-Saxon America. A more telling contrast would be hard to imagine.

Or a situation harder to reflect on with serenity. To reflect is, in Heidegger's words, "to have the courage to turn the truth of one's own assumptions and the scope of one's own goals into the object of study." This reflection, as Nietzsche said, is less limited by our intellectual capacity than by our meager "digestive" capacity to assimilate conclusions that reflect poorly upon us. But it is not only the Spanish who, for obvious reasons, have shown a tendency to avoid this reflection; neither Latin American writers nor European philosophers have had much "stomach" for it. Let us take a look.

From the South, the most expeditious way of exorcizing instead of actually "reflecting" upon this tough contrast is to declare that the relationship between the two realities is not one of contiguity but of causality. For Mario Benedetti, "the underdevelopment of the South is the consequence of the hyperdevelopment of the North..., of an oppressive, underdevelopment-producing North." "The winners," adds Eduardo Galeano, "won thanks to our having lost: the history of Latin America's underdevelopment completes the history of the development of world capitalism.... Our wealth has always generated our poverty in order to feed the prosperity of others...: the rain that irrigates the center of imperialist power drowns the vast outlying slums of the system." I naturally do not mean to deny that these arguments have a solid basis in North American policy in the hemisphere: support for dictatorships; surrender to the "sugar mentality" of their most predatory and speculative enterprises; the imposition of luxury one-crop systems on countries with a resulting break in their feed grains-food grains balance; tactical promotion of division among the countries in North America's "backyard"; direct use of force legitimized by a cheap, self-serving reduction of the area's problems to a supposed East-West confrontation, and so on. But there is no doubt that as a sort of one-shot explanation – and exorcization – of all guilt, these arguments are just as specious as the Hegelian attribution of Anglo racism in the United States to the previous criollo experience in Spanish America. (I understand that C. Rangel of Venezuela has elaborated upon this topic in *From the Good Savage to the Good Revolutionary*.)

But neither do the great European philosophers – unlike historians and travelers like Huizinga and de Tocqueville – seem to have had any more stomach for the issue, with the result that their opinions about America continue to run along the lines of those Cartesian passions *par lesquelles la volonté s'est auparavant laissée convaincre et séduire*. Indeed, from Hegel to Heidegger, and including Adorno, we find a recurring tendency to associate North America's youth with ingenuousness, its newness with unconsciousness, its size and power with archaicism. In this way, *instead of reflecting upon what they have "in front" of them, Latin Americans prefer to imagine that it is "on top" of them and Europeans that it is "behind" them.* And in this way Heidegger, disobeying his own call to reflection, is able to dismiss "Americanism": "Americanism is a European thing. It is that variety of the gigantic[59] *as yet* unattached and *not yet* emerging from the full and secluded essence of the Modern Age."

But as so often occurs, it is Hegel who first codifies this both resentful and patronizing European attitude toward America. Hegel's diagnosis of America includes "geographical immaturity" ("whose immense rivers dilate and have not come to form a riverbed"); feeble fauna ("its lions, tigers and crocodiles... are smaller, weaker, less potent"); and volatile inhabitants (who "fall back and disappear on mere contact with peoples of superior culture"). To all of this, he adds a specifically political lack of development: "North America cannot yet be considered a constituted State... nor does it offer [therefore] the slightest proof in favor of the republican system" [as opposed to the Prussian, of course].

What can this lability or flaw in the North American "constitution" be attributed to? Here Hegel uses an image from chemistry to anticipate the Toynbeean theory of the *challenge*. Just as some gases liquefy only after certain pressure has been applied to them, so natural ("gaseous") communities become "liquid" states (and the term liquidity has monetary connotations that are useful in the context) only upon application of a certain degree of social pressure. Though such pressure certainly does not exist in the Jeffersonian democracy Hegel is describing in 1830, it was very soon to rise under Lincoln (1860) with the War of Secession.

He is referring, above all, to a lack of social pressure, "for a true State can only be produced when class differences already exist, when wealth and poverty are great and a great mass of people can no longer satisfy its needs in the way in which it had before." In America, however, two factors seem to oppose this "rarefaction" or proletarianization demanded by Hegel and the English economists: the flux from the East and the emergence of the West; emigration and the frontier. For on the one hand, the existence of an open virgin frontier toward which to escape impedes "the settlement of the self-contained whole" and the resulting "reaction": "If the forest of Germania had still existed," Hegel states, "the French Revolution would not have taken place either." And on the other hand, "in order for a true State to exist, it must not be subject to constant emigration. Instead, a farming class, unable to continue expanding, must flock to the cities and urban industries – only in this way can a civil society emerge, and this is the condition for the existence of an organized State."[60] To this absence of natural and demographic boundaries is yet added the fact that "the United States lacks – for Mexico and Canada are not to be feared – a neighbor with which to exist in a relationship analogous to that which exists among the European States. That is, the United States does not have a neighbor to mistrust and in opposition to which it must maintain a permanent army...."

In *De la modernidad,* I have called this theory the "invisible German hand." According to it, a preestablished harmony would exist between the development and industrialization of any one state and the "unproductive expenses" of war to which its contiguity with other, equally expansionist states would obligate it. Hegel senses correctly that the United States needed this invisible hand, this challenge, and only a few decades later the U. S. actually begins its interventionist policy. The growth of this bellicosity and spirit of interference (held back only by the need to maintain a periphery that is not the beneficiary of North American citizenship) is meteoric from Lincoln and the War of Secession on. A few simple reminders: the intervention in Mexico in 1840 and again in 1914; the annexation of Puerto Rico, the Philippines, Midway, and Guam, and the attempt to create a buffer state between Argentina and Brazil in the late nineteenth century; the forced segregation of Panama and Guyana in the early twentieth; the intervention – *felix culpa* – in the two world wars and then in the colonies, Korea, and Vietnam. Not to mention the occasional invasion (Bay of Pigs, Santo Domingo, Grenada) or the "destabilization" (Jamaica, Chile, Nicaragua) in a continent the United States cannot seem to learn to respect as the *other* (it's *their* backyard) or to understand as its *own* (as an American problem and not a mere pawn in the East-West balance).

And here again Hegel saw the future more clearly than the Founding Fathers themselves. For Madison and the Federalists, "the laborious habits of the people, engaged in lucrative occupations and dedicated to the progress of agriculture and commerce, are incompatible with nations... like those of Europe, engaged in war and foreign competition" (1787). By 1830, Hegel could already see that neither this ideology nor its political formulation by Monroe in 1823 were to prevail in a society where development and welfare would soon be associated with the war effort. Even today, Americans continue to associate stability with conventional warfare, and economic prosperity with the nuclear arms race. Actually, the equilibrium of the North rests on the instability of the South – on Third World conflicts, where the Great Powers can size each other up, study each other's intentions, and arm wrestle with conventional arms. (In Nicaragua I have seen the crushed skulls of two children fatefully converted into the stage on which the United States decided to demonstrate its "determination and courage.") On the other hand, it is clear that U.S. prosperity is linked to the "war effort," today transformed into "defensive sophistication" ever since nuclearization no longer allows for world wars. So, even when face-to-face war is no longer possible, the North Americans have not given up on inventing or inducing a variety of ersatz stimuli for their country's war machine: wars on hold in the South, frozen in the silos, and today, finally, centrifugated out into the galaxies.

As you can see, Hegel was more intuitive economically than politically – which, by the way, has always been the hindrance of his Marxist Left, still lacking an adequate theory of the State. And so, if the United States has ended up following his economic recommendations or exigencies in order to emerge as a modern country, what it has not done is to "modernize" its federalist state and convert it into a paradigm of the Prussian model. No, the American confederation was not a still-larval and prepubescent form, an *antecedent* of the authentic European State, but an alternative to it – in point of fact, one real, live "dialectical" stage *beyond* it.

But this error, as we have seen, is the indelible mark of that European "resentment" that cannot and will not see North America as anything other than an *already* passé or *still* naive version of itself. It should be noted, however, that this resentment is the domain of the cultivated classes, while its popular counterpart is fascination with the "land of the future."

What we have seen in this section can serve as a consolation to us. We Spaniards are not the only ones who have difficulty facing North American success with serenity and aplomb. Neither Germany nor Argentina seem to have much stomach for it either. But some of the preceding considerations can also guide us. In Hegel's "geopolitical" hypotheses we have discovered some of the distinctive (and explanatory) features of the North American phenomenon already suggested in the preceding chapters. It will be in following these clues that we will try to go back to a comparative analysis of these two styles of colonization. Such an analysis should help us to go beyond the melancholic "meditation upon our being" toward a more active and objective "evaluation of our doing."

15

Interference and Contrast:
The Big Colony and the Small

But we must take one last look, albeit a quick one, at the outstanding features of what was to be the independence and immediate evolution of both colonial systems. And here even those most reluctant to admit quantitative differences cannot overlook a weighty qualitative difference: the British colony is under development from 1607 (the foundation of Jamestown in Virginia) to 1783 (Treaty of Versailles), and the Spanish from 1492 to 1821 (the independence of Mexico), if we regard Cuba and Puerto Rico as a separate case. One and a half centuries on the one hand as against four centuries on the other: the Spanish colony antedates the Anglo-Saxon by more than a century and outlives it half a century more. The difference is considerable, all the more so if you recall that Fray Marcos de Niza, Coronado, Espejo, and Oñate begin colonizing what today is North American land in 1540 (that is, eighty years before the landing of the *Mayflower*); that both colonizations coexist in the United States till late in the seventeenth century; and that the horses and arrows with which the Cheyenne and the Sioux confront the North American conquistadors in 1860 are vestiges of the previous colonization.[61] The Spaniards had in addition introduced poultry; the use of iron, copper and goldworking; weaving and spinning; the plow, the saw, and the chisel. But the most significant trace of their presence is that the Pueblo Indians retain an elective government of Spanish origin and all the rights to their land. The "spaces" that the Americans later take control of are therefore not *res nullius*, but Indian properties established according to the rules of Roman law. And in 1925, C. F. Lummins recognizes this to be so:

> When the Supreme Court of the United States expelled the Indians [here he is referring to those who lived on what would come to be the Warner ranch], they were not represented and negligence was shown in not presenting before that august Tribunal the fact that, under Spanish law, whence derive all property titles in California, it is not nor was it ever possible in any part of America, to expel an American Indian from the land where he was born.

But much as Spain had framed the American colonization process from the time of its independence in 1779, the United States would frame the last years of the Spanish colony and its emancipation. Spain, which now shared a border with the United States, feared that its example would spread and that its "provinces" would catch the North American spirit. With foresight, Aranda hastens to propose recognition of the new country and, more important, adaptation of its federal structure to organize the Spanish territories overseas and their relationship to the Crown. But Aranda's federalist proposals, sensible as they were, were no match for the rigidity of the Spanish framework, which, as is legend, "can break but never bend." No one (including Spanish America) can question the Sacred Unity of Spain, defended from the time of the Catholic Kings to the Courts of Cádiz, and whose only still positive feature (the placing on an equal footing of the "Spaniards of both hemispheres") will be bankrupted when the 1837 and 1845 constitutions deny Cuba parliamentary representation. A frenetic unity, in short, which as Julián Marías recognizes even as he exalts it, ended up costing us the very name of America.[62] Soon, however, we will see that the semantic costs are nothing next to the political ones.

What concerns us even more than the *décalage* and the mutual interferences between the two colonizations are their differences in "style," and these clearly must be sought in the respective metropolises. We have devoted a great number of the preceding pages to this, but in order to reach a clear understanding of the present-day difference between North and South America – or at least so as better to channel our resentment – it would not be a bad idea systematically to take up a few of these topics.

A schematic and no doubt caricaturesque contrast between both procedures can be portrayed as follows: (1) A country not quite formed and not yet powerful, England, (2) initiates a late and slow colonization, (3) inspired in a medieval and religious individualism, (4) which establishes a traditional and commercial structure, and (5) ends up constituting a new country that recreates the history of the metropolis, (6) paving the way for a constitution in which feudalism forges a direct link with federalism, without bowing to modern "national" or "legal" concepts, neither of which had taken root in the country of origin, just as neither Roman law nor the Catholic Church had really penetrated the vernacular traditionalism that even today inspires common law.

In contrast, (1) a more precocious and powerful nation, Spain, (2) initiates an earlier and speedier colonization, (3) carried out by (diverse) Renaissance individuals, (4) who establish a centralized political structure on a nobiliary and agricultural basis, (5) and spawn a series of progressive and enlightened nations, often as despotic as they are insolvent, who (6) reproduce by cloning the mentality of the metropolis during the reign of Isabel II.[63] We will stick closely to this outline in the present chapter and the two to come.

*   *   *

The consolidation of a feudal structure of nobles, cities, and autonomous monasteries will make it possible in Europe "after the plague and the demographic crisis of 1348, for some Inca or Pharaoh to set up a State which will monopolize and unify the figure of the landowner, the tax collector and the moneylender" (Marvin Harris). By this point, the development of those dispersed powers had laid the foundations in Europe of a multicentric society, plural and open. But is this not precisely the opposite of the tried-and-true image of a political modernity constructed thanks to national unification (James I, Henry IV, the Catholic kings) in opposition to the dispersion of privileges and jurisdictions? Indeed; and from this point of view it is less the spirit of the national state than the spirit of feudal autonomy, equally allergic to bureaucratic and administrative unification, that will culminate in bourgeois civil society.[64] Only for the purpose of eliminating other intermediary structures – guilds and above all clerical influence – will this civil society ally itself with a national state destined, as we have been informed by conservatives and Marxists alike, "to dissolve the State as such." So England offers us a textbook case of the kind of modernity in which the strength of feudalism lasts long enough to form a direct link with economicism before consolidating an absolute national state like that of the Catholic kings.

As is well known, modern monarchy stands on two feet: commerce for its consolidation, and nationalism for its legitimation and projection – two forces equally opposed to medieval Christian universalism. But although the first tends to lead to competitive individualism, the second tries to replace and reincarnate that universalist vocation (whence its chronic expansionist tendency) within a given state.* And here Spain opts for rapid spiritual unification and national expansion in the guise of the reconquest, and England

---

* Only in France do both tendencies come together from the beginning, giving rise, even before the Revolution, to the nationalization of the economy (Colbert's mercantilism) and, later, to the universalization of nationalism (Bonaparte, the Enlightenment). But French mercantilism – hélas – soon shows signs of its scant colonizing efficacy when compared with countries ruled by one (England, the Netherlands) or another (Spain) of the less hybrid systems. And finally, there are other places where this expansion of civil and mercantile society will come neither before, during, or after consolidation of the state but instead will take its place (Venice, Genoa, Catalonia).

takes the slower path of translating the national order and the new economic interests into a form of government (democracy) not based on a universal idea (the Common Weal or the Nation, Natural Law or Reason) but intended to preserve and institutionalize a vernacular "spirit of fraction" that will find in Parliament a new form of compromise and equilibrium.

By this point, Anglo-Saxon empiricism and traditionalism appear clearly formulated in contrast with the more theoretical and speculative character of Continental thought. In England, the limits of royal power will not be set by "divine law" (Boniface VIII), or by the "natural order" sanctioned by the pope (Saint Thomas), or by the "individual liberty" that derives from that order (Spanish scholasticism), or by "reason" (Grotius and Pufendorf, Rousseau and Kant). Here the legislative function of the king, and even of Parliament, is seen to be limited by *common law*, vernacular customs that only the courts can interpret and bring up to date. Rather than appeal to a mythical Nature or Reason, it seeks the support of an *artificial reason* that has been undergoing sedimentation until it constitutes an effective control not only of the absolute sovereignty of the king and his prerogative (the *soluta legibus* or *dominium regale*) but also of the new concentration of powers in the "parliamentary dictatorship" that Montesquieu would later try, more or less artificially, to "deactivate."

True, the tendency to legitimate the new absolutism never stops rearing its head, from Sir James Bacon and Cromwell's traditional formulation (royal prerogative) to Locke's modern version (sovereignty of legislative power). But from the very beginning what prevailed was the spirit of the common law, defended by Sir Edward Coke in his *Institutes of the Bans of England* against the absolute powers and "national spirit" that James I (1561-1626) sought to incarnate in the name of the natural right of the Prince.* Both the Tudors in the sixteenth century (particularly Elizabeth of England) and the Stuarts in the seventeenth will try to consolidate the absolute monarchy against both nationalist and religious dissidence (Scottish Presbyterians, Irish Catholics, English Puritans) and Parliament, where the alliance of the "dissolvent" interests of the aristocracy and the merchant bourgeoisie is acted out. In Spain, these last powers lose the battle definitively in 1521. And we have proof of the always precarious nature of their success in England, both in the religious alternation of the Tudors in the sixteenth century and the two or

---

* When James I argues that according to Natural Law, "the King protecteth the Law and not the Law the King... the one that maketh judges and bishops," Sir Edward Coke, in the name of Common Law, reponds thus: "That which has been refined and perfected by the wisest men in former succession of ages, and proved and approved by continual experience cannot but with great hazard and danger be altered and changed."

three revolutions that take place throughout the seventeenth century (1642, Cromwell's Puritans and Parliamentarians against Charles I; 1661, the restoration of Charles II against the Puritans; 1688, the alliance of Parliamentarians – Whigs – with William of Orange against James II's Catholicism).

From this mishmash of dynastic, national, and religious confrontations, at the very least two clear notions emerge. First, that Protestantism was as much a focus of diverse sects that spurred on popular revolt as it was a national religion (in contrast, Catholicism intervenes only in dynastic disputes). Second, and surely more significantly, that Parliament links feudal and commercial interests – the nobles and the dissidents – against the Crown, vindicating traditional liberties *(habeas corpus,* 1670) and never, even in its weakest moments, loosening the monarchic pursestrings.

The landowner, the tax collector, and the moneylender continue then to be distinct characters: the absolute Monarch does not exist. Private feudal and commercial interests thus ally to "bridge" the Crown: *English Civil Society takes the jump on the State. And toward America.*

The case of Spain, as we have seen, is practically the opposite. As J. A. Maravall has written, "The Spanish Monarchy, whose evolution had begun so early, gets bogged down in antiquated forms." That is also Ortega's diagnosis, which I shall quote at length.

Spain had the honor to be the first nationality capable of being one, concentrating in her kings' fist all her energies and abilities. This should suffice to make her immediate expansion understandable.... While feudal pluralism keeps France, England and Germany's power diffuse, Spain is becoming a compact, elastic body.... But, though unity had the effect of an injection of artificial plenitude, it was not a symptom of vital power. On the contrary: unity came quickly because Spain was weak, because she lacked a strong feudalism sustained by great personalities in the feudal mold.... It would be useful, therefore, to invert the usual valorization. The lack of feudalism, which was considered healthy, was a misfortune for Spain; and early national unity, which seemed to be a sign of glory, was really the consequence of the earlier weakness.

According to Angel Ganivet, from whom Ortega takes his inspiration, the traces of both this feudal weakness and this ideological power must be sought in the invasion of the Visigoths, who, "incapable of governing a more cultured people, resigned themselves to preserving the appearance of power... thereby involuntarily creating the means for the Church to seize control of the principal devices of politics, founding at this point the religious State that still persists in our land."

In England, as we have seen, local protectionist laws are progressively being eliminated so that the forces of feudal localism will be able to compete effectively in an ever freer market. In France this slow commercial recapacitation and democratic channeling of the conflict is blocked by mercantilistic controls, and in Spain by rapid political neutralization. The façade of political unity and the corset of spiritual unity inhibit and repress the living forces that ought to have given strength and content to the whole: the Jews expelled by the Catholic kings (1492); the cities and the comuneros (the Whigs of Spain) defeated by Charles V at Villalar (1521); the dissident Moors judged by Philip II (1559); and the Portuguese and the Catalonians in confrontation with Philip IV (1640).

The speed and efficiency with which the Catholic kings eliminate all those particularities and the "historic advantage" that Spain thereby acquires shape even today the notion, and the illusion, of Spanish nationalism. In twenty-five years, nobles are converted into administrators, members of the court into bureaucrats, adventurers into soldiers, and religious dissidents into converts or exiles. In Alcalá, the apprentices to the guilds will soon be transformed into university students (Cisneros) and the peninsular lingua franca will become "standard" Spanish (Nebrija).

But while the Counter-Reformation is preparing the cultural flowering of Spain's literary golden age, the political defeat of the comuneros or the Catalans signals an administrative unification that will inhibit the development of the very thing it was to administer. A sophisticated bureaucracy of chancellories, tribunals, and municipalities will overwhelm the economic and commercial spontaneity of the cities while reinforcing the local laws and discriminations that block the formation of a free market.

The *Siete Partidas* of 1256 and the Laws of Toro of 1505 mark the progressive domination in Spain of Civil Law over the Gothic-medieval tradition of local laws and privileges, the precocious passage from feudalism to national sovereignty. Under the Catholic kings, legal centralism acquires a renewed strength and prestige, which later will weigh heavily upon the development of peninsular society. For just a few years, almost miraculously, a man like Cortés manages to see his willfulness and individual initiative urged on by national and administrative growth, instead of being crushed. The very same individualistic and enterprising spirit was being defeated in Spain (Villalar, 1521) just when it was achieving its greatest American victory with the taking of Tenochtitlán. As Marx observed: "The ancient liberties were at least buried in a sumptuous tomb: those were the days in which Vasco Núñez de Balboa, Cortés and Pizarro were planting the flag of Castile on the coasts of Darién, in Mexico and in Peru; when the meridional imagination of the Iberians was blinded by the vision of Eldorado...."

But soon the Castilian centralizing spirit will also reach America, both to protect the Indians and to establish a labyrinth of positions that "paper over" all inititative and generate an intricate system of public servants, their watchdogs, bribery, sales of titles, corruption.

*   *   *

The premature growth and maturity of the State – be it of the welfare or the warfare variety – always has a price tag in the end. We saw it in the case of the Greeks (pp. 30-31), and Charlemagne's empire experienced it as well, for as Díez del Corral puts it, "it frittered away Napoleon's genius one millenium early" by organizing the form of the empire without its economic, juridical, and technical underpinnings. The same thing happens when Spain insists on projecting spatially (Charles V) or on interiorizing spiritually (Philip II) this superstructure or state shell designed by Ferdinand and Isabel (see note 50). Here too, as Paz says, we "had a State and a Church before we had a nation." From Pavia to Mühlberg, Charles V throws himself into a costly policy of European expansion and prestige. From Lepanto (1571) to the invincible Armada (a veritable symbol: in 1588 political imperialism succumbs for the first time to incipient economic imperialism, though it is more for climactic than "dialectical" reasons), Philip II is bent in turn on consolidating the "Spanishness" – the union of bloodline and conviction – of the country through the Inquisition: "I would sooner lose my kingdoms," he announces, "than be the lord of heretics." Thus they concentrate on unifying land and souls instead of unifying the market to bring about competition and the emulation of technical, commercial, and financial skills. Instead, these very skills become suspect and the work ethic is inhibited by the warrior ethic of the hidalgo – soon denatured into the conservative ethic of the officer or bureaucrat. And so the country organizes itself around that essentialist nationalism whose two variants are prefigured by Charles V and Philip II: *"antes roja* (read: Protestant) *que rota"* ("better red than divided") is the slogan when Charles V tries to contain the Protestants at Trent to assure the unity of the empire; or *"antes rota que roja"* ("better divided than red") will apply in keeping with the above lordly quote from Philip II. As Lord Keynes used to say, set ideas are even stronger than vested interests.

The taxes and levies required to sustain this ideological policy in Europe and America soon translate into the impoverishment and demographic crisis of the country. Lacking a commercial infrastructure and an economic policy that would allow Spain to use America's gold for its internal development, the flow of wealth turns into inflation or currency for manufactured goods and mercenaries. "No sooner was the nation established," writes Ganivet, "than our spirit overflowed its course, spilling over onto the entire world in search of external and vain glory, leaving the nation behind like a reserve barracks, a hospital for the wounded, a breeding ground for beggars." Still convinced that there is strength in bulk, in breadth of territory, the Spanish adopt "the system generally used by bankrupt nobles – never a thought to reducing expenses so as not to reveal what cannot be denied: that the house is crumbling. High interest loans; stupid displays of power in order to inspire confidence; marriages made in search of a providential dowry...." Everyone is on the road to the bankruptcy that will soon leave Spain in the hands of the "Swiss bankers" (the Fuggers, Welsers, and Shatzes) and of European business. "Why should you go to America?" Gracián will ask the Europeans. *"Can't you see that the Spanish are your Indians?"*

Soon, however, it becomes clear that not everyone in Spain wants to go on being "Europe's Indians." Neither the Portuguese nor the Catalans seem to be interested any longer in this Spanish enterprise that has neither taken root in nor brought benefits to their countries. Weary of the wait for a convening of the Cortes that never seems to come, the Catalans – the model, some say, for Calderón's *The Mayor of Zalamea* – stage an uprising in 1640 against a tax levied to pay the bills of an overdrawn empire and against the presence of troops and civil servants born outside of Catalonia. As is clear, "political and spiritual" unity has left its mark but has not really permeated the country at large.[65]

We have said that the modern nation-state needs *nationalism* for its legitimation and expansion, *commerce* for its consolidation, and *municipal liberties* for its democratic evolution. The early Spanish state tried to ground itself on only one of these principles, and by 1640 it was an extensive and ecstatic entity. Portugal's independence and the 1659 Treaty of the Pyrenees provisionally break, until the War of Succession, the peninsular mold. Karl Marx writes:

> How can we explain the fact that centralization has never taken root in the very country where absolute monarchy developed in its clearest form before any of the other feudal States? The answer is not difficult.... In the other great States of 16th century Europe, absolute monarchy emerges as the initiator of social unity. There, absolute monarchy was the laboratory where the different elements of society blended and associated until cities were able to exchange the local independence and sovereignty of medieval times for the general control of the middle classes and the common preponderance of civil society. In Spain, on the contrary, while the aristocracy sank into decadence without losing its most harmful privileges, cities lost their medieval power without gaining in modern importance.

...And this is how the State takes the jump on Civil Society in Spain. Toward America, it is true, but also toward the interior of the peninsula itself.

* * *

Meanwhile, England lacks the unity and coherence needed for an authentic colonial enerprise. The country is still split, as Hegel writes, "between Puritans, Episcopalians, Catholics and Quakers, all divided among themselves, taking power now one group, now another, with many emigrating in search of religious freedom." The dissidents escape from a country not yet "nationalized" and confront in turn the "barbarians" on the other side: nomadic hunting tribes still living in a subsistence economy. The lack of unity both at their source and at their destination assures them of freedom and independence when the time comes to seek salvation and personal happiness where the rules no longer apply. In Spain, on the contrary, these minorities will not be escaping to America because the state has already seen to expelling its heretics by unifying the country politically and religiously, as it will now see to organizing overseas expeditions through the *Casa de Contratación*. Commentators have insistently contrasted the private, spontaneous, popular, and even medieval style of Spanish colonization with the English, "carried out by the reflex action of powerful minorities... whether in consortiums, or by the secession of a select group that seeks lands from which better to serve God" (Ortega). And it is certainly true that in the eighteenth century, when the English and Dutch go to America, the impact on Europe of the scientific, religious and commercial revolution is quite evident, while the Castilians embark in the sixteenth century without that modern baggage. As it is also clear that the Castilian colonization – "the refuge of the hopeless of Spain" (Cervantes) – is not headed up by individuals like Raleigh or Penn but by poor, almost illiterate people with no commercial or patrimonial experience. Politically, however, the Spanish colonization is much more modern, because it transplants the new systematic, juridical, and bureaucratic national spirit, with which it builds in America a solid edifice of monuments and institutions. Linking that people and this state: nothing. Hence the contrast between the feudal, religious, and commercial *individualism* exported by the English and the ambitious Renaissance *individuals* who undertake the Spanish colonization, impelled by the spirit of independence described by Ganivet and armed with the political and strategic devices of a State. Modern and grandiose, to be sure, but also dangerous.

Cortés's *avant la lettre* Machiavellianism allows for the occupation in just a few years of an empire for which the peninsular administrative model sets up a rigid structure of *Virreinatos, Audiencias, Visitadores, Corregimientos, Cabildos,* and *Ciudades* (Vice-royalties, Courts of Law, Inspectors, Magistratures, Town Councils and Cities), while his men are being counter-conquered by the countries they are occupying, impregnated by the cultures they destroy, and seduced by the women they rape. We will find none of this in the colonization to the north: the national model or the individual strategy, the stimulation for a territorial occupation or the imprint of an indigenous cultural model (it has rightly been said that the abyss between the Aztecs or Mayas and the Massachusets or Hurons is greater than that which separated the Rome of the Caesars from the barbarous peoples of Europe).[66] In the North they limit themselves to projecting their ideals onto the American "void," to exploiting its resources and establishing their "society colonies" relatively independent from a metropolis distracted by its civil wars (they consider themselves the vassals of the king, who had conceded them their charters but not of the English nation or of its Parliament). They do not have a Crown of Spain behind them or an Aztec or Inca Empire ahead of them. What they do have (for it is now 1620 and not 1492), is a commercial and liberal drive that makes them more prone to establishing and consolidating coastal colonies than to taking up territorial conquest beyond the Allegheny Mountains.

So it is not their culture and modernity but precisely the lack of them – both of their *ad quem* and *a quo* terms – that will save the English and Dutch the trouble of facing the theoretical and practical problems, the issues of hermeneutics and racial mixture, which Spanish Americans had to face and which still have not been resolved. *What arises, in contrast to the figurative portrait painted by the Spanish with their modern political "style" and in response to a clear-cut indigenous "model," is the free Anglo-Saxon expansion and expression of a millenarian imagination that faces no conflict with an alternative local "model."*

Finally, let us compare the liberty of the English dissidents who escape to America in the seventeenth century with the meticulousness with which the Casa de Contratación organizes the expeditions and "filters" its emigrants from 1503 on (see note 21). Compare the concrete aspirations to happiness, liberty, and well-being of the Pilgrims with the ideals of imperial aggrandizement, personal fortune, and universal evangelization of the conquistadors. Compare the rudimentary colonies of Massachusetts, Providence, or Newport in 1650 with the Renaissance layout of Ibero-American cities – regular design and central square on an exact grid – from the time of Francisco de Garay in 1516.[67] Just compare these things, if you will, and think which colonization was in fact "popular, traditional, and spontaneous" and which "modern, cultured, and deliberate."

16

Gaseous Democracy and the Paradoxes of Precociousness

From there on in, and thanks to a kind of "spiritual astuteness," the tables begin to turn: a *virtuous circle* seems to link modernity with the pious and popular traditionalism of the pioneers, while a parallel *vicious circle* keeps Spain's precocious modernity from becoming contemporary.

The United States is the product of a conservative revolution (1776) that fought more to preserve its liberties than to conquer Liberty. The community envisions and organizes itself as a "reservation" that protects its autonomy and its local laws from all higher authorities. Community virtues – rational organization and salvation through labor – shall not be overridden by any power beyond the social contract itself. Both state growth and international dependency endanger this autarkic ideal that runs the gamut from Aristotle to Monroe, including the medieval-privilege (i.e., private-law) mentality. Jefferson seems to sense that only limited size and relative isolation will allow for the maintenance of the members' freedoms; hence his allergic reaction to any growth or larger frame of reference, metropolitan or American, that might lead to the solidification of the "gaseous" state of the small free community and its particular interests. From the very beginning in 1773 – the uprising of Virginia in defense of the tobacco salaries of the clergymen, the Boston tea party against the stamp and customs taxes – the defense of freedom in the United States has always been linked to particular and corporate interests: lobbies and mafias, caucuses and single issues. In 1830 de Tocqueville was already amazed at this domination of the spirit of Association over that of Mission, of Particular Interests over the ideal of the Common Good, whose paradoxical core was formulated by Huizinga in 1921:

> America was born and survived thanks to its stubborn, archaic town hall individualism – we could almost call it medieval individualism. And the fact that a continent could be conquered on these principles, when the imperialist politics of the French crown failed in the same enterprise even though its vision of the geographical possibilities of the country was broader and its

plans more vigorous and uniform than those of the English colonizers, continues to be one of the most surprising phenomena of modern history.

Indeed, a "virtuous circle" seems to unite the conservative, shortsighted individualism of the English settler with the economic expansion and political consolidation of the country. As Emerson wrote in 1844, "Feudalism has not yet come to an end. Our government is still drenched in it. Business makes even government seem insignificant." From the time of Madison and Hamilton, Jefferson's individual rights and religious freedom begin their mutation into property rights and freedom of trade. But not until the mid-nineteenth century will two great mutations – nationalism and technical development – finally transform the individualism of the Pilgrims or the Founding Fathers into the empire of big business.

In 1870 barbed wire puts an end to Hollywood's "Wild" West just as McCormick's reaper and refrigeration are favoring the concentration of property and the development of the meat-packing industry in Chicago. Howe's sewing machine initiates the transformation of this convivial household activity into industrial enterprise. The train and the telegraph foster the formation of great companies (Western Union, Missouri Pacific, and others) that subordinate the colonization of the West to capital interests from the very start. The telegraph, in turn, favors the concentration of decision centers and grand speculation. Toward 1880 the medieval society of the Pilgrims has spawned its new feudal lords – the Rockefellers, the Morgans, the Carnegies – against whom successive antitrust laws will be powerless. The process will culminate in the consolidations that unite iron, steel, mining, and transportation interests; soon oil will join them as well.[68] The only thing left is for Lincoln to unify the labor market, give a political content to the Constitution, and discover the nation's "manifest destiny." This is how the original religious freedom, transformed by the Constitution into census suffrage (you can vote only if you own land and pay taxes), is finally channeled into freedom of enterprise. For Jefferson, the business of America was freedom and happiness. For Coolidge, "the business of the United States is business." The national spirit in the United States is not born, as it was in Spain, before but after and from the starting point of that transformation of medieval piety into the cult of capital. A cult that in only a few years will turn the United States into the richest country on earth. From the end of the nineteenth century on, this fact will invert the order of events: the United States will cease to be an outcome of Europe as Europe begins its transformation into an outcome of the United States. Who, nowadays, is the epigone or the epiphenomenon of whom?

Something similar can be observed not only in the economic but also in the political and ideological transformation of the United States. Here too, local traditionalism and private interests supersede modern universal ideals. True, the ideas of Justice, Reason, and the Enlightenment resound in the Declaration of Independence. But they make their appearance only as a means – insufficient, at that – to achieving personal salvation or collective welfare. Rousseau and Montesquieu wanted to replace the old medieval values, individualistic and local, with the new republican virtue, moral and universal. Ethics and patriotism were to supplant honor and self-interest in the souls of the new men. The Founding Fathers are much less idealistic. "Reason, Justice and Equity," said John Adams, "are never sufficient reason..., only interest is, and only in it can we confide."

Private and diverging interests cannot then be glossed over with vague appeals to the Nation or to Equity. "The conclusion we must reach," asserts Madison, "is that the cause of factional spirit cannot be suppressed and that evil can only by avoided by keeping its effects at bay." For R. Herr,

> Madison here opposes virtue and patriotism as a political foundation for reasons we would now call materialistic. He warns, before Marx, that men are controlled by economic interests and that society is driven by this struggle between interests. The best government is the one that prevents the domination of one interest or party over the rest. Madison believed that the suppression of class conflict would never be possible. Marx, on the other hand, believed that after the proletarian revolution class division would disappear and all of society would obey a new morality or virtue similar to the one advocated by Rousseau.

In contrast with Marx's "scientific" materialism, the version espoused by Madison and the American Founding Fathers seems to incarnate a "vernacular" materialism that, far from believing in a Jacobinic happy ending, expresses civil society's ancestral reticence toward and resistance to the power of the State.

*   *   *

Spain offers no parallel to all this. In contrast with the conservative U. S. Constitution, which appears as the very evolution of feudalism, the Constitution of Cádiz is the prototype of a "virtuous" constitution that does not think twice about prescribing to the Spanish that they "practice love of homeland... and be just and virtuous" (Art. 6). It is from the standpoint of this pious modernity that a series of constitutions is set down, the latest always improving upon the one before it, all of them always better than they had to be. The common law tradition in the United States (something we are familiar with in Spain only as moral or theological casuism) allows for the survival, with successive amendments, of one same constitution.[69] Here the "model" of the Courts of Cádiz has, since 1918, led us through nine constitutional reforms.[70]

We have already seen the economic consequences for Spain and its colonies of having followed a course that precisely inverted the North American process: early national and administrative consolidation (four centuries separate Lincoln from the Catholic kings) before technical and commercial modernization. A paradigmatic example of this supremacy of the administrative sphere over the technical is the legislation that until the eighteenth century limits shipping tonnage so that ships may anchor in the ports of Seville and Veracruz. Rather than technically enlarge the port (or substitute Cádiz or San Juan de Ulúa), the monopoly of the former ports is legally secured, even at the cost of increasing the risks of the Atlantic crossing, and boycotting the idealistic project of making the Tagus River navigable.

In the absence of actual political modernization, America's wealth will allow Spain to go on selling principles and importing technology from Europe. The portrait Madariaga paints of a seventeenth-century royal armada unable to take to the sea until canvas and tar arrive from Holland is very expressive of the situation at hand in what Calderón once called "the Spanish ocean."

Of course, as has so often been said, the new, enlightened commercial sensibility reaches Spain and makes its way to America under Charles III. But it is precisely here that we witness *the danger involved when the state carries out the technical and ideological revolution instead of having the revolution build the state; or the danger of the new enlightened state's coming along to reinforce the centralist structures of the old patrimonial state instead of breaking them down.*[71] In contrast with the English colonies, where we saw the new commercial spirit filter into the traditional structures and crystallize, here nothing filters in; everything takes place by decree.

So, in Spain, even the joining of the new economic order must be mandated by state decree. The 1778 decrees of free trade and commerce translate, according to J. M. Delgado, into "an increase of fiscal pressure upon trans-Atlantic traffic and a liberalization of the importation of linen and cotton fabric from abroad, discouraging the investment of commercial capital in American manufacturing;... a system that bankrupted Spanish dockworkers, unable to compete with the underground trade, and overtaxed Spanish American merchants and consumers." Again by decree, the encomiendas must now be replaced along the lines of the great Basque and Catalonian companies, in turn modeled upon the Anglo-Saxon system of factories and plantations (one-crop farming with indentured labor intended to put a damper on the independentist yearnings of the criollos). The state would rent out large holdings to the companies, which would work them by monopoly of both human and physical resources (land and mines, Indians and Blacks). This placed them in conflict with both the *new* rights of the criollos and the *old* privileges of the Indian communities that, protected up to that time by the Laws of the Indies, had managed to survive and coexist until the eighteenth century. According to Paz, they had survived

> along with other forms of property thanks to the nature of the world founded by the Spanish, a universal order that admitted of diverse conceptions of property, while sheltering a plurality of races, castes and classes.... The reforms undertaken by the Bourbon dynasty, Charles III in particular, clean up the economy and make the doing of business more efficient, but they reinforce administrative centralism and convert New Spain into a real colony, that is, a territory subject to systematic exploitation and held in close check by the centralist powers.... The Bourbons transform New Spain, a vassal kingdom, into a mere overseas territory.

As we saw in chapter 3, they now try to pervert the communal system of hamlets and resguardos, which offered the native peoples an alternative to wage earning or to the new hereditary indentured servitude. Thus, conditions are created for a more efficient exploitation of the Indians by the criollo oligarchy, which manages in only a few years to seize control of those fertile and well-irrigated lands, 70 percent of which had remained in native hands until the eighteenth century.

I think that what we have said so far is sufficient to show the disfunctioning that results from this process in which political power decides, directs, and controls modernization, the formation of capital, and social transformation. There are several reasons for this. In the first place, because it causes a traumatic rupture with the process and the defense mechanisms generated by the previous system. This rupture does not occur when, as is the case in the United States, the normal road to change in the economic infrastructure slowly transforms the political superstructure and secretes a new political order. In the second place, because, though it reinforces the economic power of the bourgeoisie, it does not concede to the bourgeoisie the corresponding political power. In fact, it is this dichotomy and lack of circulation between the two powers (the political power of the Spanish civil servants, the economical power of the Spanish American noblemen who descended from the encomenderos) that, as in the Rome of Marcus Tullius, is at the core of the revolt of the criollo aristocracy against the Spanish bureaucracy. In the third place, because even those who reject Spanish power and found new nations find in this new system a model for independence that will soon degenerate into political despotism and economic dependency.

The first two points have been useful to explain the differing results in the processes of North American and Latin American emancipation. The last will now serve as our guide in understanding the contrast between the union that results from independence in the North and the fragmentation that results in Latin America.

17

Emancipation and Fragmentation
of Latin America

...to build a Greek building on a Gothic
foundation on the edge of a crater.
—Letter from Bolívar to Santander

"The groups and classes that brought about independence in South America," writes Octavio Paz, "belonged to the native feudal aristocracy; they were the descendants of Spanish settlers, who found themselves in a situation of inferiority vis-à-vis the new peninsular arrivals. The metropolis, bent on carrying out its protectionist policy, on the one hand hindered free trade in the colonies and obstructed their economical development; on the other, it kept out those criollos who in all justice wished to occupy high posts and take part in the direction of the State." In the end, it is these criollos who "break with Spain, but are incapable of creating a modern society." Why? Here, Paz's argument becomes a bit more specious. "It could not be otherwise," he adds, "for the groups that led the Independence movement did not constitute new social forces, but the prolongation of the feudal system.... Some went so far as to 'make off with the kingdoms': as if they were dealing with medieval booty. The image of the 'Latin American dictator' appears in embryonic form in the 'liberator.' "

The description is precise; I'm not so sure about the interpretation. Certainly, the figure and role of the dictator appear *in nuce* in the caudillos of the independence. However, this is not a medieval figure but quite the opposite: it is modern and idealistic in the sense that Hegelian philosophy will give the term, the result of the superimposition of Enlightenment ideals upon a social structure that, like the Spanish or German models, has evolved very little since the fifteenth century.* Bolívar and San Martín, Rodríguez de

---

* I have tried to show (in *De la Modernidad,* pp. 175-82) how only idealistic "mediation" allows the humanistic idelogy of the Enlightenment to turn into the model or *engineering* of the modern world. During the Middle Ages, Theory fled from reality and constructed an ideal world apart. It was now coming back to this

Francia and Francisco de Paula Santander represent *an sich,* more purely than Napoleon, that stage in the evolution of the Spirit that, according to Hegel, always precedes its theoretical formulation. Bolívar is Hegelian before Hegel in the same way that Cortés had been Machiavellian without having to read Machiavelli. This distinguishes them as greatly from the provincial spirit of the North American Founding Fathers as it does from the "Guadalupismo" of Hidalgo or Morelos, who, as Paz himself points out, "never showed the aspiration to universality that is at once Bolívar's greatness and his blind spot." This is how Spain spawns a series of nations as progressive as they are impotent, reproducing Latin American clones of Spain's own dilemma. We saw that a strange *List der Vernunft* seems to connect the local sensibility of the Pilgrims with the American federation and union. Well, it is this same *List,* but in reverse, that leads Enlightenment nationalism and centralism inexorably into Latin American fragmentation. Traditionalism and commercial spirit in the North try, in the words of Hamilton, to reap the rewards of the history of England without having to repeat it;[72] the caudillo spirit in the South repeats the history of Spain without reaping any of its rewards. Thus, just as the North American union is being consolidated, Latin America is undergoing definitive fragmentation (Mexico, 1836; Ecuador, 1841; Chile, 1844; Venezuela, 1845).

In just a few years, the four Spanish viceroyalties (just one of which covered all of South America until 1779) are transformed, but not into the three great nations proposed by the Count of Aranda. Nor into the confederation of provinces, assemblies, or nations that could easily have emerged from the extension of citizenship by the Courts of Cádiz, the insurrection against Bayonne, or Bolívar's proposals. Instead, eighteen "free and sovereign" nations rise up, fruit of the conflicts that in Spain are the result of Bourbon modernization grafted onto an already bureaucratic but still patrimonial structure.

The emancipation of America is above all a civil war between Spaniards. The issues and alternatives at stake are the very ones that are tearing apart the metropolis. There are many "Americans" – particularly Blacks and Indians – on the loyalist side, just as there are many Spanish liberals and free trade advocates who support the insurrection. The very temperament of the insurgent caudillos seems to reproduce the diverse stages through which the Spanish "spirit" has passed: Bolívar's quixotic and conquistador spirit (which, as he confesses to Gual in Tegucigalpa, aspires to completing the insurrection with the liberation of the Philippines or the reconquest of Spain); San Martín's spirit of independence (he, who goes back to America to

---

world, no longer to illuminate it but to define and represent it as Nature, Reason or State – that is, to endow it with universality.

"consummate" his participation in the Spanish war against Napoleon); the free trade passion of Artigas. There are very few Indianist, fringe, or "single-issue" groups – Mexico aside – among the personalities who head up the emancipation. Or among the places in which it is cooked up: the patriotic councils *(juntas)* and the municipal cabildos – about which we will have more to say on the next few pages.

The *juntas* that protest the "Bienamado" (well beloved and even better depicted by Goya) defend – in keeping with Suárez's *pactum translationis* – a Spanish sovereignty that neither Iturbide nor San Martín question. Only the singular shortsightedness of Ferdinand VII could have wasted the opportunity to use this new integrating principle from 1814 to 1864, the years of Spanish recovery in America. Adding mercantilist orthodoxy to the old centralist and patrimonial tradition, Ferdinand VII does not extend the right to trade to the new juntas. On the contrary, he vindicates the most worn-out rights of the Crown, among them, the "presentation of bishops." In this way, the pro-Spanish sentiment of the first juntas is soon traded in for criollo nationalism honed in confrontation with the Crown delegates or officials installed to permeate and control life in America. Among these, we find the officers of the regular militia created by Charles III, the Catalan merchants of the companies (who want not only to "unload" their products but also to control distribution and sale), the new Sevillian civil servants and Castilian bureaucrats, and so on.

The municipal cabildos, the other great focus of the emancipation, arise in turn from the modern urban structure that, as we saw, characterized Spanish colonization. To gain control of the viceroyalties or tribunals in the hands of the *gachupines* (derogatory terms for Spaniards in Mexico, referring to their sunburned cheeks), the criollos do not forge alliances in the countryside (Mexico, once again, is the exception) but instead seek control of the cabildos or municipal assemblies, from which they try to make life difficult for the servants of the Crown. The rural world is evoked in speeches and invoked in proclamations, but never or hardly ever convoked to the assemblies. Once more it is the very superstructural modernity of the Spanish system – now municipal – that interferes with a coherent and homogeneous modernization. A Renaissance marvel of laws and urban planning is superimposed emblematically upon a rural and traditional hinterland,[73] prefiguring the "parallel economy" (Cardoso and Furtado) characteristic of underdevelopment.[74] All of which only worsens with the shift from a Renaissance city-state structure to the Baroque state-city: a city of landowners, prelates, and civil servants, in which, as the saying goes, "Everything that is not palace is poverty" *[todo es miseria lo que no es palacio]*. (In contrast with the comfort and elegance of the country homes of Virginia or Carolina, here the poverty of the towns and haciendas is juxtaposed with the spectacular magnificence of the churches and official buildings: Tepoztlán, Santa Rosa de Querétaro and Santa Prisca in Taxco, the Academia de San Carlos, the Casa de la Moneda.)

Along these lines, the emancipation inspired by the cabildos can be understood, to use the words of J. A. Maravall, as a revolt of the Renaissance city, "which had lost its free municipal initiative and been converted into an administrative nucleus incorporated into and governed by the State." But the citizenry that is now rising up is also the product of this now-baroque city. On the one hand, untenured civil servants and criollos economically ruined by Bourbon mercantilism will see in the Jacobinic ideas a means to transsubstantiate their resentment into nationalism. On the other hand, rich absentee landlords and the landed urban aristocracy, more accustomed to living off the fat of the land than off industrial productivity, will be confronting an innovative, rationalistic government in Madrid.[75] The nationalists of the *juntas* and the civil servants and *rentiers* of the *cabildos:* their union, catalyzed by Enlightenment ideas, the Revolution, and the Napoleonism of their caudillos, could not help but favor the purest of idealisms and the most perfect of political fragmentations.... As a result, just as pragmatic traditionalism is forging North American unity, ideological modernism begins to fragment the Latin American continent: a *real* atomization of Latin America is the result of nothing more and nothing less than the multiplication of the *ideals* of national or continental unity.

For these magnificent imported nationalisms, the fluid American reality – which in good Hegelian fashion is to be "elevated to the level of concept" – is not quite enough. Which means, as we have seen, repeating the history of Europe instead of reaping its rewards: transplanting and reconstructing in America – just like Eiffel's "iron house" erected in mid-Peruvian jungle – Spanish or French political ideals. In the space of a generation a national *unity* more intense and cohesive than that of North America is to be established by decree ("It would be better to adopt the Koran than the government of the United States," as Angostura's speech goes). And also more extensive and ambitious: a confederation of Latin American states that, following Philip of Macedonia's model, would have its Corinth in Panamá. The result of all this passion for unity is, naturally, the chaos so succinctly described by J. H. Parry: "The liberators and their successors killed and expelled one another with the same ease with which they had fought the viceroys.... In the 1820-1830 decade almost all the countries of Spanish America were already destroyed by civil wars among rival caudillos. In some, the only possible result was their partition; in others, dictatorship. Spanish America was finally free."

But this multiplication of nations is even further replicated by the fracture within each of them between the real country and the official one: between the system of habits and beliefs of the people and the system of concepts and ideals of their leaders. The progressive nationalism of the urban politicians confronts the conservative and religious particularism of the peasants and natives. Traditional religious intolerance now evolves into the doctrinaire intransigence with which "positivists" or "liberals" brutally repress the revolts of *religioneros y cristeros* in Mexico (1873-1875, 1926-1929) or that of *os sertões* in Brazil (1885-1897) – this last so brilliantly recreated and reinterpreted by Mario Vargas Llosa in *The War of the End of the World*. The complicated bureaucratic procedures established by the Crown to control distant subjects become the liturgical objects of the new politicians and administrators. One need only set foot in a Colombian or Mexican office nowadays to see how the cult of the official seal and the fetishism of the quintuplicate persists. A cult that the people can only reappropriate, either by taking its formalism to the extreme of creating a new baroque filigree around the official seal, or by perverting and personalizing it through the *"mordida,"* the bribe.

But still, *something* had to hold together those creations decreed before they were constructed, just as *something* had to assure the connection between a too-enlightened politics and a too-illiterate population. *Militarism* and *caciquism*, endemic from that time on in Latin America, are the "something" that was to bridge the gap between words and things, between institutions and populations: the capillaries that in one way or another (and charging no mean fee) connect the proclaimed order with the social, economic, ethnic, and geographical reality of the country. This is how the landowner becomes the Governor, and the local boss, the Mayor. To control the country, the new formal power, concentrated in the capital, depends on the accords it can reach with the local influence brokers, who demand and now receive the official recognition that the Crown had started out by limiting and then completely eliminated by the late sixteenth century (Parry). In much the same way that the lands disentailed by the decrees of *desamortización* now go on to swell the patrimony of the wealthy, these suddenly emancipated countries also go on to depend upon these local tyrants "of all races and colors" whom Bolívar already warns of when he refuses the presidency of Great Colombia.[76] Whence Parry's theory that the emancipation recreates a situation much like the first years of the conquest, before the Crown had managed to prevent the conquistadores' setting themselves up as permanent governors.[77]

But those conquistadores went on to become soldiers, and then, when Charles III formed a permanent army and militia of the Indies, they were further transformed into a professional *military*. The military became all the more necessary and powerful in these new "nations without nationalists" (Bryce Echenique), where soon they will turn out to be the only real unifying factor, militarizing the state and initiating the tried-and-true coup d'état tradition.[78] The "speculative" nations constituted by the enlightened politicians and caudillos are in fact territorial expanses that only an army or an outstanding military officer could even begin to control and pull together. Soon the 1910 proclamation by General Obregón will not be an isolated incident:

> "By these pistols of mine, I proclaim myself candidate for the Presidency...,
> without prior offering of a platform: let him who wants me follow me."

The charisma of the new colonels and generals is further reinforced by the symbolic value that the army itself acquires in a world in which the signs of monarchical power have been lost. "The power of obedience to a personal monarch had disappeared," Parry concludes, "but the idea of loyalty to an impersonal and abstract republic... was slow in taking root. The army thus became the nucleus of real authority. It came to be considered (or it considered itself to be) the guardian of national interest and integrity, both in government and in defense...." The military acts as the alternative to the monarchy, just as the Spanish monarchy has, since 1975, acted as the alternative to the military (later we shall see the lesson that can be derived from this). Such a military establishment, however, will seem from that time on to be destined for command in these countries, because it constitutes the most coherent caste with the best technical preparation and greatest independence from the vagaries of politics and favoritism.

This is, in fact, how the caciques and the military class bridge the abyss between the real country and the country on paper when the modernization of the economy and the administration break with Habsburg colonial tradition (and in this sense it is more a case of what distinguishes the Consejo de Indias from the ministers of Charles III than of what differentiates the latter from the Rivadavias or Portales who emerged from the emancipation). This is not, of course, to deny that many of the flaws that have henceforth weighed upon the countries of Latin America originated in the distant colonial tradition. But their breadth and consolidation can be fully explained only by the doctrinaire rejection – first by the enlightenment, then by positivism or liberalism – of that tradition and its compensatory devices, whether ideological or legal, which had assured a relative tolerance, humanitarian concern, and anthropological sensibility in the colonial period.

The contrast established by Paz between the liberators or reformers of the nineteenth century and the evangelizers of the sixteenth is illustrative of this:

> The impotence of their intellectual agendas in the face of real events corroborates the fact that our reformers had neither the imagination nor the sense of reality of the 16th century missionaries. Impressed with the fervent religiosity of the Indians, the *padrecitos* sought and found points of contact

with Christianity in the pre-Columbian mythologies. By becoming Indianized, Christianity took root and bore fruit. Our reformers should have learned from this approach.

*   *   *

Three examples, each quite different from the other, will perhaps be useful in reinforcing this argument *sensu contrario*. Mexico, as we have seen, becomes a coherent nation and an original political system (plagued with favoritism but popular; not very democratic but not military either) precisely because it is not based on a modern revolution undertaken in the name of Liberty or Equality but, rather, on a traditional revolt headed by priests and manned by peasants: "One of the few genuinely popular outbreaks," says Octavio Paz, "inspired more by hunger for land and resentment of poverty and indentured servitude than by the desire for political independence." True, soon "positivist" or "scientific" caudillos will appear there as well, and, from Iturbide to Porfirio Díaz, they will do their best to "modernize" and usufruct the revolution. But it will be too late to redirect it along the lines of the modern enlightened model, first progressive and then uniformed. The result is "that open and basically amorphous organization – the Partido Revolucionario Institucional – led by a political bureaucracy born of the popular and middle classes [through which] Mexico has been able to escape for over half a century that circular fate which consists of swinging from anarchy to dictatorship and back."

Here the Enlightenment came late. At the other end of the continent, on the pampa, we can see what happens when it comes too early. Argentina offers us a bitter laboratory model of a pure Enlightenment colonization without the compensation of Spanish political tradition or Anglo-Saxon empiricism. On the one hand, *latifundism:* Starting in 1840, Manuel Rosas, the caudillo, repeals the Spanish laws (later known as "emphyteutic") that established the inalienable character of the public lands, thus hindering the formation of enormous landholdings. Rosas hands out concessions among his cronies and supporters, who create the great cattle-raising *estancias* or ranches – later converted for raising wheat or corn. This situation is not unlike that of the North American West in 1870 but, without the technical development or the commercial spirit of the latter, it will not make the changeover to great companies or financial trusts, clearing the way for overseas dependency: from the British companies to the European wars. On the other hand, *racism,* where the Argentines are certainly on a par with the Yankees. The Indians of southern Buenos Aires and of the pampa had been catechized but not really colonized under the Spanish. In the second half of the nineteenth century, under Rosas, Balcarce – the "hero of the desert" against the Pampas Indians – and the two pedagogue-presidents (Mitre and Sarmiento), these Indians will be efficiently and systematically colonized modern style, that is, persecuted and exterminated just as in the wilds of Arizona. Perhaps this is the source of that "immigrationist" spirit of the Argentinians, who have had to replace the indigenous mind they repressed with the analysis of their unconscious Oedipal mind. For, as the Mexican joke on Argentine bigotry goes, "Man descends from the apes, but Argentines descend from ships." Did Argentina's first quarrel not face off the "friends of France" and the "friends of England"? In any case, the single example of the situation of the pampa can give us an idea of what the Latin American cultures might have been like had colonization been undertaken with the mentality of some of the *Libertadores* .

Brazil, the third counterexample. It is well known that here independence is less traumatic and its consequences are less devastating. The heroes of the independence are not left wandering around in search of a "mission" and, in the area around São Paulo, single-crop latifundia are discontinued in favor of middle-range, mixed-crop *fazendas* or small manufacturers. E. Caballero's explanation may seem exaggerated, but it is the best *a contrario* illustration of what we have been saying:

> After the earthquake of the Independence, Spanish America fractures into numerous peoples. Brazil, in contrast, remains firm in its multifaceted unity. All because the Braganzas were able to lift anchor for Bahia while the *majos* of Madrid immobilized the carriage of Ferdinand VII, "el Deseado." Whence it becomes clear that the aspirations of the grand old men of July 20 in swearing obedience and submission to the Bourbons were not so wild, as long as they were willing to come and take their place in Cundinamarca. The consequence is that today Brazil constitutes a common market, while the nations of Spanish origin believe that they can reconquer lost time by making timid efforts toward partial integrations: the Andean Group, the Central American Common Market, Alale.

In our final chapter we will point out how and to what extent – now that Latin America is freeing itself of its political spectres but has not quite been able to cancel its debt or integrate its groups and social classes in a national project – the present-day Spanish monarchy could compensate today for the previous shortsightedness of those *majos*. In this chapter I have simply stressed the fact that what I called the deeply superficial modernity of Spanish power must assume the most direct responsibility for the fragmentation of this heritage forged between the caciques and the military. In contrast, the trans-Atlantic monarchy for the Brazilians, or the Church for Hidalgo or Morelos secure to a certain extent both their *liberation from dependence* and their *independence from liberators*. In the next chapter I will expand the discussion to show that paradoxical as it may seem, the basis of the profound union that in spite of it all continues to exist among the countries of Latin America is the classicism, vulnerability, and malleability of Spanish culture.

18

Present Imperfect

As is often said of the dinosaur, you can also perish from an *excess* of bulk. Nowadays we hear psychologists, economists, and biologists say it as well: an excess of productivity turns out to be counterproductive; premature growth often dulls the ability to adapt and develop; early comprehension inhibits experimentation.[79] We have seen it in this book as it related to the Greeks, to Charlemagne, and above all to the precocious political modernity of the Spanish: their early nationalism and imperialism turned out in the long run to be less efficient than the slower, more spontaneous, and traditional Anglo-Saxon colonization.

Now, from a cultural point of view, the situation is exactly the inverse and the shoe is on the other foot: success corresponds in this case to a more classical and traditional culture like the Spanish, which, by its very nature, is able to convert and be converted, to translate and be translated into the reality of an "other." Provincial and linear, Gothic culture is insensitive to anything prior to it or foreign to it, which it tends to relegate to "nature" (call it "the frontier") until it learns to consume it as folklore. The arrival of this culture to the most backward zone of America could not help but reinforce this tendency. More reticent and slippery, Spanish classical culture (and I shall soon justify the use of the word *classical)* is more permeable and integrationist.

Europe on the whole had advanced in the modernizing process traditionally associated with individualism, disenchantment of the world, secularization of relations, a clear distinction between subject and object or between facts and ideas, the conception of knowledge as control of reality and of morality as a personal affair, and the like. This process was literally "blessed" by Protestantism in the sixteenth century, and from that point on followed a linear progression: rationalism, the Enlightenment, transcendental idealism, historicism, Marxism, and so on – where each stage demythified the previous one by extracting its "rational nucleus" and leaving out its "mystical gangue" (Marx). As we saw, the United States, lacking an institutional past (church, crown, nobility, army) to defend traditional values, and with no strong autochthonous cultures like the Aztecs or the Incas to confront, can take this tendency all the way to its paroxysm. The weightlessness of what has gone *before* favors and has as its complement the inability to perceive what is *outside*. Puritan culture effectively "purifies" its surroundings until they become a mirror in which all it can see is itself.

In Spain this process of "modernization" is different. Disenchantment of the world does not occur in a linear way. Rather, it generates reticence and provokes resistance. The world of appearances does not let itself be easily reduced into its new abstract "truth": profit and predestination, pietism and pragmatism, instrumental reason and moral imperative, intellectual subject and *res extensa*. The external forms of Truth or Faith are never seen as inessential. This clearly generates a certain stiffness or "clumsiness" in their conduct. As Chandler says, "There is something mechanical about the Spanish, as if they were moved by an automatic principle." And there is a certain formalism in their thinking, never entirely absolved of sensible images or traditional categories. But it is this very same thing that permits them actually to assimilate other forms instead of "extracting their rational or spiritual nucleus." And this is how the Spanish friars come to translate and be translated into the new cultures. We saw in chapter 2 that what distinguishes Spanish from classical colonization is the seed of Christian universalism, and we shall now see how Spain's classical sensibility prevents it in turn from razing or ignoring the cultural forms in its path, as the purely interiorist colonization of the Protestants will do. A difficult and precarious balance.

The British and Dutch dissidents who flee their countries do not bring along an institutional culture. They come only with their ideal of freedom and a pious yearning for worldly salvation. In contrast, the Spanish do not come in flight but, like the Romans, bring along their laws, their institutions, and their monuments. In the very act of destroying the rites or institutions of the culture they are confronting, they cannot help but feel the need to "convert" it. In their tradition, external forms of worship are never dispensable, and a place must be found for them among one's own. The Franciscans will start out by respecting them, Jesuitic laxism will try to integrate them, and the hermeneuticists, from Durán and Sahagún on, will labor toward their translation. It is no exaggeration to say that the cultural relativism of these men of the sixteenth and seventeenth centuries has not even been surpassed by modern anthropology. Nor, in fact, could it have been, because the search for the single, profound "truth" of forms has replaced that classico-scholastic sense of, and interest in, formal analogies. The reduction of rites or myths to their functional (Malinowski), logical (Lévi-Strauss), or pragmatic (Harris) truth is much more ethnocentric and reductive than the actual "conversion" that the evangelists applied to them.

Sacrifice turns into sacrament, the cult to the corn goddess is converted and protected under the mantle of the Virgin, and fertility rites mutate into votive processions. The Spaniards understand and are impressed by that indigenous dignity, so close, if offended, to pure nihilism, as Father Gumilla relayed in amazement ("The men do not go near their women so as not to engender slaves," and so on.). Or even by the pathetic integrity with which, according to the accounts of Bartolomé Colón and Juan de Zuma, the natives of Veragua commit suicide rather than accept captivity: "When the Spaniards awoke the following morning, they saw the most horrifying sight. All the prisoners, men, women and children, had hanged themselves, using any rope they found at hand, and as the bridge was not high enough, some had had to hang themselves from a kneeling position."

Their empathy with the indigenous world doubtless had to do with the "imperfect" modernity of Spanish thought and disposition in which the split between an interior world (made sacred by the Protestants, then universalized by the Enlightenment) and a more and more disenchanted exterior world never quite caught on. When this split takes place, both moral and gnoseological categories abandon the figurative daily world to be shut away in the world of pure "concepts" and "intentions." Spontaneity and efficiency, work and drinking sprees, piety and rigor characterize this modern spirit, for which, as de Tocqueville says, "figures and symbols seem to be puerile artifice and ceremonies leave it cold." But where this spirit has not quite made the split, forms of conduct – style, bearing, and figure – continue to sustain the classical aspiration to *Kalós Kagathós* [80] described by Xenophon, though it be only in the simplified yet exacerbated form of the Spanish "genio y figura hasta la sepultura." [Akin to the British "stiff upper lip," this refers to maintaining intact both character and the forms and manners that correspond to this character right to the grave.]

This is the formalism of a Captain Meneses, who, when his ship is about to go under, dons his finest regalia and faces death reading Lope de Vega in a display of what Ortega characterized as "tragic sumptuary formalism." Or of the condemned men described in *Guzmán de Alfarache* who "steal the last hours from the salvation of their souls... to finish and commit to memory the speeches they intend to make from the heights of the gallows."

The morality that refuses to abandon the classical *Palestra* in order to plumb the depths of the Augustinian *Abyssus Conscientiae* is left at midpoint: the point of honor.[81] Hegel understands this "Spanish honor" to be the feeling that all subjectivity is at stake in each one of an individual's outer manifestations, in one's appearance, one's bearing, one's name. In America, and particularly in Mexico, this sentiment blends in with the strict courtesy and etiquette characteristic of a ritual society. Spanish honor, the tendency to fear the loss of one's dignity, tinges Aztec formalism with tension and soul. The slightest suggestion, suspicion, or insult can wound this thin-skinned personality whose only protection is Form. This, says Octavio Paz, is why impassibility and suspicion are espoused for Mexicans with the love of form. "A form which contains and encloses intimacy, preventing its excesses, repressing its explosions, separating and isolating it, preserving it. The dual indigenous and Spanish influences converge in this predilection for ceremony, formulas and order."[82]

One enigma persists: If Spanish honor indeed demands nothing less than the *purity of lineage* peculiar to the old Christian, how could it merge in America with the honor of a pagan race? How was it that an even more aristocratic and exclusivist style of colonization than the Anglo-Saxon did not emerge? The paradox can be resolved if we realize that the above "nothing less" is in truth "nothing more": Spanish *purity of lineage* is, as Alcina Franch puts it, a minimalist, popular, and democratic demand, in contrast with European society of that period, constituted in veritable watertight compartments protected by lineage and form. More accessible than "purity of profession," less rigid than the often- "tainted" noble ancestry,[83] purity of lineage gives rise to a minor and populous nobility of hidalgos and squires that does not require prior titles or present-day privilege. What thus characterizes Castile is not so much its "hidalgo spirit" as the banalization of this idea: its association with the individual and his works rather than with his family background. This is very clear in the theater of the period. North of the Pyrenees the villain or rogue is never more than a secondary comic character: the casuism of honor is reserved for the higher classes. In Spanish theater the townsman occupies center stage to the extent that the defense of his honor is combined in *El alcalde de Zalamea* with the class struggle and the vindication of municipal liberties.[84] As was only to be expected in a country whose theology had confronted predestination, here the concept of the old Christian is not so clearly associated with purity of lineage as with honorability of attitude. Whence Sancho Panza's "I am a Christian, and I need nothing more to be a count," or Quevedo's commentary in the "Dreams": "Though he come from low and vulgar men, if through divine habits he becomes worthy of imitation, he creates lineage for others." From Calderón:

> *...here blood is exceeded*
> *by the place one makes himself*
> *and seeing not how he is born*
> *how he behaves is seen*

to Alarcón, the examples multiply:

> *One need only behave*
> *like a gentleman to be one.*
> ....

> *Regardless of their birth*
> *the feats of illustrious men*
> *have honored their inheritors.*

Alarcón, born in Mexico, has his own reasons for reminding us that true nobility is not a question of inheritance but of destiny.

No wonder, then, that within this framework and in this language – a language that started out by setting down and saving "for memory's sake" the vernacular legends or customs in Bernardino de Sahagún's bilingual code – criollos, mestizos, and Indians alike could eventually bring honor to themselves and their descendants. Sahagún additionally showed his respect for the native languages in the very courts of justice,[85] finally creating a vehicle for mestizo sensibility: Garcilaso's allegorical version of neo-Platonic texts, or Sor Juana Inés de la Cruz's aspiration – Gongoresque and feminine all at once – to integrating the entire Cosmos in a Dream :

> *El mar, no ya alterado*
> *ni aun la instable mecía*
> *cerúlea cuna donde el Sol dormía;*
> *y los dormidos, siempre mudos, peces,*
> *en lechos lamosos*
> *de sus obscuros senos cavernosos,*
> *mudos eran dos veces...**

We have already seen how this cultural porousness manifests itself when Bernal Díaz, the soldier, recognizes in the recently conquered city the art of the three Indians he compared to Apelles, Michelangelo, and Berruguete. This sensibility soon will begin to carve out the images of the saints and climb the façades of the cathedrals, while Genesis is infiltrated into the Popol Vuh and the notes of the *jota* take on a new sonority in the *jarabe tapatío*. Using first Plateresque and then Baroque elements (though, mind you, in layouts that are more Renaissance or even Herrerian – Antigua, for example – than truly Baroque in the way of Borromino), an original variation on peninsular style begins to blossom in America. One element that the Spanish Baroque seems to have rejected proliferates: the *stipitate* pilaster or truncated pyramid with the base on top. Mixtilinear arches that can be traced to the Mudéjar style multiply as well, Arabic inspiration seemingly forging a direct link to indigenous sensibility. In a completely original fashion, tiles cover the dome of Santa Prisca de Taxco as well as the façade, portal, and columns of San Francisco de Acatepec. These tiles also appear for the first time alongside flat

---

* The sea, no longer turbulent, does not so much as rock the unstable cerulean crib where the Sun was sleeping; and the fish who, in the limey seabeds of their obscure caverns, are always silent and sleeping, were doubly silent.

bricks in the churches and public buildings of Puebla, or in sage contrast with the stones or volcanic *tezontle* of Cholula. Themes of vegetation, exotic motifs, pre-Hispanic tracings, and angels' sly smiles are all equally demonstrative of the imprint of indigenous experience and sensibility on Spanish American decoration and iconography...

In this chapter we have seen how pure Protestant subjectivity forgot classical form while in turn wiping out any alien forms that crossed its path. In contrast, Catholic spirituality would still cling to certain formal vestiges of classical paganism while embracing those of the new American paganism.[86] In the next chapter we shall see how this urge to translate figuratively such disparate elements – Christian, pagan, barbarous – could not help but produce more and more abstruse and overwrought forms, for as the classics put it:

> *around here if holy calm is to be our goal*
> *we have either too much matter or too much soul.* *

The first great attempt to introduce the "conscience malheureuse" into classic figures had already produced the grotesque capitals and fantastic gargoyles of Romanesque art. The new attempt to make this simultaneously traditional and national, capitalistic and colonial spirit fit into them would now generate the emblematic symbolism of the Baroque, in which causality and analogy, concept and intuition do their best to cohabitate.[87]

---

* aqui para vivir en santa calma/o sobra la materia o sobra el alma.

19

The Baroque: Frontier of the Classical World

As Plato said in his Seventh Letter, comprehension requires not only being *attentive* to things but also becoming *disposed* toward them: "We must adopt an affinity toward the question... until our soul takes on a resemblance to the objects it wishes to know." Let this reference stand as justification of the doubtless very baroque interpretation of the Baroque that follows.

The Baroque generally – and more singularly in Spain – seems to be an attempt to retain the classical ideals in a world in which everything seems to overwhelm them; a portentous effort to contain elements intent on overflowing any figurative perimeter. Against all odds, Baroque artists try to offer a tangible translation of a world torn apart by Christianity, aggrandized by the Church and disjointed by the State, disqualified by monetary economy, and thrown off center by cosmological and geographical discoveries. Calderón expressly manifests this desire

> *ver en un día...*
> *sombra y luz como planeta*
> *pena y dicha como imperio*
> *gente y brutos como selva*
> *paz y quietud como mar*
> *triunfo y ruina como guerra*
> *vida y muerte como dueño*
> *de sentidos y potencias.* *

But how were they to keep so many planets and so much empire "in sight"? What form to give to so many new phantasms and so many modern ideas? How, indeed, not to expect – here on the geographical and historical "fringes" of classicism – forms to become pompous, expressionistic, and

---

* to see in one day.../shadow and light as the planet/sorrow and joy as the empire/people and brutes as the jungle/peace and quiet as the sea/triumph and defeat as war/life and death as the master/of senses and possibilities.

wrenching in shape and feeling? In fact, baroque *Form* prefigures and anticipates what will soon occur with Hegelian *Being:* by dint of wanting to define itself not by exclusion but by inclusion, or of trying to stuff all temporal or contingent reality into its breast, it ends up showing the very features of all those things it has swallowed up, thus becoming a restless, changing, historical, labile Being.[88] Whence, as Antonio Regalado would have it, the simultaneous baroque affirmation of the world as everyday life (Murillo) and as chimera (Hieronymous Bosch), as will and as representation *(Don Quixote)*, as truth and as error, that is, as image. Not as a Diltheyan "image of the world" constituted before the subject but rather as a Heideggerian "world" constituted in image by the very reciprocity of consciousness. A phenomenology of illusion that includes the subject – "Is it my eyes that lie to me, or desire?" is the way Calderón poses the question – in which "truth and untruth are sisters engendered by the same mother, the Mind, fed by the Idea, with Language as the midwife."

But rather than lose ourselves in this phenomenology, we must stop and say a few words, both about the "classical ideal" (whose last bulwark we mean to identify with the Spanish baroque), and about the physical and cultural framework to which it responds. What most amazes us about the classical world indeed is the equilibrium or "ideal" reconciliation it achieves between the individual and the collective, the theoretical and the figurative, the intellectual and the sensorial. In the classical city there are neither individual Subjects nor universal Men; just citizens (as well, of course, as slaves). In classical art there is neither literal Reproduction nor Abstraction; just ideal types, archetypes. Its philosophical "dialogues" inaugurate Western reason, without ignoring mythic narration. Its theory still takes into account fables and gods, rites and traditions that it cannot cut off – nor does it want to. Classical thought imposes limits upon the interpretation of reality as its art imposes limits upon the stylization of appearances. Its capacity for abstraction is never cut off from a figurative conception of things. *Theoria* means "vision": the *sense* behind things always has to do with what our *senses* tell us about them. Hence in Greece they never jump from theory to the purely ideological frenzy that characterizes modern philosophy-theology since Hegel. Hence also the Greeks' capacity to ponder appearance and linger over form, not only over meanings or formulas. Hence, finally, their creation of an archetypal and symbolic world midway between sensibility and intelligibility, in which everything is related to Everything, but not to anything else.[89]

Now, this classical ideal required a perfectly defined social and cultural environment, wherein the connection between the intuitive and the rational, the natural and the cultural, the speculative and the imaginary, the figurative and the expressive would at once be conceivable. Plato and Aristotle are perfectly aware of this, and in more than one place refer to and champion these "objective conditions" of classicism. Plato, in the artistic sphere, criticizes art too given to amiability and verisimilitude that generates, he thinks, a merely passive and hedonistic appreciation: a consumer of sensations instead of a participant in ideals. Aristotle, in the political and social sphere, denounces the dangerous change of scale that is taking place in the city and the economy. The ancient city has to have an "imaginable" size, as Lynch would put it nowadays, within which citizens can recognize one another. Further on, with cosmopolitanism, the ecumenical and torn spirit of the Stoics would arise. The economy must be related, in effect, with the *oikos* (the home), so that, for Aristotle, lucrative activity *(krematistiké)* not intended for the satisfaction of domestic needs is no longer in fact "economical." Thus, before Marx used "exchange value" to analyze capitalism, Aristotle had discovered and rejected it, as an assault on classical principles.

And the least that can be said is that Plato and Aristotle's intuition was right: classical and figurative culture was not compatible with such an enlargement of their experience and magnitude. Beyond a certain threshold, the polis gives way to the State and citizens grow a Soul, the studded sky of Empedocles turns into the infinite Cosmos, Destiny becomes Duty and Guilt – the categorical imperative – and the oikonomía turns into the economy – exchange value. In turn, ontology becomes epistemology, eros or philia turn into love – courtly or romantic – and the hygiene of the gymnasium gives way to the sex of the bordello or the *libido sentiendi* of the Jansenists. The inability to grasp the environment, the anonymity and anomie of the city are clearly at the heart of economic, erotic, or moral individualism. Just as they are at the core of the "arts of artfulness," which Gracián's Discreet Man will apply to survival in this labyrinth.[90]

Now, an extensive State and an intense Soul emerge and ally to cancel definitively any chance of canonical or figurative "reconciliation." The ancients did not have either State or Soul, and this is why they were classics. But how to maintain their synthesis and equilibrium in a world torn between Christianity and Capitalism, Colonialism and Urbanism? How still to maintain the global image of a world in which new autonomies – the autonomy of faith (Protestantism), reason (Cartesianism), experience (empiricism), or wealth (mercantilism) – are emerging daily? This is the outsized task that the baroque shoulders following the practical failure of the Renaissance project in the seventeenth century.

The classicist message still fit rather comfortably into the visual and figurative world of the *Quattrocento*. The free republics of Genoa and Venice still retain a "human" scale not very distant from that of the *polis* and its ideals of proportion, simplicity, and symmetry. Science appears in close association with art in the anatomical tables of Vesalius or Leonardo. The *virtù* of their *bravi* still has more to do with strength and demeanor than with guilt or holiness. The ideal, as in Greece, still fits inside the real: in the "marvelous Necessity" sung by Leonardo or the "sacred harmony of the parts" that Michelangelo discovers in man, and Copernicus or Galileo recognize in the stars. However, the unification of the real and the ideal will not be carried out here, as in Greece, through the "archetype" but rather through the pupil: "That wondrous place where the colors and the images of the entire universe are concentrated in one point; the new place of all things" (Leonardo). Thanks to Andrea del Sarto's bold invention of linear perspective and pyramidal composition, the Renaissance will now be able to systematize the world from this unitary "point of view": to paint a perfectly continuous and homogeneous space.

But soon it would be felt that Gozzoli's, Bellini's or Perugino's space was actually more geometric than natural or atmospheric. And that is why, by the end of the sixteenth century, we are witnessing the transformation of Masaccio's solid figures into Raphael's *certa idea,* of Ucello's precise planes into Leonardo's *sfumato,* Donatello's equilibrium into Michelangelo's *terribilità,* Alberti's flat façades into the *maniera* of Vignola's buildings. Man no longer seems to trust his "regular," perspective vision to be the truth of the world around him. In the art of the sixteenth and seventeenth centuries, the eye-mind that used to be the center and place of all things begins wandering about lost, bouncing from one side to the other. The change is as dramatic as it is easy to recognize. Although the enlargement of any detail of a work by Masaccio or Botticelli is in itself a painting on which the gaze can rest, in a baroque painting the angel on the right is nothing more than the counterpoint of (and remission to) the other angel on the left. While in Brunelleschi's Piazza della Santissima Annunziata, each building constitutes a formal, self-sufficient unit, in the Piazza di Spagna the buildings are organized on the basis of the parietal continuity they are to form with the square as a whole, an effect that can be perceived only by a moving pedestrian. Alberti's buildings were also composed of "elements," while Palladio's Villa del Zeno is a latticework of references in which no single element can be perceived except in its relationship to the rest.

This crisis of Renaissance forms certainly has its "social history." It includes the invasion of Italy in 1493 and Savonarola's significant discourse; the occupation of Italy by Spanish troops and the sacking of Rome; the Reformation, dynastic quarrels, and the Thirty Years' War; the rash of nationalisms that will last a century until the absolute monarchies are stabilized. The Modern Age certainly does not come up with political and social solutions so quickly as the Renaissance ideally established its cultural foundations. And this *décalage* between cultural and politico-social modernism is what, according to Hauser, heralds *manierismo* and paves the way for the baroque. The formal equilibrium of the Renaissance is torn asunder in the seventeenth century by polarized and contradictory forces: Reformation and Counter-Reformation, asceticism and the work ethic, rationalism and empiricism, the state and consciousness, ecstasy and sensuality, Cano and Rubens. These contradictions can no longer be rendered in the terms of Renaissance equilibrium or reconciliation between matter and spirit, reality and the ideal, experience and reason. The particular ceases to be a case of the general, passion to be a mere motor of the rational personality, and reality to be a made-to-measure macrocosm in mystical correspondence with the human soul. Valdés Leal paints Death, and Murillo, Glory; Bernini depicts Ecstasy, and Ribera, Poverty.

The crisis of the "objective conditions" of Greek classicism and of their rebirth in *quattrocento* Italy thus brings about a rupture of forms that then begin either (1) to be resolved externally in exalted *images* or rhetorical figures, or (2) to dissolve internally into abstract *ideas*. Let us look at each of these two moments so that, in the next chapter, we may begin to sketch out the original approach of the Spanish baroque to this crisis.

1. The *modern* expansion of the State, the Church, or the Capital posed new rhetorical and symbolic demands. The art commissioned by the Athenian *eupatridae* or the Florentine *maecenas* is addressed to their peers: to persons whose culture they share and who possess the same keys to its interpretation. The audience of the new popes and emperors is by now much broader and more heterogeneous. As a result, they must take care that their message be efficiently broadcast, understood, and consumed in the most remote places – and that it prevail over concurrent messages from other nations or religions. This is how the forms and signs of classical art are now transformed into trompe–l'oeil images and grandiloquent symbols. The distance from power, the abstraction of its message, and the scope of the audience call for a change in emphasis: from "production" to "promotion." The symbolic demands of the Capital (be it national, ecclesiastic, or imperial) are also imposed upon the formal or structural demands of the buildings (R. Venturi). The front colonnade of Saint Peter's is not meant to reflect or express its labyrinthine interior of hallways, anterooms, offices, and chapels but, rather, to camouflage it in order to offer the homogeneous and monolithic image of the "One, Holy, Catholic, Apostolic and Roman" Church. The works Olivares commissions for the Palacio del Buen Retiro – the *Rendición de Breda* (Surrender of Breda) and the *Toma de Bahía* (Taking of Bahía) – both try to convey the image of a magnanimous victor who "is twice triumphant" for he also triumphs over himself. And this is how the real world carries out the orders given by the Author to the characters of *El Gran Teatro del Mundo* (Calderon):

fabricate appearances
to turn doubts into certainties

The triumph of *effect* over *form* fulfills the need for persuasion that arises when power overruns certain limited thresholds of expansion and abstraction. The passage from "democracy" to the civil or ecclesiastic "republic" made unfeasible the Aristotelian appeal to the citizenry to join together and discuss its decisions. As Bodin writes, this is no longer possible, "given the existing difficulties for gathering a citizenry together in a determined place, the disorder that a multitude signifies and the vanity and inconstancy of the people." Such a multitude, Quevedo will add, "confuses instead of comforting; is a burden and not a bounty..., becomes stirred up, like the sea, at a mere breath, and drowns only those who trust in it."[91]

As was to be expected, in this milieu the function or "truth" of the artistic forms wielded by the ruling classes will no longer be found in their genesis or structure but in their destination: in the impact "those vividly painted images that almost batter the unwary senses" (Pacheco) will have on the casual user, parishioner, or consumer. An "aristocratic" culture (Nietzsche) linked to *origin* had given way to a city culture founded upon *coherence,* only to give rise now to a state culture legitimated by its *repercussions.*

But the State and the Church do not grow only in Europe: they also spread throughout America. And what may be necessary in Europe to transmit the message of power, is fundamental in America to introduce European culture. And so in the Indies we witness the paroxysm of what I have called a "Baroque situation": *the need to amalgamate disparate realities and communicate with unknown audiences.* And also its brilliant resolution in churches made to "lure" the new Indian audiences through the seductive power of their magnificent choruses, their liturgy, their images, and their metaphors: all those elements that, according to Father Lejeune, S.J., "inspired a profound admiration in the mind of the Indians, leading them to embrace, without pressures or constrictions, the beliefs of those they admired." A good example of this Baroque "way-of-preaching" is Father Curiel's 1768 description of the entrance of a Jesuit into the city of Asunción:

> From two leagues away, where many people had come out to see him, he entered the city unshod of foot and leg with a crucifix in his hand, preaching the entire length of the road to the multitude that grew greater and greater the closer he came to the city, and when he reached the square, on a dais they had prepared for him, he began his sermon with the fervor of a Saint Paul by saying: *terra, terra, terra, audi verbum Dei* , upon which the audience was terrified and filled with remorse, and the remorse and mending of their ways grew in the sixteen days that the sermon lasted, for it bore abundant fruits.

2. The *counterpoint* of this external overflowing of forms into *images* and *effects*, I was saying, is its internal dissolution into *ideas*. State policy, the Protestant religion, the monetary economy, or Copernican cosmology have all presupposed an "energumenic" (both "gigantic" and "ruled by ideas") development of everything that art was now called upon to express. The etymological meaning of *energumenic* is "ruled by ideas," and ideas, indeed, and not tangible things are the anonymous City, the absolute State, mining or colonial Wealth, Protestant Guilt or Piety, the pietist God, the "Great Sun" of astronomy that Descartes opposes to the "little sun" of sensorial contemplation. They are ideas that can certainly be thought, felt, and even calculated but no longer seen. Everything they have gained in significance has been stolen from intuition. This is why both classical "representation" and traditional analogy now become problematic and a Protestant Baroque appears (cf. Rembrandt) in which the individuality and idiosyncrasy of the characters aggressively breaks down all canonical beauty or equilibrium. The reconciliation of man and his medium in the polis is split between fear of the *homo homini lupus*, metaphysical trembling before "the system of infinite spaces," and the agonistic doubts of Shakespeare's soliloquies. The representations upon which Aristotle based the knowledge of the world now become the deceptive *idola* of Bacon. The figures on which the Catholic Church founded the knowledge of God seem to the Protestants to be mere *anecdotes* that humanize and blur the pure *esjaton* or divine message. Thus the method that will now be followed to deal theoretically with this energumenical swelling of new ideas first sets out and gathers momentum. Rationalism and empiricism separate the "signs" from the "world" in which they no longer seem to fit, and relocate them (in complicity with a Cartesian or Berkeleyan God) in pure Reason or Sensation. Knowledge no longer seems to depict the order of things but to express the order of one's own thoughts or representations. Now signs stand only for the "categories" of understanding and will (Kant). Or even less: they are mere "conventions" as they had also been for the Stoic thinkers in a period of analogous political and social energumenism. In any case, the device behind all these works and theories turns out to be one and the same: to separate the sense from the figure, the essence from the anecdote, reason (or revelation) from image, emotional experience from its sensual vehicle.

20

Spain: A Numantian Classicism

But the Baroque is and continues to be Baroque so long as it is not resolved in that separation between representation and meaning, so long as it carries out a Numantian defense of the *naturalness of the supernatural.* (The inhabitants of Numantia defended their city to the death against the Roman invasion. A Numantian defense has thus come to mean a desperate and unflagging resistance.) Spain seems now to be the last bulwark of this now impossible classicism, which "adores expression for what it has in it of concretion and contour... and feels the constant temptation to domesticate what is transcendent, reducing it to clear and concise forms. All of this in contrast with the Nordic spirit, which is familiar with the infinite, and lacking in that Catholic affection for myth, for the figurative and sensual, inherited from Greece and Rome." Hence the refusal of our Baroque to ignore forms, to divorce its phantasms from its figures, economy from weights and measures (the just price), morality from religion, and responsibility from its external manifestations. Hence also Suárez's espousal of the concepts that would give rise to modern idealism while stopping short of renouncing an objective and individual idea of Being.

The Spanish baroque still wants to give a visual figure and a profile to both the Gothic soul and the Indian spirit, to capitalist economy and state policy. It thus has no alternative but to force and distort classical forms to their very limits in order to make a place in them for modern ideas (in an analogous way, Picasso would later distort modern figures to make a place in them for contemporary ideas). This is forced and overwrought realism trying to represent visually all that is most abstract (or to "classify" what is most modern and Christian: "the death, coronation and ascension of the pagan soul in the Christian arena," as Vossler says of Calderón), which many, particularly in the North, will perceive along with Nietzsche "as a punch in the eye, as a cynical mockery of the symbol." I understand, of course, that all those souls who entertain such familiarity with the infinite – with Life, the *Ganz Anders*, the Will to Power, historical Reason, *und so werter* – will forever find ridiculous or perverse this Gongoristic pretension to translating

123

characters into images and combining verses "in a manner both invented and sensual" (Paz). Or, they might feel shocked by this endeavor to constrain in more and more extreme forms and subtle silhouettes this new world of abstract experiences or sublime ideas.[92] Personally, I must recognize that I have mixed feelings about it. The admiration I feel as a classicist for the enormous plastic and hermeneutic endeavor of the Spanish baroque is dampened by the fear I feel as a liberal of its totalizing and holistic purpose.

A peculiar kind of cultural viscosity hinders the quick and unilateral conversion of Spain to "modern ideas" – a process that required ignoring both what was *prior* and what is *external* to them. We have already seen a sample of this inertial classicism in the Guaraní reductions of the Jesuits. We will wrap up by referring to two artistic and literary monuments that attest this same temperament or tradition.

In order to express visually a situation that engulfs all human scale and intuition, artistic forms become complicated and go out of proportion. To give form to the double infinity discovered by modernity, both cosmic and psychic, perspectives must multiply and intersect, proportions must break down. Bernini and Borromini thus insist on an illusionistic and scenographic use of the classical elements of architecture. In Titian's paintings the point of convergence is not in the center but up and off to one side, so that the "point of view" is no longer that of man but of Power or God. One across from the other in the National Gallery, we can compare the still frontal, neutral, and geometrical space of Vicenzo Catena's *Warrior Adoring Jesus* with Titian's *Vendramini Family* or Veronese's *Joys of Love*, in which that eccentric point of view gives the characters a new movement and grandeur. At this point, Flemish art will try to delve deeper into the representation of the domestic cosmos (the Arnolfini family), penetrate intimacy (Rembrandt), and encompass the metaphysical infinity of the *amorphos* that lies beyond Florentine Neoplatonism.

The phenomenon arises in Italy and spreads through Europe. How does it take shape and what are its nuances in Spain? It has been said that here it acquires all the exuberance and immoderation of the Counter-Reformation spirit. However, it can be seen as just the opposite: not as exuberance but as the will to keep in check this proliferation of Nordic or exotic infinities that metaphysics and painting are now hatching. Let us take a look.

According to Menéndez Pidal, there is a common traditionalistic and realistic bias in the three peninsular literatures: from Gonzalo de Berceo to the *chansoneta breu i plana* of Guillem de Bergadà; from the "topicality" of the *Romancero* to the "triviality" of *Tirant lo Blanc*, the chivalric novel in which, according to Cervantes, "the characters sleep like ordinary men and die in bed after making their wills" (trans. note: This in contrast with the traditional chivalric dragonslayer and savior of damsels in distress); from the *Chronicles* of Alphonse the Wise to Don Quixote himself describing his only truly fantastic adventure (in the Montesinos cave) as "surely apocryphal." It is this distaste for chimaeric artifice or for magical elements (reinforced no doubt by the religious fanaticism displayed toward witchery) that allows Menéndez Pidal to speak of "a brand of sobriety and realism that extends like a brushstroke from East to West across the map of the Iberian Peninsula, broader toward the East, more tenuous in Portugal, but firm throughout its length." More than a desire for "realism," I would call it a desire for "realization," i.e., an effort to translate into reality or assimilate into the sensorial everything that appears to exceed its bounds. And that is why it becomes hyperbolic and outlandish when it tries to absorb the forces conspiring from the four corners of the globe to proscribe figuration, make imagery abstract, break with classical proportions, and substitute feeling or concept for form.

Of course, this is only one possible interpretation of the Spanish baroque. Schematic, no doubt, but also "apropos" in the sense I have previously given the term (see chapter 9). From this vantage point, for example, Spanish constructions from different times and places seem to take on a family resemblance and even to form a system in their common penchant for working within the borders. The Church of Santa María del Mar in Barcelona or the University of Salamanca – Catalan Gothic and Plateresque, respectively – try to control Gothic or Arabic excess while keeping the most extravagant motifs within a classical subordination to unity. The Escorial reduces the Renaissance itself to a theorem. The Royal Alcázares, the chapel of the University of Salamanca, or the Church of Belém – Mudéjar and Manuelino – all strive to "figurate" Moorish arabesques or Indian frets. The cathedral at Puebla and Santa Prisca of Taxco fit native themes into rigorous Renaissance floor plans. From this standpoint the Plateresque style of the 1600s no longer looks like an overflowing of *manierismo* but, rather, like an effort to contain it within a Renaissance structure. Just as the Churriguerism of the 1700s will reveal itself to be a maneuver to maintain the mobile forms and asymmetrical rhythms of the Baroque within a severe constructive framework.

It can be said that Calderón's theater is very theological, but it is surely more just to say that his theology is very theatrical. It is not that his characters are ideas but, rather, that ideas, in his hands, turn into characters. The baroque process is deductive, not inductive; it is not the three-branched tree that becomes the Trinity, but the Trinity that is incarnated in the Tree – and in Nature at large. Spanish art expresses in an exemplary way this classical-deductive aim to translate the very idea of *the World* into a tangible and external image (Góngora's "Labyrinth," Fernández Ribera's "Inn of Fools," Calderón's "Theater," Quevedo's "Dream," Tirso's "Republic in

Reverse"); to wedge it into sober (Montañés, Zurbarán) or laconic (Quevedo, Gracián) form; to gather it up into a unity (Herrera, Cervantes); or even to bring it close to vulgarity: to paint "with bravado" as Gracián tells us was Cervantes's intention, in contrast with Raphael or Titian.

The zeugma ("Deceit is very superficial and only those who are fall into it," Gracián) is the most perfect formal expression of this tendency. In its humorous guise, it gives rise to a *baroque sarcasm* that is the exact counter-point of *romantic irony*, more akin to the cynical and stoic spirit. In effect, from Menippus to Diogenes and from Schlegel to Heine, romantic irony tries to stress the irreducible distance that separates the subject's soul from all objects or anthropomorphic representation: even from its own work, even from its own body. It is this pure subject that Diogenes seeks with his lantern in plain light of day. It is also expressed in Posidonius' dialogue ("You can do what you will, oh pain!, but you will not bring me to confess that you are evil"), or it speaks through the mouth of the Holy Martyr ("Disjoin his members, pummel his body though you may, you will never reach Eusebius"), and who, at the very limits of irony, goes so far as to give his torturers technical advice:

> *"Go easy there, you're going to break my arm."*
> *Crack!*
> *"You see? I told you so."*

In contrast, Baroque sarcasm tries precisely to show the *reducible* and *compatible* character, in a spatio-temporal unity, of the most disparate elements (the objective and the subjective, of course, but also the Sancho-topical and the Quixote-utopical, the sublime and the ridiculous, the elegiac and the lowdown) or their definitive identity in the heart of nothingness. Irony labels things with names and images that are "contrary to the commonplace" (Aristotle) as a viaticum to another vision of those very things, while sarcasm (from *sarkasmos,* to skin) immediately strips them of their aura by means of a semantic device. The first step is to introduce a peculiar or noble trait which is immediately revealed either as nothingness ("in earth, in smoke, in dust, in shadow, in nothing," from the sonnet by Góngora), or as a distinct reality with which it communicates through figurative or grammatical form. In the first case Baroque satire is more *radical* than romantic irony – as well as less *solemn* – in the second case, it tells us how...

...Don Clemente was always said to be of good stock, and the way he drank, it could hardly be a lie. *(Life of the Buscón,* 1,2)

...He had trouble meeting women's eyes, but not other parts. *(Buscón,* VI, 3)

Under the commandment 'Thou shalt not kill,' Master Pedro included partridges and capons.... and it seems he considered it a sin to kill hunger. (IV, 3)

Fernando... squeezed me in his arms... and with that and turning and leaving the room of this maiden, I no longer was one. (Quixote, I, IV, XVIII)

There have been no few attempts to see even the *Quixote* through the lens of "irony." Moreover, like every great work, it certainly admits of multiple "uses," though rarely does it allow itself to be trapped within a single interpretation. Heine tried to reduce Don Quixote to the type of the romantic hero who "struggles not only against the books of chivalry but against all forms of *enthusiasm.*" Don Quixote thus becomes the symbol of the *exceptional* individual who sees the world as the inessential territory – the *côté aventure* – upon which he ironically projects the figures of his mind. Hegel himself had seen Don Quixote as a symbol of the modern "unhappy consciousness" that does not believe any more in an "enthusiastic" world (*enthusiastic* meaning filled with God), thus losing all confidence in any external truth or happiness, apart from oneself. And we could go on in a similar vein, attributing to Don Quixote everything from the sublime irony of the saint who seeks suffering and temptation in order to confirm his infinite superiority, to the astute irony of Odysseus who confronts all the figures of passion in order to temper his character, save his soul, or construct the "new man" in his struggle with them.

Ortega and Unamuno both tried to mine Don Quixote's "deep core." For Ortega, however, this core is not ironic but ethical; and for Unamuno the hero is no longer romantic but existential or tragic. Ortega proposes that we demythify this "Gothic Christ lacerated by modern anguish," in order to find in him the conquest of lucidity and consciousness. Unamuno asks that we identify with this "existential hero" in his struggle against all the baccalaureates, priests, and barbers, all those creatures of bigotry who ask for a "user's guide" to life. They coincide, then, in their wish to rescue the *Quixote* from the ambivalence that, as María Zambrano has indicated, constitutes its great ideological and formal novelty. The first ambiguity obtains between Don Quixote and his squire, the "mirror of consciousness that looks upon and takes the measure of the genial knight." And the other ambiguity (that both Ortega and Unamuno wished to obviate) between the author himself and his work: "Cervantes, who never bares his soul, who is not prodigal in his use of the first person, is nonetheless present at every moment of the work." In reading the *Quixote,* "we will feel as we do in life: hesitant under the omnipresent gaze of an author who, expressing himself with the greatest clarity, still leaves the mystery intact for us." And M. Zambrano concludes that this is precisely what reveals Don Quixote to be a "symbol of something we imagine to be eminently Spanish, but which soon shows its universal purport: ambiguity...." No doubt, we have here a moral and liberal conception of Spain quite distinct from the "imperative and assertive" Spain of Ortega and Americo Castro that we examined in chapter 12. An image that further shows itself in the formal and ideological kinship between Cervantes's *Quixote* and Bernal Díaz del Castillo's *True Story:*

> "What does it mean," M. Zambrano asks, "for the Spanish epic myth to be precisely a novel like the *Quixote?*" "In the *True Story...,*" responds Carlos Fuentes, "the epic is torn between amazement at the discovery of an enchanted world and the bellicose obligation to destroy it. This is a *hesitant* epic. And a hesitant epic is not an epic: it is a novel."

Ambiguity, doubt, hesitancy: a flexible and receptive attitude that gives natural course to the novelesque way of inhabiting the world. Of course Don Quixote also keeps his distance from *this* world. Not, however, like ironic or stoic heroes, for the purpose of saving his soul or establishing his unique personality, but precisely in order to live nigh on this reality. To *exist* (not by chance so close to *exit)* signifies to "be outside." So it does not mean conquering an "authentic existence" (that romantic sublimate of life lived in the heart of the *conscience malheureuse)* but, rather, walking among things – sinning all of its sins, acting as the playing field of all of its reasons – until nothing of this world is alien any longer. (Something that surely, and without my intending it, has happened to me with this book – written between Catalonia and Spain, between Spanish scholasticism and English common law, between the American Dream of the North and the Hispanic Labyrinth of the South – which for this very reason is a baroque example of the very thing it *says).* Don Quixote does not pursue the figures of his passion and his conscience in order to set himself apart but to integrate himself "into a world understood as will and as representation" (A. Regalado). From the romantic hero we thus move on to the classical "Knight of the Sad Countenance" wandering about this ambiguous and disjointed world where souls border on nations and fiefdoms on empires. A modern world in which personal "virtue" can be embodied only either by making of it a purely subjective matter or – if the classical ideal of objectivity is to be retained – by becoming oneself the object, the playground, of the events confronted. The latter is the path followed by Spanish Quixotesque reality. This is a morality that certainly does not partake of the romanticism of irony or of the lightness of a sportive, "fun" morality. This is not a play-morality, but a toy-morality.[93]

Don Quixote does not try to save any of his ideals or phantasms from Popperian "falsification"; he does not imagine the real but, rather, realizes the imaginary; he does not idealize the world but tries to embody its ideals. As a result, of course, this figure becomes complex, baroque. Just as the book itself becomes formally complex and participates in this very same *experimentum crucis.*[94] The mixing of levels, the assimilation of ongoing events, the representation of the impact of the work-in-progress upon its own environment, all these things form a rare and rich literary tissue where no dimension of reality is ignored, or released. The book also does what it says by means of a sophisticated play of curls and metalanguages, managing not only to describe but to incarnate in the narration itself the complex tangle of a world – the negative of the Renaissance picture – in which appearance has lost its credibility, words and things no longer resemble one another, similarities deceive, and perspectives multiply. And all of this, which in other works of the period produces hallucination and delirium, is here embodied in a knight who tries to retain the adventure – in gesture and in *geste* – in a world now ruled by the profundities of physical determinism and self-consciousness.

José María Valverde has pointed out that something similar happens in *Las meninas*. It is difficult to imagine a more equivocal and ambiguous work, one more replete with tropes and paradoxes per square inch. The everyday realism of the theme blends with the illusionism of its pictorial treatment; the baroque "dissolution" of objects in the light merges with the "reflection" upon the very act of painting them. We see a painting from which the painter, in turn, sees us. But the mirror in the background does not reflect us, for it is already "wearing" Philip IV and Doña Mariana. As a result, they take our place or that of the artist himself (Valverde has called this the "toady hypothesis," based no doubt on Velázquez's reputation as a social climber). The possibility that the work may be a self-portrait cannot be ruled out, but in that case the artist would have to have a mirror in front of him, nor could the faces of the monarchs appear in the background mirror. The places of the artist, the spectator, and the model thus seem to be interchangeable in this visual aporia in which each interpretation both remits to and cancels out the next. The enigma of *Las meninas* is unsolvable, for its space "does not duplicate the scene as in Dutch painting, but rather what is outside of the scene, what would be seen if the canvas were extended" (M. Foucault). Thus, Pacheco's commandment is obeyed: the image must leave the frame. And in this way the Renaissance perspective is also inverted: we do not see the painting, but the painting sees us; it is not the perspective view that orders the space, but the pictorial space that organizes and recreates the series of views giving rise to a new, more radical and paradoxical, objectivity.

We could go on finding examples. But I think that these two works suffice to show the classical and autoplastic bias of Spanish culture that (in vivid contrast with its political centralism and religious intolerance) we have already traced in the legislation of the Indies or the Guaraní reductions. That is, its ability to open up spiritually and absorb formally what surpasses it.

In the introduction I suggested that Hispanics and Anglo-Saxons, Anglo-Americans and Latin Americans should each learn from the conservatism and traditionalism – not from the modernity – of the other; that we should take a page from Anglo political traditionalism and they should take one from Hispanic cultural traditionalism. Now, I think the challenge has already been taken up in Spain, and it would be good – even urgent – for the North Americans to do their part. These are the topics that I will begin to set out in the last chapter. They would undoubtedly call for another book.

21

Encounters in the Labyrinth

From 1975 on, Spain has run more or less the following course. There has been a move to add to the liberal and radical values of peninsular tradition those of a pragmatic and democratic tradition that until now had been quite distant from us, if not indeed foreign. And so we have seen two heads of government and one president of an autonomous nation (Adolfo Suárez, Felipe González, and Josep Tarradellas) behave more in accordance with reality than with their own origins (Phalangist, Marxist, or Republican), not hesitating to sacrifice their principles in order not to betray their country. And we have also seen an electorate that, no longer in thrall to any one party or doctrine, has stopped delivering an unconditional vote. Now it merely lends its vote and ponders carefully the condition in which it has been returned before deciding who will be its beneficiary in the next elections. In both cases, a doctrinaire notion of political options is giving way to the recognition of the symbolic and conventional character of politics. Eugenio Trías writes, "To the dismay of tourists and Hispanists, passions are being 'recycled' into reasons, beliefs into opinions, and vehemence is being contested by intelligence." A new sense of "expediency" – as far removed from cynicism as it is from dogmatism – has begun to permeate Spanish politics.

But not without enlisting the efforts of many and incurring the outrage of a few. The passage from one political *imaginaire* based on the solidity of principles to another based on ever-precarious balances and approximations required a delicate psychological retraining. This retraining, still going on, consists basically of

- Recognizing, in contrast with traditional Hispanic moralism and political grandstanding, that political conflict is more a question of interests than of principles, and that by the same token the fractionary spirit cannot be dissolved through vague or sublime appeals to Justice or the Common Weal, Patriotism or Republican Virtues.

131

- Knowing, though, that the interests that come to replace these principles will meet with passions – be they national, ethnic, or religious – that either disguise or exalt them; that beyond any doubt the "emotional agenda" of political life is still made up of gut feelings and reactions that are better given entry, with open eyes, through the front door than allowed to slip in, tacitly, through the back door.

- Recognizing, then, that the passage from "charismatic" to "rational" legitimization is less linear or automatic than we had thought; that the new fundamentalisms, common today in both under- and overdeveloped countries, set down for us both the limits of techno-economical legitimization of the state and the need for a, shall we say, "monarchic" principle to balance the two extremes.

- Assuming an ironic attitude that will allow us to make political choices without demanding a manufacturer's guarantee, that is, without needing to believe that when we make a political judgment we are conjugating the very language of things, or that in order to decide we must coincide with History or Progress, Tradition or Revolution. This attitude, which draws the slim but important distinction between faith in politics and the politics of the faithful, shows the passage into a lighter, more ironic or patronizing tone, of a sensibility that used to swing back and forth from enthusiasm to sarcasm.

- Managing, finally, to make that irony or intellectual distance compatible with personal commitment to the rules of a political "game" that is to work out social conflict by means of its dramatic representation in the houses of parliament. And not only that: recognizing that this game deserves to be championed with passion *precisely* because it is conventional, for a power not based on brute force or pure superstition can be founded only on a conventional pact.

Still, it should not be forgotten that this profession of democratic faith is a conquest as revolutionary as it is fragile, and all the more so in a country addicted, as Nietzsche said, "to wanting too much." This is why, for the psychological recycling of the country, a "mythical" groundwork had to be laid to provide traditional legitimization, binding force, and popular verisimilitude. This is precisely the role that the constitutional monarchy took on in our case, and continues to play nowaday.[95] We shall now take a look at how this came about.

- Bertrand Russell said that democracy is strong and secure only when it has become traditional. Only then, indeed, does it cease to be something under discussion to become the framework and medium of the discussion itself. In 1975 Spain, the social and economic "conditions" for democracy did indeed exist. But after so many years of abstinence, the idea of democracy appeared as more a mythical object of desire than a fair way of resolving conflict, as a transcendental referent rather than a methodological one. Certainly, in the very beginning, an ancestral "logic of submission" (I. Sotelo) may have played perversely in favor of democracy, for many people who voted in favor of the new democratic constitution did so because "they were just following orders," because the Army High Command, the Central Committee or the Episcopal Assembly said so. But it is clear that, in the long run, the consolidation of democracy could not be constructed on the basis of this habit of obedience.

– Lacking this traditional legitimization, could Spain not find other grounds on which to build its democracy? Did the history of ideas not offer a good list of nontraditional grounds, either civil or religious, social or rational? For Locke, the solid basis on which a democracy could and should be founded was an entity of private law: Property.[96] For Kant, it was a law of practical reason: the Categorical Imperative. And for Fichte, it was Life itself: the natural impulse for Happiness.[97] According to Bergson, it had to be an an ancient and express mythological reference; and today, for Habermas, a linguistic commitment. [98] These and other principles have been called upon to legitimate democracy. The problem with all of them, to my mind, is that they are either too mythical, too intimate, or too explicit to constitute the tacit convention that ultimately works as the actual foundation of a democracy. They are not really useful as the basis for an agreement that must be neither merely personal nor exclusively legal; as a device that has to be "naturalized" until it becomes the "a priori synthesis" of public life; as a kind of tact or civility working both as a subjective distillate and as an objective consolidation of political coexistence. What we need is the "good taste" of *"el hombre en su punto"* ("man at the golden mean," Gracián) in whom the knowledge of the rules and the sense of expediency, community feeling and intellectual freedom all come together. A good taste that Kant conceived of only on an *anthropological* level (in the "aesthetical judgments" without a leading concept) but which Gracián sensed as a *social* construction or conquest.

And so it is. Before and beyond Freudian "interiorization" exists the social transmission of tribal imperatives precipitated in uses and customs. "Etiquette and tact," said T. W. Adorno, "presuppose an uninterrupted and ever-present convention: the (Kantian) reconstruction of what was subjectively obligatory." A reconstruction as variable as culture itself, but in which, at the same time, we can recognize the limit of all cultural relativism, i.e., the absolute superiority of a civilization in which vehicles stop to allow pedestrians to cross, over another in which convention, and survival, require the exact opposite.

Or inversely, the absolute limitation that comes from, as Juan de Mairena (pen name of Antonio Machado) warned in 1938, "a certain lack of vital tact and irony which had made the Germans, a great metaphysical people, into a politically deplorable community."

– If any of this is valid, then, the Spanish situation in 1975 could not have been more difficult or paradoxical. On the one hand, as I have argued, we could not dispense with any of the traditional-conventional kind of legitimization. On the other, after forty years of the Franco regime, we were lacking precisely in a tradition on which to found a democratic process. Only an "a priori synthetical" convention could resolve the dilemma. A convention like the new democratic monarchy, which could serve to *fill in the missing continuity and democratic legitimization with its own dynastic continuity and institutional legitimation.*

A traditional institution thus helped us break with our most immediate and dramatic tradition. The monarchy was an "a priori" reality, and its radical commitment to democracy endowed it with a "synthetic" character. From this standpoint, freedoms usually acquired only through democratic continuity and the habits that it creates were recovered in a few short months. Its role was and is, therefore, that of a *symbolon* in the etymological sense of the word: a nontraumatic mediation or suture between two tissues, between two continuous yet contrasting periods of our history. But why, you may yet ask, this need for a mediating convention to act as the catalyst for the changeover? A long genealogy testifies to the fact that people have always sensed that conventions are an indispensable "viaticum" in times of radical change.[99] One day in February 1981 (the day of the takeover of the Spanish Cortes by an army officer, Antonio Tejero, in a failed attempt at a coup d'état, which finally subsided when King Juan Carlos addressed the nation, expressing his support of the Adolfo Suárez's democratic government) we confirmed exactly how this monarchical convention blocked the "rejection syndrome" and the attempt to revert to the past. Today we are finally beginning to experience its capacity not only to neutralize attacks on democracy but also to sustain its development.

This is a capacity our monarchy can still demonstrate by acting as a bridge or joint – once again, as a symbol – between two conceptions of the state that the early and superficial unification of Spain was not able to meld; by making flexible and real what had been a rigid and ideological unity. The "Castilianization" of the Spanish monarchy under Philip II and its "courtification" under Philip III seemed to trap the monarchy within these narrow and rigid boundaries. But it is also true that this same monarchy was often able to remain sensitive to and respectful of the rights and freedoms of the diverse peninsular states even as it confronted them.[100] Hence the well-founded belief that in the new monarchy we can still find the features of an institution that, according to Elliott, "conceived of itself as integrated by different individualized States, each one linked to its sovereign by traditional legal bonds, which continue to lead independent lives according to their own historical systems of government." What is certain, in any case, is that the monarchical tradition turns out to be much more capable than the Jacobinic tradition of the modern absolute state to deal with both internal and external diversity: to recognize Spain as a labile reality, which is both *more* and *less* than what the Spanish state contains and whose identity is none other than the overlapping or "logical product" of its colonial adventure and its national plurality.

What is more, only this ideal of a new and flexible unity with Latin America can help us to overcome the hysterical obsession with a "vertebrated" and "integral" Spain (Ortega) that we saw emerge precisely after the loss of the colonies (see chapter 12). Only by going beyond the Spanish "frame" will we learn not to saturate its canvas. And to do this, it will suffice to recover an ideological and institutional tradition that at a certain point was able to articulate this country instead of imposing upon it a rigid isonomical structure whose perverse counterpoint is the residual *casticismos* or the made-to-order autonomous communities. This, then, is the tradition that links up and harmonizes with a country that is more and less than a State: the tradition of a monarchy that can put an end to integral Spain and give us back a Hispania that is both plural and intercontinental.

I have already stressed the role of the monarchy in neutralizing the Spanish attempt at *in*volution. But just as dangerous or even more so was the tendency in the country toward *ex*volution, toward converting rapidly and expeditiously to "Democracy" just as it had converted to the Enlightenment in the eighteenth century, to Liberalism in the nineteenth, and to Revolution in the twentieth. In order for history not to repeat itself, the new laws had to be able to drag the old structures along with them; democratic ideas had to come to be real convictions and be consolidated into republican habits. *The maximum of formal continuity compatible with substantive change* had to be achieved in order to keep those idealist reflexes at bay. And to bring this about, the new monarchy could seek inspiration in the successes and failures of its own dynastic tradition. Alphonse XIII had tried to confront the cacique mentality of southern Spain and create an opening for Catalan autonomy without betraying the 1876 constitutional framework. International and social conditions were not favorable and his attempt was a rueful failure. In 1975 conditions were indeed more favorable, but the immediate ideological and "constitutional" tradition (General Franco's *Principios Fundamentales)* was much less so. Franco. How to reap the fruits of tradition and simultaneously break with *that* immediate – and still lively – tradition? The task Adolfo Suárez took on to dismantle the system and achieve the formal self-dissolution of the Franco regime drew up the guidelines of a bold and prudent process in which the Spanish monarchy took the lead it has maintained ever since.

*   *   *

The Spanish experience – as everyone from R. Morse to Octavio Paz has agreed – constitutes a model in which anyone can pick and choose the orientation or inspiration that best suits him. In Poland, Adam Michnik, a leader of the KOR and Solidarity, was already referring to Spain in 1986 in his proposal for a "compromise between membership in the Warsaw Pact and the transformation of the political and social structures. The Spanish model," he concluded, "represents a great hope for us. Spain provides us with a viable model of a way to move from dictatorship to democracy..." Michnik was most likely not taking into account that the Church would not be able to play the role in Poland that the monarchy played here – nor indeed that the USSR of the time was not the United States. Let us hope that with perestroika it moves a little closer, so that the model can also take effect there.

For Latin America, which has shared with Spain its lack of democratic tradition and consolidation, the Spanish monarchy can offer an incentive for seeking a point of reference both traditional and open-ended, both immanent to social reality and transcending immediate political struggle. The American republics must find this principle in their own experience and on their own turf and terms, from their own traditions and liturgies, so as to confront this other tradition of coups d'état, bureaucracy, and corruption that constitutes our most shameful legacy in America: the true Spanish *leyenda negra*. Even more to the point, the historical memory of the protective role of the Spanish monarchy, so plainly alive in many indigenous communities, could make of it one of those shared references that the Latin American community ought to recover. Let me state outright that this is not an attempt to vindicate any rights of the Spanish sovereign in Latin America. Instead, quite to the contrary, it is a defense of the rights that the Latin Americans – just like the Sephardim, the Gibraltarians, or even the peninsular independentists – can claim of this monarchy: their right eventually to share this institution with the Spanish and use it for their own projects and goals. Now that Latin America need no longer fear the threat of Spanish hegemony, there seems to be no reason that, as Juan Carlos I has suggested, "united by our brotherhood in language, a common past and a shared world view, we should not seek jointly to resuscitate the importance and specific weight that our peoples once enjoyed on both sides of the Atlantic."

On another, more circumstantial level, perhaps it could also be instructive for Latin America to examine the peculiar path, midway between voluntarism and empiricism, social democracy and populism that Spanish democracy has taken. The loyal virtuosity of Adolfo Suárez, and the tenacity of Fraga or Carrillo in converting the most reluctant among their clientele to democracy was followed finally by the controlled boldness of Felipe González and a new generation of politicians or union leaders able to move naturally from clandestine activity to the negotiating table with an exquisite respect for the rules of the game; able also to establish a tense and effective pact between their own socialist body of ideas and the economic, autonomic, corporate, and professional interests that make up and must also dynamize the country. A pact that considered, among others, ideas so "unorthodox" within socialist tradition as an industrial and technological modernization meant to avoid the savage social costs of similar liberal modernizations or the eschatology of the "visible saints"; a break with the cysts of interest-group and corporative spirit (a spirit that has yet to be confronted within a university recently saturated with new tenure seekers and within a political party to which no challengers are emerging); an economic and social liberalization that took on the privatization of public enterprise and the deregulation of the productive sectors (and that was willing to bet, less boldly in this case, on pluralism in television and on "that necessary irony of Sovereignty and the Motherland," to quote F. Umbral, "known as the State of Autonomies"). All of this suggests that the damned pendulum that kept swinging back and forth from dogmatic and messianic faith to passivity and indifference has at last been broken. Finally, Maeztu's declaration that "we Spaniards just weren't meant to be Kantians" seems about to be refuted.

This option was particularly daring and apropos at a moment in which the generalized trend seemed to be in the other direction: economic "liberalism" paradoxically or perversely allied with a new national and moral fundamentalism (in which preferential credits were allied with moral arguments, the application for public concessions with declarations of faith in civil society or the market, and the imposition of prayer in schools with the "officialization" of the English language in California). And it seemed even more apropos in the Latin American countries where the formation of capital and productive structures had always been subject to the mediation of a State that declared itself to be modernizing before actually being modern, that rarely was able to stimulate development or the formation of a middle class, and that is directly responsible today for 67 percent of the foreign debt in those countries.

None of which means that greater unity and cooperation must be achieved on the basis of a one-way influence of the Spanish transition upon the Latin

American process. The struggles for liberation from Mexico to Nicaragua, the present-day political evolution of Brazil, Uruguay, or Argentina, the independence that the OAS has begun to show since Acapulco, the interregional pacts and parliaments meant to create a united front and market, all offer examples for us to learn from. And above all, Spain should also learn in turn from the infinite skill with which these countries tackled and resolved the problematical tradition we left behind: the way they absorbed, preserved, and enriched the genius of the language; assimilated Hispanic shame and native tact to found upon them an exquisite courtesy; achieved the metamorphosis of the colonial complex into a new identity that, in 1939, was even able to offer refuge to an intellectual elite under persecution in "mother Spain," and so on. This versatility produced in Mexico the first synthesis between Anglo-Saxon pragmatism and Latin positivism (the *científicos*), the first popular revolution of the modern age and the original synthesis of avant-garde art and criollo iconography represented by Mexican mural art.

Under the new monarchy, Spain seemed to initiate the recovery of its traditionalism; to finish it up, it must leave behind only its centralist reflexes, the most pernicious remnant of a precocious state allied with social backwardness. Under the socialist government, in turn, it seems that the classical and neoscholastic ideal of a "non-Calvinist" modernization has been revived; the only thing left is for the Socialists to pay the country its ultimate tribute by finishing the task. Of course, this ultimate tribute will not be rendered until they have lost an election and thus demonstrated that, in Spain, as is fitting in a democracy, there is neither a new ideology of salvation, nor an eternal generation of politicians, nor a charismatic option of deliverance. But in the meantime, in order to define their task, the Socialists will have to have learned to be both purposeful and porous; to recover the traditional Spanish cultural permeability and not merely the reflexes of its more or less enlightened despotism. Only then will they have lost the obsession with "vertebrating" Spain and recognized that political homogeneity must emerge inductively from society and not deductively from the state, nor even from a single political party. Only then will they no longer personify a socialism that is invincible in small rural towns, so well prepared to win elections in noncombative autonomous states, and so impotent in its leadership of the well-established, industrialized historical states like Euskadi and Catalonia. Only then will the Spanish government be able to look at Europe without that "effervescent thrill and hunger of the convert" (Jaume Lorés), i.e., of those who seek a "new identity" by which to forget the genuine reality – experienced as nightmare – of its equally plural and transnational dimension. And only then will Spain be able to teach and bring to Europe; still in its "Visigothic" stage, that uninhibited and invertebrate crossbreeding *(mestizaje)* of origins and of destiny from which Spain was able to invent a cultural reality whose discourse, narrative, or theology now challenges us as a European project undertaken from an original perspective, with another blood and in different latitudes. If nothing more, let these notes of mine serve as evidence that the pathetic reflection of Spain upon its own identity can become still more complex and Baroque if combined with a Catalan and Latin American reflection.

*   *   *

But an encounter such as I proposed in Washington could not come to a close without posing this last question: Does Spanish experience, whether colonial or present-day, have anything to offer North Americans? Aside from the "values" it may incarnate, can it draw any guidelines? Symbol that it is, can it also be a guide?

Up to now we have observed the contrary: the private and sectarian nature of North American colonization gives birth to the liberal and dynamic bias of its society, in contrast with the impotence and grandiloquence so often served up by the official apologetics of its Latin American counterparts. The severe religious principles that inspired the Founding Fathers turned out to be more attuned than Catholic dogma to the provisional pacts and compromises among interests of bourgeois ethic. This ethic may well be, as Ortega thought, "morally and vitally inferior to the integral solidarity" of the dogmatic or warrior ethic, but it was certainly the one that founded both modern democracy and a more relaxed and efficient imperial politics, led by economic rather than moral or ideological principles.[101]

Necessary and practical as it was, this secularization of principles did not come about without taking its toll, or generating its own mumbo jumbo. Have we not seen that in Europe itself the old myths of Divine or Natural Right were not eliminated but replaced by the new myths of State or Reason, more earthly but no less energumenic myths than the ones they replaced. In the United States this secularization did not take place without a process of historical amnesia and metaphorical impoverishment that has come to pose practical problems for North Americans in their relationships with the world and among themselves. These are the problems, as we shall see, for which the Spanish experience can nowadays provide not only valuable historical testimony, but also practical guidelines.

The most important problems appear, of course, among North Americans themselves. The values or ideals expurgated from an activity theologically oriented toward efficiency now reappear – in a sort of Freudian "return of the repressed" – transmuted into more secular but no less "ideal" values: Openness, Informality, Communication, and the like. Now the eager and systematic attitude previously adopted toward economic and social values is reproduced in the "conquest" of the new ones. And so, the anxiousness to feel or to experience comes now to take precedence over the more traditional will to power or desire to possess.[102]

"Sometimes they call me an idealist. Well, that is the way I know I am an American. America is the only idealistic nation in the world" (Woodrow Wilson). And so it is, indeed: pure interests soon hatch pure ideals; the grossest pragmatism, the most sublime idealism. Hence the growth in the United States of an economic liberalism that doubles as religious fundamentalism; a behavioristic positivism that forms a system with the broadest assortment of therapies and industries for intimacy. The Swami and the Guru right next to the Manager or the Executive: pure piety in the heart of pure efficiency. A literal copy of the structure that, according to Hegel, presided over Oriental thought: empiricism "made up of infinite details and additional, dull enumerations," alongside a "cosmic and sublime spiritualism in which the subject is definitively lost."[103]

I must add that I do not consider this mixture of irony and condescension with which the American attitude has tended to be judged in Europe from Hegel on to be fair. If nothing more, because this attitude reflects an original American experience that Europeans – under the shelter of American power and warmed by their own "discourses" – have often not even had to confront. But it is no less true that those intellectual "discourses" and social conventionalisms that may be a burden in Europe are just what American society needs to cushion its tendency to move expeditiously, and without skipping a beat, from statistical data to mystical fantasy, from pragmatism to utopia, from technical "know-how" to an iconic "way of life." It is a fact that American power has not so much been spread by arguments or theories as by the diffusion of an image or a way of life that nowadays has become ecumenical. An image of immediacy and universal compatibility in which wickedness goes arm in arm with candor, in which man seems able to connect directly with Nature or the Future and in which his most contradictory desires miraculously become complementary. Beyond the Hegelian "thesis and antithesis," beyond the Freudian "discontent with civilization" or the Kierkegaardian "either/or," today we are witnessing the triumph of the American "not only but also," in which our most conflictive aspirations seem miraculously to be reconciled: both more civilized and more sensitive, wiser and more ingenuous, more powerful and more vulnerable, more individualistic and more community-oriented, more tribal and more universal.[104]

I do not know whether this mythology is better or worse than its predecessors. But I do know that, just like them, it has a price. It is a fact, for instance, that the lack of a model (class, history, creed) to which to "refer" one's own success or failure, leads an individual (and his family) to experience his failure as the stigma of his *personal* inferiority. In the same vein, the rejection, in the name of "spontaneity," of socially recognized conventions transforms sociability into a compulsive and imperative intimacy, or childhood education into an imposition of conventional values thought of as "facts." (My six year-old son failed a test in a Boston school when he did not "understand" that the most important aspect of a story was that "the child came back home at the right time" and not – as he answered – that "the child caught five fish on his trip.") And this very "social empiricism" that reduces education to strict indoctrination or manipulation is what in turn transforms courtesy into something like the "rules of face-to-face interaction" described by E. Goffman or into the *Games People Play* analyzed by E. Berne.

In this way, the dark underbelly of the professed behaviorism and cult to the "casual" in the United States is revealed to be the most elementary psychologism. Why does this happen there, in contrast with Europe? I think the explanation is simple. What helps Europeans to relativize education, socialize guilt, and relax manners is their bulk of well-established (and lively) "forms" of rhetoric, liturgy, or ideology. As it is the very absence (or rejection) of these forms that spurs Americans to run around looking for *the real thing*. Hence my conclusion, that if we can learn from their traditional ability to give body and entity to political conventions, they should in turn learn from our ability to generate social conventions that preclude their insensitive slide toward the intimate or the mythic, toward fundamentalism or utopism: toward the postindustrial "return of the repressed."

Nor should anyone find it strange that the individualistic and competitive Puritan temperament on which American prosperity was founded has begun to pose problems in the New Industrial State. In *Organization Man,* W. White explained how the great American corporation had tried to replace the "Lone Ranger" self-made spirit praised and fostered by schools and the media, which had become a hindrance for the cooperative teamwork spirit that was now needed. V. Packard gave a journalistic account of the methods used to change the Puritan conviction that saving was a virtue and consumption a vice ("a *purchase* today means one less man on the unemployment line: maybe *you"),* and to invert its principles of moral causality whereby effort must precede compensation and you can only enjoy what you have already earned. Galbraith and D. Bell have stressed in turn that the very orientation of American corporations and policy toward short-term immediate returns has often hindered their actual efficiency and development. Thus, we see a new prestige among the American establishment of the cooperative and compassionate spirit of a Catholic tradition seen until recently as linked to, and liable for, the underdevelopment of the Latin American countries.

But if utilitarianism left on its own has often turned out to be quite inefficient, neither has the complementary moralism of American society turned out to be more ethical. For Richard Sennett, the surprising and truly scandalous thing about the great American political scandals is that they are not focused so much on the character or efficacy of the political decisions as on the eventual sincerity of the actors, on their good or bad, better or worse, intentions. Kennedy was saved from the disaster of the Bay of Pigs because he "sincerely" admitted to the fiasco. "I will never lie to you," was the slogan that gave Carter the presidency. "Did he know? Did he order it? Did he agree to it?" were the questions discussed after Watergate or during Iran-Contragate, and which seem more appropriate to a Hispanic confessional than to the U. S. Congress. The practical effects of policy are never so passionately debated as the purity of intention with which it is carried out. Hence that mixture of moralistic incompetence of the policymakers and of barbarous indifference toward the effect of their policies upon the world. Hence that lack of theoretical and historical sense that leads them to judge rather than understand, to switch from a social vision to a moral or pyschological one "which looks at the world as it were from the pulpit, always ready to judge it and even to impose its armed will upon it" (B. R. Barber). Hence, finally, that strange and disquieting mixture of candor and arrogance, of goodwill and cruelty, of Machiavellianism and clumsiness of U. S. policy. Or, as Octavio Paz asks himself, "In a democracy which constantly reveals itself to be fertile and creative in science, technology and the arts, how and why can the mediocrity of its politicians be so overwhelming?"

I suppose the answer lies in the fact, to put it in Kantian terms, that a pragmatic imperialism with no theory is "blind," if not obfuscated, in much the same way that an amnesiac moralism without a sense of history is "empty," if not, simply, cynical. In this area, both the theoretical faculties and the cultural sensitivity of Hispanic imperialism could still teach a lesson to North American imperialism. As a British historian has written, the Spanish colonization produced "a fruitful collaboration which gave intellectuals a powerful stimulus for formulating theories and for focusing their attention on the pressing concrete problems." We witness it in the attempt to locate events within the framework of a critical reflection on one's own acts and a theoretical comprehension of others. We witness both perplexity and observation, both projection of programs and absorption of attitudes. Everything that has been lacking in the North American tendency to see or use the other as no more than a land mass for the exploitation of natural resources or a surface for the projection of its cultural prejudices. Prisoners of both their (traditional) project to make the nation a private reduct away from the world and of their present-day capacity to make this world over to meet their needs, Americans have never acquired the experience of otherness that Hegel had long ago diagnosed as their Achilles' heel. Their growing addiction to Instant therapies and Videocults has done nothing but reinforce this very narcissism and self-indulgence in their own "view" or "experiencing" of things. "Hence," O. Paz has written, "the reluctance they affect when they must confront the outside world, their incapacity to understand it and their clumsiness in dealing with it."

But this attitude, which may have been fitting and practical as long as the United States was still an "autonomous community," became counterproductive, not to say extremely dangerous, when it turned into the center of the world while continuing to entertain a provincial and manichaean vision of everyone else. At that point, the erstwhile time-honored liberties of the small community tend to become today's excuse for oppression or alibi for the exploitation of others. The very melting-pot ideology expressed in the "movement to Americanize the immigrant" begins to fail once the pre-1924 rhythm of selection, quota, and migration, which assured the progressive assimilation of the new arrivals, can no longer be sustained. Today's massive Hispanic immigration, the boomerang result of Yankee "behaviorism," is generating a new North American style that adopts its ways but remains reticent regarding its goals or ideals. Thus, they find themselves with a "difference" incrusted in their very heart, which they will have to learn to deal and coexist with, instead of segregating it as they did with the Indians and the blacks, or metabolizing it as they did with the successive waves of Europeans. It is in confronting this experience that they can find a new guiding power in a Hispanic empire that did not give birth to a manifest destiny, instead elaborating a hesitant epic, and becoming assimilated to what it had conquered to the point of actually forming part of it. The Spanish colony, instead of just extending Europe's dominion, was able to induce a new "version" of the West that two centuries of Anglo-Saxon domination did not produce in, say, India or Namibia.[105] Indeed, the only thing still lacking in the formidable power of fascination of today's United States is the Hispanic capacity for conversion and seduction that never confused its will for theoretical clarity and distinction with the pathos of cultural distance.

Or this, at least, is what I wished tendentiously to stress in the colloquium in Washington. After all, one way of neutralizing the perverse effect of prejudices is to make them explicit. This is what I have tried to do with my own in this book.

Notes

1. Antonio Regalado has developed these aspects of the Spanish baroque:

> Spanish Baroque society is not fundamentally closed, for it contains subsystems which reveal an open society that enjoys great artistic freedom and implacably analyzes the relationships between the individual and society. Thus, it both incarnates and serves as the critic of the incipient yet modern process of rationalization, of reason as social control.... Now that modernity is in crisis and even Marx has been reviewed, the Spanish Baroque can offer us an alternative model for reason, and not rationalization as repression. It is clear, for example, that neither French theater nor the European literature of the period ever question the authority of the father or the king, while in the Spanish Baroque this authority is implacably analyzed and polemicized.

2. Much has been written about both Columbus's knowledge and capabilities and his mistaken beliefs or superstitions, but only M. Polanyi has seen fit to analyze the psychological "profile" – a mixture of *naiveté, credulousness,* and *stubbornness* – that makes of him the great "Discoverer":

> The ability to pursue commonly-accepted beliefs beyond the limits of their contemporary implications is in itself a preeminent force for change and scientific advance. This is the type of force that sent Columbus off across the Atlantic to seek the Indies. His genius consisted in taking literally the fact that the earth is round – something that his contemporaries maintained vaguely and as a matter of speculation – and using it as a guide to practical action. The ideas elaborated by Newton in his *Principia* were also common in Columbus' time; and once again his genius revealed itself in his power to coin these vague beliefs in concrete and precise form.

3. These descriptions are undoubtedly intended to justify using the crucifix to beat the Indians into conquest and evangelization, but they are unrelentingly contested from Spain by theologians and jurists alike. *"Tam barbarae gentes inventae non sunt,"* wrote Suárez in his study of the "right of intervention." *(De Fide,* disputatio XVIII, n. 1566). No idolatry or brutality legitimates war against a people, adds Vitoria, so long as it does not deny other peoples (or those among them who convert) the rights recognized to all people by the *ius gentium.* As Sánchez Ferlosio has rightly pointed out, the criteria by which

Zurita or Vitoria consider the Indians still "primitive" (inconstancy, nonuse of money, and so on) are fundamentally economic. "What the Spanish saw as a phylogenetic age difference between themselves and the new conquered peoples, was in fact a difference in the place of economics in the daily and social life of both and, in consequence, a distinct configuration of both time and the individual."

4. Withal, both the anthropological vision underlying these analyses and the theory that frames them have recently been questioned. I refer to the theory that considered to be perfectly linear historical processes the passages from *status* society to *contractus* society (Maine); from *Gemeinschaft* to *Gesellschaft* (Tönnies); from "primitive" collectivism and dogmatism to "modern" individualism and pragmatism. Mary Douglas has demonstrated, in contrast, that both "modern" competitive behavior and the individualistic analysis and valorization of behavior have always existed in certain "low-grid" tribes, which she calls the "New Guinea type" as opposed to the "African type." (In the supplement to article I of *Das Kapital* we find a wonderful description and enthusiastic valorization of this same primitive "individualism.") We must not forget, moreover, that at the time of the conquest a merchant class of businessmen that might eventually have replaced the dominant warrior class had begun to form in Tenochtitlán. In his *General History,* Sahagún tells us that the "gentlemen of Tlatilulco" had already won the right to sacrifice their "bought slaves" on Huitzilopochtli's altar after the warriors had sacrificed the "prisoners captured" in combat.

5. This is also, though mitigated, Julián Marías's thesis in *Encuentro ¿con quién?* (Encounter with whom?): "América... existed only for the new arrivals; it began to exist in someone's mind precisely in that year (1492). The inhabitants of that continent had no notion of their existence, of their entirety, of their scope. They did not know one another, they had not traveled its length, they could not speak with one another. Hundreds, perhaps millions of languages were spoken.... The American Indians only began to speak to each other beyond their different ethnic groups, when they were able to do so in Spanish." But in 1804, W. von Humboldt, who reckoned the number of languages to be between 500 and 2,000, had interpreted the phenomenon quite differently, comparing it to analogous European situations. And O. Paz has recently stressed the *unity* and *continuity* of pre-Columbian culture, sometimes greater than that of Europe:

> There was not only a continuous interrelationship and influence among the different societies and epochs – Olmecs, Mayas, Zapotecs, peoples of Teotihuacan and Tajín, Tula, Cholula, Mitla, Tenochtitlán – but also a

similarity in their forms and cultural expressions, from the cosmogonic myths and artistic styles to the political and economic institutions. In addition and as a complement to this unity there was an extraordinary continuity of more than two thousand years. Naturally, there were changes and alterations in Mesoamerica, but not the brusque ruptures and revolutionary transformations of other continents. Mesoamerica did not suffer religious mutations like the abandonment of pagan polytheism by Christian monotheism, or the appearance of Buddhism and Islam. Or the scientific, technical, and philosophical revolutions of the Old World.

So, if we are to speak of "cultural limitations" at all, they do not so much derive from the fragmentation stressed by Marías as the magnificent isolation and coherence sketched out by Vargas Llosa and Paz. To quote the latter, "The immense and prolonged historical solitude of Mesoamerica is the cause of its greatness and its weakness. Greatness because it was one of the few truly original civilizations of history: it owes nothing to the others; weakness because its isolation makes it vulnerable to the principal experience of both social and biological life: that of the *other.*"

6. After demanding their surrender, and recognition of the kings of Castile and Aragon as their sovereigns, the requerimiento drawn up by the theologians of Valladolid continues as follows:

> If it were not done thus, I certify that, with the help of God... I will wage war upon you in all places and manners, and subject you to the yoke of the Church and of his Majesty, and I will take your women and children and make slaves of them and as such I will sell them and dispose of them as his Majesty should order; and I will take your goods and I will wreak upon you all the ills and damages that I may, as befits vassals who obey not.... And I protest that the death and damages that might proceed therefrom, are your fault and not His Majesty's or ours, nor that of those gentlemen who accompany me. And just as I state and demand this of you, I ask the present scribe to give it to me in signed witness.

The response of the Carib Indians to this requerimiento, taken by Enrique Caballero from Enciso's *Summa Geographica,* states that "the Pope must have been drunk when he gave [the king of Castile] what was not his, and that the King, who asked for and took such merchandise, must have been mad, for he demanded and offered what belonged to others."

7. In fact, the classification of gods or devils follows a general rule in which classical tradition often takes precedence over Christian. Thus, in Book II of Sahagún's *General History,* those beings who rule over the city and war are usually called "gods"; the domestic spirits who preside over the hearth and individual funeral ceremonies are known as "devils."

8. Modern anthropology has come to add an "ecological" explanation of human sacrifice to this first "theological" justification. The sacrifice and ingestion of prisoners is, in fact, the most efficient way of controlling growth and obtaining required protein, above all in a country that has become urbanized without access to protein from pigs, cattle, sheep, or horses (M. Harris). The only domestic animals that existed there were very small – the turkey and the *escuincle* (small dog) – and, exceptionally, the llama in Peru, where for this reason human sacrifices are more unusual... We should not forget, moreover, that the Spanish conquerors, despite having access to those large mammals, did not refrain from eating the thighs of their own countrymen (who had been hanged precisely for having eaten their horses) on the feast of Corpus Christi in 1536, "when there were no more rats, or mice, or snakes left, and they were crawling about on the ground, dying" (E. Caballero).

9. The human sacrifices of the Canaanites of Byblos, the Carthaginians, and the Semites are well known... Even Father Brébeuf's travail has a precedent in the torture applied by Pompina in Rome to Philologus the freedman. With a single difference: in this case anthropophagy becomes autophagy, for Philologus himself is obliged to swallow his own roasted flesh. And let us not forget that Montaigne establishes a significant comparison between the American sacrifices and those that are being carried out in *contemporary* Europe in chapter 30 of his *Essays*.

10. "The scholasticists," J. H. Elliott observes, "were not gratified by the idea of the Empire," which they attempted to delegitimize by various means. On the one hand, "Vitoria devoted part of his work *De Indis* to refuting the argument that the Emperor could be the lord of the entire world." On the other, "the rejection of the doctine of the direct power of the Pope by Vitoria, Suárez and other important scholasticists of the 16th century had so weakened the Spanish position that by the end of the century it was almost impossible to reconstruct it using other lines of reasoning."

11. Eugeni d'Ors's reticence toward Spanish evangelical style is based precisely on what he calls its lack of "snobbery" in contrast with Islamic missionary style. He writes in *La Ciencia de la Cultura,*

> Reasons have occasionally been sought for the more rapid and efficient results which Islamic missionary activity tends to achieve among the pagan populations of Africa when compared with its Christian counterpart. Upon consideration, it becomes clear... that while the Catholic missionary struggles to place the principles of the faith within the grasp of the natives, even of

those whose mentality is most rudimentary, even seeing fit to silence some of these principles for the moment, as too difficult, and using at every juncture the most accommodating equivalencies – "Your name for our Mother of God is goddess X," etc. – the Moslem missionary, proudly, adopts the air of one who condescends to teach the native a special style, imbued with hermetical distinction, with which to read or chant the texts of the Koran and pronounce them. The result is that, just as the pagan *lowers himself* in submitting to the humiliatingly basic nature of the Catholic teaching, he is caught up by the prestige in the note of superiority that the possession of that style and that phonetics seems to garner him among his peers: snobbery comes into play.

The sense of equality, the willingness to adapt and to be comprehended of Spanish evangelization would thus have been the cause of "a diffuse, sustained, experientially uncurable disappointment, experienced by a sector of the Exoteron (the colonized territories) in their – more or less secret, more or less conscious – aspiration to rise and be incorporated into the Ecumenon (the Metropolis)."

12. Still, the good reasons proffered by those who defend "easy baptism," baptism en masse and almost by obligation, must be taken into account. In a 1555 letter to Charles V, the Franciscan friar Toribio de Benavente, also known as Motolinía, refers to the tradition that from the time of Gregorius Magnus prohibited Christians from enslaving one another. "When baptism was rapidly imparted," A. Armani observes, "the natives were converted *ipso facto* into free men, and could thus not be subjected to slavery, according to the exact same principles adopted years before regarding the inhabitants of the Canary Islands," and applied as well, as L. Hanke observes, in the colonization of the Philippines from 1570 on.

13. As we have seen, Cortés is just as prone to manipulate signs or use psychological warfare as he is to use arms – or even more so. He is able to dialogue from the very start with Moctezuma's messengers, thanks to "La Malinche," who translates the words of the Indians from Nahuatl and communicates them to Aguilar in Maya, who in turn translates them into Castilian for Cortés.

14. Slavery is a general practice in Europe, where from the thirteenth century on the Germans take captured Slavs into slavery (whence the term "slave"), the Christians take the Moslems and Saracens (and vice versa), and the English develop their industry on the basis of the slave trade. It is in this context that Humboldt's admiration must be understood: "The legislation in the Spanish Republics of America will never be sufficiently extolled for its prudence. From the very beginning it has seriously sought the total extinction

of slavery. In this respect, this part of the world offers a great advantage over the southern part of the United States, where the white men, during the war with England, established freedom for their exclusive benefit, excluding a slave population of more than a million and half men." For Román Arciniegas this orientation comes into being in eight decisive days. On April 12, 1495, the Catholic kings write a letter to the bishop of Badajoz giving instructions for the sale of the Indians brought from the Antilles by Columbus. Four days later, on April 16, they decide to suspend the sale because "we wish to consult their fate with lawyers, theologians and specialists in canonical law, to see if they can be sold in good conscience." Within four more days, the decree of April 20 is released, ordering the Indians to be freed and returned to their countries of origin.

15. A meticulous development of the topic I have been discussing in this section can be found in *Los grandes conflictos sociales y económicos de nuestra historia,* by Indalecio Aguirre (Bogotá, 1980).

16. This is the same device by which Caesar attempts to drive a wedge between Cassius and Brutus in Quevedo's *Julius Caesar* when both aspire to the post of *praetor urbanis* and he sentences, with calculated ambiguity, "Cassius' claim is more just; however, the best is due to Brutus." Quevedo thus interprets the action: "By giving hope to each of them in their claims to the urban praetorship, he divides them with ambitious enmity...; as he wants them both to be his friends, it was to his advantage that they be mutual enemies."

17. Aristotle defines these men of unbending political vocation as "individuals who seize upon public posts as if they were afflicted with a sickness that could only be cured by continuity in power" *(Politics,* III, 8).

18. A similar device had been in use in Spain, but with the inverse purpose of protecting the common people from the hidalgos in the elections to municipal office. The records of the 1618 Cortes testify that "so that elections will turn out in their favor, the farmworkers... try to elect the poorest and most wretched hidalgos, with the least talent and ability, either to annihilate said estate or because in this way they... come to hold control of the offices of the estate of the hidalgo, to the prejudice of the nobility and of the notables of blood and lineage...."

19. To understand or "make sense of" what they see, the conquistadors take recourse to their handbook of classical utopias (the Atlantis of the *Cratylus,* the Fountain of Youth, the land of the Amazons, the city of the Caesars) and

to the images offered up by books of chivalry or fantastic zoology (the country of Cinnamon, Eldorado, the White King, the Silver mountains).

20. The legend of the effective exclusion of the Catalans from the conquest and colonization has been definitively refuted by C. Martínez Shaw in *Catalunya i el comerç amb Amèrica: final d'una llegenda* (Catalonia and American Trade: The End of a Legend).

21. Here we begin to appreciate the paradoxical drawback to America's development that the very modernity and efficacy of the Castilian state and administration would represent. If the Casa of Contratación had not controlled the data on travel to America with such administrative efficacy, many more Jews, Moors, or Dutch could have slipped through this customs house, even though in principle it was closed to all foreigners and even to "all those reconciliated with, or Moors and Jews recently converted to, our Catholic faith, and their children, and the children or grandchildren of those burned or condemned as heretics, on either the male or female side." With fewer posts to buy and sell, those who went to America would have had to seek their wealth through work, and not through monopoly and sinecure. With less capacity for centralization and control, the structures of the patrimonial state would not have been empowered by those of this incipient and precocious modern state through the creation of a system of institutionalized corruption (a common practice in those days), which still persists in Latin America as the most sinister inheritance of the Spanish, the symbol and the safeguard of the continent's underdevelopment.

22. Judaism is at both the theoretical and practical heart of modern rational and mercantile development. On the one hand, its rejection of all forms of superstition in the name of a transcendent God freed the daily world of the religious density that in still magical or animistic societies blocks rational manipulation and systematic exploitation outside all ritual or liturgy. On the other hand, Jewish tradition and its "eccentricity" within European society (the Jews could not be landowners) forced them to devote themselves to manufacture, trade, and finance. Jewish piety rewarded knowledge of the law, the study of which also served as mental training, for other, more secular dealings. Furthermore, the Church still prohibited monetary commerce as usury, but because it had become indispensable for commercial traffic, even the clergy had to appeal to the Jews for many of their transactions. Now, if in spite of all this the Jews stayed at a level of "capitalism of pariahs, not moving on to a rational capitalism" (Weber), this could have been due to the fact that they still retained a "primitive" residue of a *double* morality, while credit and financial operations required a *universalist* morality in which it no

longer mattered whether the signator was a Jew or a Gentile. Hence the specific capitalistic need for a Christian morality. This need began to be conspicuous when it became common for merchants to associate with a priest who would sign their credits and bills of exchange for them. Still lacking a law or state administration to guarantee payment, the Christian "morality" of the priest was sufficient guarantee for the creditor.

But this function of the medieval priests or monks also shows why Catholic morality and ideology could not actually satisfy the needs of universality required by the new emerging economic system. The Church still opposed allowing that spiritual universality to percolate into this world, giving way to the absolute profanity – profanation – of secular time and space. Shrines, holy offices, and pilgrimages continue to organize the space without and to mediatize the piety within. The liturgical calendar continues to impose an ecclesial rhythm upon "the works and the days." The Church also shares with the old guilds their aversion to the free market, to the loss of the sense of one's own work associated with the division of labor, and to the impersonality of relationships to which a monetary economy leads. Bartering or gift giving, even robbery or slavery, are "personal" relationships between "whole men." The formation of market prices is, in contrast, an impersonal process ruled by money, that "egoism in the abstract" to which the Church still opposes the *iustum pretium* ("just" price, "necessary" salary, "legitimate" earnings, definitions that resist the passage from *oikonomía* to *krematistiké*). In opposition to the "creditor morality" of the newly rich merchants for whom opprobrium derives from nonpayment of debts, the Church still holds to a "debtor morality" (Tawney), according to which shame derives from the exploitation of poverty through speculation and usury.

Of course, the Church had created certain nuclei of rational organization and systematic labor: the monasteries. In fact, the monks provide a great proportion of the civil servants of the Middle Ages, and it has even been said that the doge of Venice fell when the "war of the investitures" prevented him from continuing to utilize them as agents in his overseas enterprises. But these nuclei of "rationality" were in the service of a Knowledge understood as the laborious exegesis of texts and the passive "contemplation" of Truth, not as Protean or Kantian manipulation and transformation of reality. Even more to the point, the Church tacitly recognized that the pure, ascetic life was an unachievable desideratum for the ordinary mortal, whose weakness was both exploited and pardoned through the sacrament of confession. As a result, a "double morality" was to take on a new force with the "extenuations" and "exemptions" of Jesuit laxism.

23. First expected only to form part of the audience (see Appendix III), Laureano López Rodó later participated with an *ad hoc* speech in the meeting

at the Wilson Center in Washington.

24. Neither atheists nor, as Hegel said, even Catholics: "The Protestant religion encouraged mutual trust, for in the Protestant church religious activity constitutes one's entire life. In contrast, among Catholics the basis for a similar mutual trust cannot exist, for [among them] violent power dominates profane matters... and those forms known as constitutions are not sufficent to protect against this mistrust."

25. Keynes continues:

> On the one hand, the working classes either accepted – out of ignorance or lack of strength – or were obligated – persuaded or pressured by custom, conviction, authority and the well-established order of society – to accept a situation in which they could lay claim to only a very small part of the cake that they themselves, nature and the capitalists had produced in collaboration. On the other, the capitalist classes were allowed to consider the greater part of the cake to be theirs and were theoretically free to consume it, under the tacit, fundamental condition that in practice they should consume only a small part of it. The duty to "save" turned out to be nine-tenths of the virtue, and the increase of the cake was found to be the goal of a true religion. All those instincts of Puritanism which in another period would have retired from worldly things and forgotten both the arts of production and those of pleasure were now developed around the non-consumption of the cake. And so the cake grew.... Individuals would now be exhorted not so much to abstain as to postpone and to cultivate the pleasures of security and anticipation. Savings would be for their old age and for their children (but only in theory). *The virtue of the cake consisted in its never being consumed.*

26. "In London," Cadalso states in his Letter XXIV, "there are cobbler's shops that have passed on from father to son, assets increasing over five or six generations till they include the acquisition of country homes and estates.... But in Spain each father wishes to see his son in a higher position, and if this does not occur, the son takes care to leave his father in a lower one... all seeking with incredible zeal to situate themselves in one way or another among the noble class." He then makes an exception of the Catalans: "Manufacturing, fishing, navigation, commerce and trade are things almost unknown to the other peoples of the peninsula.... Some call them the Dutch of Spain...but they will flourish only so long as personal luxury and a penchant for ennoblement among the artisans does not take hold among them: these are the two vices opposed to the genius that has enriched them thus far."

27. Take a look at the enlightening line of reasoning set forth in 1780 by Father José Cardiel of the Jesuits to excuse the "subsidiary" intervention of the fathers in this process of development and modernization:

But, are there no men of good will among the lay people who can carry out this task of modernization with rectitude and piety, taking good care of the Indian and, even more, giving him sustenance? Certainly there are; but men of good will find it easier in America than in Spain to get along comfortably without working very hard, and they do not seek the task of caring for the Indians. That job, if it is to be done in good conscience, involves a great deal of work. Dealing with the Indians, a coarse, slovenly, inactive people, unenterprising, and very lax in character, is a torment for a man of good will, and thus he who is of this sort does not wish to take upon himself so much work, and if he does his work as he should, it will redound in much less benefit to him than what he has, or can have with greater tranquility.... This is the cause of our having lost so many Indians, so many townships, which is cause for complaint for everyone, even to the Tribunal and the Viceroys. May God remedy this and shed His holy light upon all. The Jesuits persevere in Italy [where they have been secluded after their dissolution and expulsion]. In silence, patiently carrying out their tasks, they commend themselves to God, to the King and his ministers and await what Divine Providence might dispose for them." *(Compendio de la Historia del Paraguay,* 1780).

28. In the pleading of the Guaraní case before the Crown, the "Jesuitic" style of argumentation can be seen at its best: it consisted of an astute combination of precedents and jurisprudence (the privileges conceded to the Cañaris of Cuzco and to the Indians of Darién), of the merits earned by the Guaraní in the defense of "His Majesty's territory" against the Portuguese, and of the benefits that a more direct control of the frontier might suppose for the Crown in the future.

29. The Jesuits were also accused, and justly so, of (1) not eradicating polygamy by force – indeed, they tolerated it while educating the youth in the new Christian practice of matrimony; (2) being more concerned with the economic development of the Indians than with their evangelization; and (3) strengthening "pagan languages" in detriment to Castilian. Voltaire himself recognizes that the Jesuits are not so much seeking the immediate conversion as the education and instruction of the natives: "The Jesuits took a few savages when they were still children, educated them in Buenos Aires and then employed them as guides and interpreters.... They taught them to plant, to make bricks, to work wood, to build houses.... Their children became Christians."

30. In fact, the legal basis for this protection or segregation is already present Spanish legislation. The Jesuits only carry it to its extreme. Bishop Zumárraga had recommended that the Crown not permit Spaniards to spend more than one day in the reductions. Both the ordinances of Viceroy Mendoza

and those of 1536 in Peru limit their stay to two days, and finally the 1680 *Recopilación* of the Leyes de Indias establishes the limit at three days.

31. Only the Indians and the popular classes appear to disagree with the expulsion of the Jesuits. The *Instrucciones* of the Count of Aranda regarding the methods to be used in containing the pro-Jesuit rebellion speak of "placing the severed heads of the Indians who had taken part in the uprising in the most public places." Both the exhortations of Archbishop Antonio de Lorenzana, railing against "the abominable opinions maintained by the Jesuits regarding regicide and tyrannicide" and the last words of Galvez's decree expelling the order from New Spain are enlightening: "... as once and for all the subjects of the Spanish monarch must know that they were born to keep silent and obey and not to ponder and hold forth upon the high affairs of government."

32. It should not be overlooked that these Jesuitic theories are often simply more psychological elaborations upon the Aristotelian-Thomistic "natural order of the world." The present topic – *property* – can help both to point up this tradition and to contrast it with the theoreticians of the new bourgeois state.

For Saint Thomas of Aquinas, the right to hold property has its foundation in the ordering of the world: that which is most imperfect (things) yields to that which is most perfect (man), who can then make use of them *(Summa Theologica,* II, II, 64, 1). But this right must be made compatible with another principle of natural law that reads: "all things for all men" (ibid., a. 7), whereby the individual can be only, so to speak, the usufructuary of these things, respecting in any event their "social end." Property is thus a "natural law"; private property, on the contrary, is merely the "law of the people" *(ius gentium) (S. Th.,* II, II, 66, 2, ad. 1) or, as the Jesuits were already putting it, a pacted and relative right (Suárez, *Defensio Fidei,* III, II, 130). In good Aristotelian style, Saint Thomas defends this private property but only for occasional purposes or reasons of convenience (stimulation of production, guarantee of social peace, condition of exercising liberality, and so on.). He never ceases to insist on the ideal of "common property" as the early Christians practiced it, and as the mendicant orders of the day, which Saint Thomas courageously defends, continue to practice it. In fact, the Jesuits will add only a more subjective tinge or nuance ("enjoyment," "private happiness," and the like) to the arguments already put forth by Saint Thomas, while developing their casuistic interpretation.

The position of the new "contractualism" will be exactly the inverse, beginning with its valorization of private property as nothing less than the only and fundamental "natural law." Even Bodin, the defender of the Prince's *puissance souveraine* over all other uses, customs, or laws, stops his power short of private property. With Locke, the theoretician of the absolute "legislative bourgeoisie," this private property becomes the basis of and natural justification for the entire political edifice because "it cannot be supposed that God would wish us to maintain [lands] in common without cultivating them…, hence he has given them for industrial and rational use and not for the covetousness and caprice of the lazy and quarrelsome." The Right of Property then precedes Society and the State, for "the greatest and principal end… that brings men to join in society and place themselves under a government, is the preservation of their property," whereby "if at any time the legislators attempt to destroy or affect that property, they place themselves, by their own acts, in a state of war with society, which, in consequence, is absolved of all obedience" *(Second Treatise,* VIII, 95; IX, 123; XI, 134).

33. This is also the source of Suárez's critique of monarchy as the natural and necessary form of political organization: "Power is necessarily in the whole community and not in one part of it: thus there is no reason why it must correspond to one person (the prince) or to one group (the aristocracy) more than to any other within the community" *(Defensio Fidei,* III, II,105-6). "Nor is one sole monarch absolutely necessary for good government. There are other sufficiently effective forms of government… so that, when we speak of a sole sovereign, we may understand a tribunal or unique power, whether it reside in a single head, in a physical person, or in a council or reunion of several, like a moral person *[persona ficta sive mystica]"* (ibid., II, I, 73).

It would also be enlightening further to compare what constitutes "civil society" for Suárez in *De legibus ac Deo Legislatore* with Bodin's *Six Books* and Locke's *Second Treatise,* as well as with the eclectic synthesis Hegel makes of them – happiness and religion on one side, property and business on the other – in his *Philosophy of Law.*

34. This is the very point of Carlos Fuentes's keen observation to the effect that here Suárez is to Rousseau as Machiavelli is to Bodin. "Bodin can invoke the rights of the middle classes," Fuentes writes, "because the basic problems of Foundations, unity and equilibrium have been resolved in France. Machiavelli must invoke the rights of the revolution because those objectives – territorial unity, national identity – have yet to be achieved in Italy."

35. Once more the distance between Saint Thomas's doctrine and what I have called "radical-Thomism" is revealed. For Aquinas, disobedience is licit "when the prince has been excommunicated" – the only result being that the absolute authority of the State is supplanted by that of the Church. For Father

Mariana, it is sufficient for "the governor to have taken power without the consent of the citizens," and for Suárez, that he not have just title, whereupon he can be "judged and executed individually by any citizen" *(Defensio Fidei,* VI, V, 1670).

36. Later, Pufendorf will establish a distinction, within the contract, between the *pactum unionis,* which establishes passage from isolation to community and the *pactum subjectionis,* by which this collectivity takes on a head. Only the first creates a permanent tie, according to Mariana, Vitoria, and Suárez.

37. This is surely the reason behind his not developing a *positive* theory of constitutionalism such as that suggested by Vázquez, Covarrubias, or Father Mariana himself when he advocates fundamental laws or "tutelary action presided over by justice," which must not only limit but also define the powers of the prince. Another element of the new concept of freedom not elaborated by Suárez is the effective participation of the people in the elaboration of the norm. What interests Suárez most is not a new legitimation of power but, rather, its limiting function: the right to resist the law "in good conscience," the retroactivity of the pact of sovereignty, the limit to the *ambitus* of both the law and the state, which can never intrude upon the realms of individual happiness, religion, or humanity in general, to the extent that it is not – nor should it be, as Kant too will state – constituted in a single, worldwide political government. This bias of Suárez's can be understood as an early, and justified, reticence regarding any persons or institutions that wish to interpret and usurp these concepts – always either too gaseous or too codified – that later would be known as the "Spirit of the People" (Montesquieu), the "General Will," (Rousseau), or even the "Opinion of the Majority" (Locke). This is the other side, the critical side, of an apologetic doctrine that, in contrast with other philosophical tendencies of the period, "was not a method of exploration of the unknown, but a system to defend what was known and established." "The Modern Age," as O. Paz concludes, "begins with the criticism of the first principles; the neo-Scholastic age was determined to defend those principles and demonstrate their necessary, eternal character."

38. This Christian split is what Spanish scholasticism now tries to protect from the new absolutist tendencies, just as Ockham had done early in the century against the theocratic tendencies of Boniface VIII *(Breviloquio sobre el principado tiránico).* The limits Suárez sets on the prince's would-be monopoly on the legitimate use of power can be classified into two types:

   1. *Synchronic.* The equilibrium between, and mutual neutralization of, the

different prevailing rights and laws – divine, natural, traditional, positive – which we already saw in Father Vitoria's argument ("nothing which is licit by Natural Law is prohibited by the Gospel," and so on). This "equilibrium of laws" confronts the formation of the absolute State understood by Descartes and Spinoza to be a "substance."

2. *Diachronic*. The exercise of power is also to be limited causally by natural law, and teleologically by its objective of necessary adaptation to the "common good." Both limitations oppose the *summa potestas* of the Sovereign (Bodin), the Will of the Prince (Machiavelli) or the Action of the Government (Hobbes) as the *soluta legibus* unencumbered by any limits. In opposition to all of these, Suárez's people "transfers power to one or many... but always retains the right once again to assume it and once more to tranfer it." Only with Locke will this "right to retract" reappear in public law.

39. If in the last note we saw Spanish scholasticism defend individual freedom and will in a still medieval way, in this one we shall point out its new foundation in a metaphysics clearly oriented toward the Renaissance and rationalism. Both mysticism (Eckhardt) and logic (Duns Scotus) foster a univocal conception of being that is distinctly, but also integrally, "attributed" both to God and to his creatures. The defense of the "analogy of attribution" as against the "analogy of proportionality" sponsored by Cayetano and Juan de Santo Tomás supposes that metaphysical intelligibility is transferred from generic to individual subtance. From a world arranged in a meticulous hierarchy on diverse levels where each individual has a "proportion" or quota of being, we go on to a world tilting more and more between Being and the Individual, between God and the Subject. As I did in the last note, I shall try to sum up Suárez's position in two points:

1. Following Franciscan tradition, Suárez vindicates the primacy of the "singular concrete" both in the nature of Being and in that of Knowing. *(a)* Being is nothing more than the singular reality of things, in which there is no real distinction between essence and existence ("entity is the same as existence," "I take for granted that we understand Being to be the actual existence of things" *(Disputationes metaphisicae*, II, S. 9, and XXXI, S. 1, 2). There is no distinction between the being and the existence of the creature except in "the conception of mind" (ibid., XXXI, S. 2, 12, 13), that is, insofar as the mind asks either "Is it?" or "What is it?" By this means, Suárez anticipates the position of both Spinoza and Kant, who will no longer see in the essence/existence distinction anything but the distinction between the possibility/reality modes. He is in this sense one of those most responsible for the "forgetting of Being" and the "ontological difference," which for

Heidegger characterizes Western metaphysics. *(b)* In correspondence with this idea of Being, Suárez supports direct or intuitive intellectual knowledge of the singular. And here again his definition of Science – "clear, evident and perfect knowledge or perception of the object" (ibid., XXX, S. 15, 2) – is a direct forerunner of the Cartesian version. *(c)* Finally, his ontological pluralism – which has a definitive influence on Leibniz – is extensively developed in his study of the "contingent being" (ibid., IX, 1, 1-19) and in his explanation of individuality as a *modus substantiae,* that is, as constituted not by matter but by formal or modal structure. A thing is composed of *this* matter and *this* form, both of them individual. (Radicalizing Suárez's position, I have defended in *De la modernidad* that it is not a question of form's *also* being individual, but of its being the *only* individual reality, in contrast with the basic stuff or raw material of which it is made up.)

2. Both Vázquez and Suárez in turn take on the rationalization of "divine law," detaching it from theology and associating it, as the Renaissance will, with the "rational nature of man." In so doing they prepare the way for an autonomous ethics that "would exist even if God did not" (Grotius) or which is His very condition (Kant). To this already natural and relational idea of law Suárez adds the unequivocally modern component in the comprehension of both human and divine law: Will. Suárez thus begins by reducing and domesticating – more properly "demagnetizing" – the Aristotelian-Thomistic concept of an absolute God (ibid., XXX, S. 15, 1) to make room in Him (like Bruno or Eckhardt) for freedom and love. Then he goes on limiting divine omnipotence and sovereignty to give rise in turn to human freedom in contrast with both the Protestant and the Thomistic-Dominican theses of predestination. Báñez of the Dominicans still maintains that for a human act to be free it must bear the influence of a divine act ("Divine concourse"). To this idea Molina and Suárez opposed "simultaneous concourse": God intervenes only in the very moment of action and cannot in any case determine it for He endows it only with being and not with any specific quality or direction. His theory of possibilism (which nowadays we would call indeterminism) seeks to save free will a place for itself against Divine Providence and Omnipotence.... No wonder Jesuits were acused of "not being concerned with the state of original sin, trusting to overcome even the worst misfortunes by their will and claiming that free will can produce good moral works without the aid of Grace."

40. "This is," according to O. Paz, "the mask of the tyranny and intellectual origin of Jacobinism and Marxism-Leninism. It is revealing," he goes on, "that in Spanish and Spanish American thought of the modern age the presence of the two Spanish neo-Thomists should be hardly perceptible, as

they were the first ever to see in social consensus the foundation of monarchy itself. This insensitivity is one more example of a well-known fact: the adoption of modernity coincided with the abandonment of our tradition, even of ideas like those of Suárez and Vitoria which were even closer to modern constitutionalism than the speculations of the Calvinists."

41. Veblen sensed early on that economic differences were much less radical than those established on the basis of education. And in our times Bordieu and Sennett, Illich and Zaid have been the ones to argue that the theoretical access of all to knowledge and culture tended more to reinforce than to compensate for differences of origin and class. I do not believe that either the neo-Frankfurtian or the countercultural critiques of public education have always been just – but I do believe that they are sufficent to put an end to its Jacobinian mythification. I have gone further into this topic in *Metopías* (chap. 1) and in *De la modernidad* (chap. III).

42. When I asked the Jesuit historian Father Miquel Batllori to give this text his *nihil obstat,* he replied by pointing out a few minor errors, which I have corrected, and by making this request: "I would ask you to present your theses as hypotheses, so that I may respect them as it is my wish to respect all opinions, and as I tend to reject all theses." I must add that his marginal comments were often critical regarding my defense of the Jesuit *reducciones,* "which I," Father Batllori indicates, "can only partially share. Was it indeed humanitarian to leave them forever in that childlike state?" And finally, his notes tend to underscore, in contrast with my text, the continuity of the "political ideology" of the Jesuits in the Thomist and Dominican context.

43. It has been said that the *aesthetic intuition* of the unity of the world and its laws preceded and prepared their *scientific analysis* during the Renaissance. In a similar vein, we could argue that here the mythical or eschatological vision of history that begins with Saint Augustine and culminates with Marx has served – which is certainly no small feat – to endow historical events with the breadth or universality needed to move on from mere description to comprehension or even to "scientific analysis."

44. Clearly, if one takes the State or the Market to be the "adaptation of things to their concepts" (like politico-economic reality "becoming conscious of itself," or like the "epiphany of Reason in time," which separates Prehistory from History), then any process not leading to their consolidation was seen to go "against History" and to be doomed to failure *ab initio.* Just as nowadays "merely empirical revolts" that did not see themselves as the Revolution (Marxist, of course), or "merely geographical" countries (Hegel)

that were not moving toward this "incarnation of Law and Morality" known as the State (Prussian, of course), would be equally doomed. It is symptomatic, moreover, that among these countries that "will never achieve the ideal perfection of the State" Hegel includes, for reasons we will see further on, the United States of America.

45. Now that Heidegger's "post-modernity" is being stressed, it is useful to note that both his *reflection upon technology* and his *theory of shepherding* contain many characteristically "modern" elements – elements I would situate very precisely between Hegelian and Marxist tradition.

46. In both *El arte ensimismado* and *Teoria de la sensibilitat* I analyzed and challenged this "modern thought," but the last chapter of both works was an exemplary, almost caricaturesque, case of more of the same. Only in *De la Modernidad* did I offer a theoretical alternative to this modern thought (pp. 29, 34, and Book IV) first suggested in *Ensayos sobre el Desorden* and whose systematic development I offered in *Filosofía y/o Política* (chap. II). In this book I try to tell a story following in part the method proposed in those works: just describing the repercussions that news or events have upon a "non-Fichtean" self.

47. "Events are one-way," writes M. Gardner, "not because they cannot go another way but because it is enormously improbable that they would go backwards." So stated, what definitively distinguishes the future from the past is nothing but its component of chance, and in this sense S. Hernáez refers us to the notion of Eddington's time arrow: "Let us arbitrarily draw an arrow: if on following it we find more and more hazardous elements in the state of the world, the arrow is pointing toward the future; if the hazardous elements decrease, the arrow is pointing toward the past. This is the only distinction that physics recognizes."

48. This is what I have tried to argue for in *Europa y otros ensayos* and what Vattimo develops in the prologue to *The End of Modernity* where he explains the present-day "multiplication of the horizons of discourse" as "an emptying of the notion of progress resulting from progress itself."

49. What starts out under the Catholic kings as a struggle against internal subversion (Jews or Illuminists) becomes under the early house of Austria a defense against external ideological subversion. As Elliott observes, "By compensating in many respects for the absence of a Spanish nationality, common religious devotion had clear political repercussions and, as a result, a practical value that Ferdinand or Isabella were quick to make use of." For

Charles V and Philip II, the Inquisition is "deliberately reduced to a department of the State" which is to control a Church "whose function has been nationalized" (J. A. Maravall) and to fight the "other" European ideology. This political root and function of the Inquisition is particularly clear in Catalonia and Aragon. When Philip II fears that Catalonia will form an alliance with France, he uses the Inquisition to prohibit the French from teaching in Catalan schools. In Aragon, the Inquisition prison is used by Philip II as a "federal prison" to which he attempts to have Antonio Pérez moved in order to remove him from the jurisdiction of the Aragonese courts.

50. Several factors appear to join forces in Castile to inhibit the development of medieval pluralism, favoring, in contrast, this early and expeditious political unification. The very aridity of the Meseta (central plateau) fosters shepherding over agriculture and the concentration of power over its dispersion (Harris). The process of the reconquest further weakens agriculture, always vulnerable to shifting frontiers, and loosens the feudal ties that now begin to respond to personal loyalty rather than to territorial dependency. The collective struggle against the Moors in turn reinforces the tendency toward military and religious unification over and above economical or commercial unification. The "public enterprise" of the reconquest favors the domination of the aristocracy and of the Crown to the detriment of agricultural or commercial "private enterprise." To these factors must surely be added the reaction of the Crown to the contrary circumstances that tended to limit royal power in Spain and that Karl Marx himself summed up in the following way: "On the one hand, during their long struggle with the Arabs, the peninsula was being reconquered in small pieces which become constituted in separate kingdoms. During this struggle popular laws and customs were adopted. Successive conquests, carried out mainly by the nobility, invested excessive power in them, thus undermining royal authority. In addition, while inland cities and populations were taking on great importance owing to the need the people saw of residing in strongholds as protection against the continuous incursions of the Moors, the configuration of the country and the constant interchange with Provence and Italy was giving rise to the creation of first-class commercial and maritime cities on the coasts." J. H. Elliott has recently stressed the ideological or religious nature of this unitary obsession:

> Spain had to deal with a much more complex problem than was posed to any other Christian State. Only Spanish society was multiracial, and the interpenetration of Christian, Jewish and Moslem elements created constant problems of national identity. The insistence... upon the most rigorous orthodoxy represented a desperate attempt to combat a problem of unequalled complexity and no one should be surprised if religious unity seemed to be the only guarantee of national survival for a society characterized by the most

outstanding racial, political and geographical diversity."

51. What is often cited to demonstrate the closed, xenophobic, and reactionary character of the comunero revolt is its rejection of both Catalan influence and the Flemish role in the economic affairs of the court of Charles V. I believe, instead, that the Castilian comuneros had all the reasons in the world to oppose these influences that came to Castile from above: as the allies of a power unwilling to concede in Spain the freedoms they enjoyed in their countries of origin. In fact, the comuneros had to oppose the Catalans and the Flemish in Castile in order to vindicate the very open, municipal, and commercial spirit these peoples represent. This is a typical double-bind situation, which explains the contradictory interpretations given to their revolt. What was a ferment in Catalonia and Flanders is imposed as a rule in Castile.

52. Whose nature, as M. Batllori specifies, "Américo Castro – radical separatist that he was – believed to be Spanish."

53. In chapter 20 I will elaborate on the specific "subduing" that, to my mind, characterizes Spanish Baroque sarcasm in contrast with Romantic irony.

54. When from the seventeenth century on, Catalonia and Valencia reappear as vital forces (less affected than Castile by inflation and the demographic crisis), Castilian Spain – vested in and bogged down by the success of its early centralization – will not know how to accommodate the political organization of the country to the new structure and balance of forces. "The national State," writes Octavio Paz, "was a late reality in Germany and Italy.... The case of Spain has been the exact opposite but the results have been similar: the different peoples who coexisted in the Iberian Peninsula were trapped from the 16th century on in the straitjacket of a centralistic, authoritarian State."

55. In fact, "Napoleon was not only a foreigner who knew France in a purely objective way and used it as an instrument... but, by moving his armies around as if they were naval squadrons, [he was like] an island that fell upon the Continent."

56. For Menéndez Pidal,

> In ancient times, as always, the Celtiberians [the territory of preunification Spain that compromises the great part of the present-day provinces of Zaragoza, Tercuel, Cuenca, Guadalajara, and Suria] represent the totality of Spain. Celtiberia [the territory of preunification Spain that comprises the greater part of the present-day provinces of Saragossa, Teruel, Cuenca,

Guadalajara, and Soria], in conjunction with Andalusia, produces all the significant men that the Peninsula offers to culture and politics, with none appearing in the extreme northeast or northwest; and the same thing occurs in the 16th and 17th centuries, when the center and the south produce the essential men....The cultural map of the Peninsula is the same as the Spanish empire: the regions of fecundity bear the same color and point up the same shocking atony of the northwest and northeast in those periods of powerful universalist ideals, an atony in marked contrast with the fecund tonicity that these regions show in other less culminating moments....

There is also no dearth of examples of an equally caricaturesque – and peculiarly resentful – Catalan vision of the problem, the almost perfect negative of the opinions of A. Castro, Menéndez Pidal, or Ortega y Gasset. Thus, even from such an evenhanded writer as Josep Carner we can read a text like this: "No human force can put an end to the Catalan phenomenon. Not even the hatred of the Castilians who indeed have been living by our side for centuries, but have always felt a deep spiritual distance from our people, for that essentially poor, fatalistic, and immobile race feels a kind of repugnance for evolution, work and prosperity."

57. Sánchez Ferlosio has pointed out the difference between the theoretical will to "vertebrate" Spain and this effective concern for keeping its people and nations "in line."

58. A schematic – almost stenographic – history of this series of "disencounters" between Catalonia and Castile could read as follows:

1. *Content and form.* In the late fifteenth century the material and formal conditions for the modernization of Spain show up in different places: the political will and demographic substratum in Castile, the social and mercantile foundations in Catalonia. Here a commercial bourgeoisie had developed, an assembly with legislative power, a pactist political theory, diplomatic experience, and even an ideal for Hispanic unity that emerged in the Catalan assembly under Juan II, though it would be carried out only by his son, from his throne in Castile (J. H. Elliott). Castile was, in contrast, a seignorial cattle-raising country where "monarchical-seignorial absolutism" prospered. The king reinforced his power by forming alliances with the aristocratic and ecclesiastic classes rather than with the peasants, artisans, or bourgeoisie. Instead of "gentrifying" or going bourgeois, the nobles became bureaucrats. In this way the sectors that ought to have infected and permeated the new State in a more consistent process fell under formal and legal control: the Jews and the municipal assemblies, the bourgeoisie and the merchants, the *germanías* and the Catalans. And so begins the Castilian tradition of neutralizing social and territorial conflicts from above

instead of letting them be expressed in the Cortes.

2. *Castilian separatism* (sixteenth century). Till the time of Charles V an itinerant monarchy that respects both the states and the constitutions of Aragon, Catalonia, or Valencia remains in place. The system that emerges under Philip II from midcentury on involves both the sedentarization of the court and a renewed defense of the American territories as the exclusive patrimony of Castile. This new Castile does not care to occupy Catalonia, rather ignoring the region and the anarchy growing within it. This period of Castilian "separatism," which comes to an end when Philip II intervenes in Aragon in 1591, is blessed at very least with coherence. The disencounter between Castile and Catalonia-Aragon persists, but for once political and economic power, institutional leadership and social vitality all come together in Spain. And here that is no small feat.

3. *Catalan separatism* (seventeenth century). But this harmony does not last long. From 1630 on, the coastal lands begin their economic recovery, while Castile remains bogged down in the financial and demographic crisis that resulted from its Euro-American policy. Less affected by "social hidalgoism and the tax bureaucracy" (Pierre Vilar), Catalonia tries to recover its lost political protagonism. We have already heard the Castilian "meditations upon one's being" maintain that this is where the story of "Invertebrate Spain" begins. I believe, on the contrary, that what begins here is a "Calcified Spain" that lacks the reflexes to respond to a new situation. It no longer knows how to run an empire and profit from it, so it turns its very inferiority complex into a self-assertive "imperative spirit." Castile, which is no longer medieval but is not yet modern, is not able to adapt to this new situation – neither by accepting the traditional *plurality* of powers, nor through the modern *division* and *balance* of powers. Thus Catalonia ends up confronting and defeating the "spirit" of Olivares on Montjuïc (1640). When, ten years later, the Catalan ruling classes look to Castile to fight the French, it will not be the result of the Olivares spirit but rather of the much milder spirit of Philip IV or Haro (see note 71). Once more Castile and Catalonia can reach an understanding only of convenience, not of conviction: a common enemy takes the place of the common project they lack.

4. *Castile discovers France* (eighteenth century). As the Catalans feared, Castile will recover the will to dominate with the entrance of the new dynasty from Bourgogne, which the Catalans reject (1702-1713), not because it comes from Castile but precisely because it is French. One more disencounter: now that the Castilians want to be French, the Catalans become the defenders of Spain. As they will be once again a century later when Spain finds itself facing off with France. In Castile

this dynastic alliance will soon translate into a conversion – the first in a long series – to the spirit of the Enlightenment. Catalonia is now more guarded and less vulnerable to that spirit. A new ideological disencounter whose political correlative is the *Decreto de Nueva Planta* will now pick up the baton of the already exhausted and decrepit imperative spirit. Elliott writes, "Now a centralized government was arbitrarily imposed upon the richest zones of the periphery.... And the result was a tragically artificial structure which constantly created obstacles to Spain's political development, for political and economic order were to seem permanently divorced for the next two centuries. The center and the periphery would therefore be following antagonistic paths...." An ironic corollary to this series of disencounters: "The sweeping out of the fueros and privileges *(Nueva Planta)* unexpectedly benefited the Catalans not only because it obliged them to look to the future, but because it opened up to them the same possibilities enjoyed by Castile in the common bosom of the Monarchy" (Vicens Vives).

5. *Two more centuries of conversions.* The early administrative and ideological unification of Castile marks its future proclivity to conversion to all the messages of modernity: its unrestrainable faith in ideas. Just as quickly as Castile had become enlightened in the eighteenth century, it became liberal in the nineteenth. This is where the liberalism of civil servants – as superficial as it is centralist – crops up (the analogy with Erasmianism in the sixteenth century is worthy of note), confronting a "country which, save a few urban masses, continues to subscribe to the traditional credo" (Vicens Vives). The contrast between the country decreed and the actual country is absolute, and Catalonia resists this ideological euphoria that carries with it a new pedigree for a unilaterally Castilian vision of Spain. The popular movement of the *malcontents* (1827) and the more aristocratic version of the *Carlistes* (1833) incarnate this revolt against a state that is beginning to display all the features of a South American nation. The radical constitutions (1812, 1837, 1868), Mendizábal's disentailment (1839), or Espartero's populistic militarism (1840) are not only the prologue to the *Cartas* and the destruction of the *resguardos* in America but also to the caudillo model and the providential militarism that followed them. The moderate periods (1844 and 1876) offered in turn the model for the caciquism and corruption that will blend so well with the first, in Latin America as well as in Spain. Castile stops making America to make itself over in America's likeness – and to take its distance from Catalonia, which goes off with its own vernacular, familiar demons on a solitary drunken spree.

Thus, this unreconciled counterposition between a progressivism as idealistic as it is doctrinaire and a traditionalism as pragmatic as it is cowardly will persist into the twentieth century. Only this century's repeated and spasmodic "conversions" to anarchism or fascism, to

Marxism or national socialism will come to unite us once more against a common enemy – only now it will not be the French or the British but our own countrymen in the opposite trench. As Machado wrote from Barcelona in 1938, "There are some things that only war allows us to see clearly. For example: How well we understand each other in different mother tongues when, on this side of the Ebro River, swamped in a flood of iniquities, we each say: 'We have not sold our Spain'! And that we say it in Catalan or in Castilian in no wise lessens or increases its truth." What I find most disturbing is that nothing less than a civil war should have been necessary to arrive at this realization.

59. Heidegger here takes gigantism to be "the large become quality, both incalculable and unrepresentable."

60. Hegel here reflects the concern of his day about the excessively easy terms that could prevent the formation of the needy (and therefore proletarianized) class required by capitalist "civil society." It was only then, when this class had taken definitive shape, that the existence of a *lumpen* would begin to be valued "economically" (though not politically, as is clear in Marx) as an external supply of cheap labor that would assure that salaries did not rise more than benefits and that prices were competitive. Henceforth, to offer a more recent example, economists will no longer study, say, Spanish, Portuguese, or Turkish emigration to Europe with the same eyes Hegel used to see emigration to America, for they will see in it instead the basis for the rapid development of Europe in the 1960s. In any event, the theory that, in opposition to Hegel, seeks to explain development and growth from the viewpoint of the influx of immigrant labor, doesn't hold water, even in the recent European case (vid. David Landes, *The Unbound Prometheus).* This theory would not, for instance, account for the growth without immigration that also took place in Sweden and Austria, nor for the fact that the relative rise in the price of labor that it entailed for countries like Spain did not hold back the spectacular development of those same years. Only one explanation seems to do justice to both the "Hegelian" and the modern thesis: it is not the flow of labor that produces development and growth – it is more likely development that generates the flow.

61. Even the toponymy is often Spanish, though North Americans, quite symptomatically, do not distinguish it from the Indian, as the following Whitman poem illustrates (note italics):

> The red aborigens... syllabled for us names
> Okonee, Koosa, Ottawa, Monongahela, Sauk, *Natchez...*
> Leaving such the States, they melt, they depart, charging

the water and the land with names.

62. "If the territories of the Monarchy up to Texas, Florida and Louisiana were called 'Spain,' the denomination 'American' was freed up, so to speak, to be chosen by the founders of the United States – thus 'American' becomes synonymous with citizen of the United States and the others are soon defined as 'Latin Americans.' " As I. Abelló and M. Montero have pointed out, this latter denomination – dashed off by France toward 1860 in order to dilute the Spanish past and neutralize the plans that Bismarck's pan-Germanism might be nurturing – also began to seem comfortable for the United States, "not only because it lumped all its southern neighbors in a single mold but because, in addition, it allowed for a distinction between the two categories of Americans: them, and the others, the Latins."

63. The first point synthesizes the conditions of the Metropolis; the second, the Conquest (which in the North blends in with the colonization); the third, the Colonization proper; the fourth, the established colonial System; the fifth, the Emancipation; and the sixth, the Independence of the American republics.

64. As G. Parker points out in his *Spain...*, "The bourgeois ideal in the 16th and 17th centuries was to return to the days of greater autonomy, not of greater participation in general affairs. That is, to maintain a traditional regime of participation in what medieval law had called *dominium regale et politicum*, as opposed to the absorbing and unique *dominium regale.*"

65. In effect, both Olivares and Vélez are defeated by the Catalans in 1640 at Montjuïc, and only the greater guarantees for their privileges that the Castilian crown ends up offering convince the Catalan aristocracy to support Spain instead of France in 1652. The story is briefly as follows: the breaking of the peace treaty with Holland (1621), the opening of the front of Mantua (1627), and the war against Richelieu (1635) create the overwhelming need for new troops and tribute that the Crown of Castile demands of the other peninsular states. The ruling classes in all of them are reluctant to collaborate because they believe not only that their internal problems have been ignored (banditry in Catalonia, the defense of Brazil in Portugal, the Moorish problem in Aragon) but also that they have been discriminated against in the distribution of honors and imperial posts. Olivares tries to kill two birds with one stone by sending the duke of Braganza's troops out against Catalonia, but the Portuguese stage an uprising and name the duke king of Portugal. The troops Olivares finally sends to engage Catalonia in the war with France are met by the local population, which rises up, takes Barcelona, and, under the command of Pau Claris, forms an alliance with the French to fight the

Castilians. From then on, internal factors undermine Catalan independence, which, in contrast with the Portuguese scenario, offers a rather sad portrait of the capacity and national will of Catalonia: the Catalonians face tensions between the nobility and the people, foreign alliances formed to resolve class problems, and lack of support from the Aragonese and Valencian quarters (which in turn had received no aid from Catalonia during the revolt of the *Germanías* or in 1591). But if the Catalan *consellers* and aristocrats go over to Spain instead of France in 1652, it is also because the Spanish monarchy of Philip IV and Luis Haro seems more disposed to accept their local laws and privileges than does Mazzarin's France. Catalonia's "French" experience is traditionally conflictive. Proof of this is the fact that its reaction, fifty years later, against Philip V owes more to his French dynastic origin than to his role as king of Spain.

66. These are nomadic tribes, that live from hunting and grazing in a subsistence economy and still lack the strength and bellicosity with which the Apaches, Navajos, or Comanches will confront Kit Carson in the nineteenth century. The proverbial "fierceness" of these peoples comes out only when the Spaniards introduce horses. For a long time the radical distinction between Indians on foot and Indians on horseback will be maintained in both North and South America. As José Cardiel, S.J., says in 1780, "All the infidels who make war in these provinces [of Buenos Aires] are bandits on horseback who do not work the land.... The nations on foot, who are almost all farmers, do not make war. The horse makes the Indian insolent."

67. Cortés, more sensitive and "cross-over" than Garay, wants to adapt the plan of the city to the Aztec temples, which he wishes to preserve "for memory's sake." The Crown, conscious that symmetry is the geometry of imperial power, insists however that they be carried out "in such a way that once the foundations are laid, the town should appear orderly... thus in the place where the church shall be, thus in the order followed by the streets... because where order has been laid from the inception, places shall continue to be orderly with no work or effort, while others shall never achieve order...."

68. As a result of the issuing of high-risk bonds – junk bonds – great mergers have been in the news again in 1985: General Motors acquired Hughes Aircraft for $5.2 billion; General Electric bought RCA for $6 billion; Philip Morris, which already manufactured Marlboro cigarettes, Miller beer, and 7-Up, bought General Foods for $5.7 billion; and its competitor R. J. Reynolds (Winston cigarettes) hastened to absorb Nabisco Brands. In the end, then, only *Superman III* could impede the consolidation of the world monopoly on oil and coffee, which the Sherman Act and the Federal Reserve Act of 1913 could

do little to remedy.

69. In contrast with the conventional image of U.S. modernism and lack of a sense of tradition, it is not out of place to remind Europeans that U.S. political institutions were chartered before 1800, and that no new ones have been created since then.

70. This discrete and nongradual process of Spanish charters or codes was complemented by their discretional application, governed by a series of exceptions that always allowed the ideal perfection of the norm to remain in place. Ganivet had this observation to make regarding the Spanish penal code: "The punishment of criminals is apparently regulated in Spain by a Code, which in fact is a Code and a systematic application of pardon. In another country, the Code would be modified and accommodated to principles of greater temperance and moderation. In Spain we prefer to keep the Code rigid and later annul its effects through pardons.... We punish with solemnity and rigor to satisfy our desire for justice, later pardoning the convicted quietly and in silence to satisfy our desire for mercy."

71. "Under the Austrias," writes González Fernández, "the nation still made the State; when the Bourbons came along, the State tried to manufacture a nation."

72. "Near by the closed cities," Hegel also states, "places rose up in Europe where the same trades were practiced, but without corporative coercion. North America finds itself in a similar position vis-à-vis Europe. Many Englishmen have left to set themselves up in that land, where the taxes and tariffs that weigh upon commerce and industry in Europe do not exist; they take all the advantages of civilization with them and can practice their trades without disturbance."

73. Once more we witness the contrast between a vernacular and a classical colonization whose cities, as Braudel writes, "proclaim, not a functional necessity, but the transparence of space inhabited by men, the victory of order over shadow," of the *nomos* over the *physis,* of the aerial and rational gods over the chthonic spirits.

74. *The Economist* (February 22, 1986) attributed Latin America's loss of export capacity throughout the 1970s – in contrast with the same period in Southeast Asia – to its urban structure. In Latin America money retained a high parity, because devaluation, though it would have helped rural workers, would have penalized the urban workers, who consume manufactured and

imported goods. The fact that 72 percent of the inhabitants of Latin America live in cities (in contrast with 32 percent in Southeast Asia) would thus explain the 40 percent difference between black market and official rates of exchange (as against 6 percent in Southeast Asia). The city would thus have brought about a monetary "idealism" that was to end up making Latin American countries less competitive and more consumerist than other less "urban" poor countries. And this is what a penetrating study of Mexico City by Gabriel Zaid confirms and illustrates:

> Cheap dollars were only possible as an imposition of import centralism over the exporting periphery since Mexico City imports between one-half and three-quarters of the national total, while only exporting between one-eighth and one-fourth of the total.... Thanks to those cheap dollars, the capital city consumes not what its own country produces, but the machinery, spare parts, raw materials and agricultural products produced by other countries.... As a result, from 1958 to 1981, in spite of the fact that oil exports rose 750 times (in dollars), Mexico City wallowed in a bottomless pit of expenses that not even the oilpits could satiate: it imported four times what it exported and the city deficit was the fundamental cause of the national debt.

Hence, still according to Zaid, the effective modernization of the country requires the inversion of its centuries-old centralizing tendency by means of a progressive "deurbanization." And as the great "natural resource" of the capital city is nothing less than power itself, Zaid proposes to begin by "devolution" of eight ministries (among them, Agriculture, Urbanism, Education, Fishing, Health, Tourism) onto the governments of the states. In a well-known earlier book, Zaid had developed the thesis that the urban and bureaucratic concentration of power leads only to "improductive progress": "Bureaucracies believe that concentrating resources unproductively, rather than spreading them around represents progress." But, in reality, "a million pesos transferred from the bureaucratic sector to small producers yields twice as much and creates eight times as many jobs."

75. Many agree, according to Fontana, "upon cutting the ties with a metropolis which seems to have lost the capacity to keep order within the empire... replacing the consensus of the divine right monarchy with that of nationality, and pursuing the exploitation of the indigenous population under new conditions, now tied in with the world market through the intermediary of British trade."

76. As F. Chevalier points out, these are very powerful and "generous" characters – along the lines of Sarmiento's *Facundo* or Gallegos's *Doña Bárbara* – who immediately base their power upon relationships of personal

dependency. Now then, in order to understand the psychological and social mechanisms of the cacique system, like those of peonaje por deudas (indentured servitude), Mauss's explanation is certainly more useful than Marx's: the most dangerous and powerful person is not so much he who takes away increased value (plus value) as he who gives it – he who acquires the monopoly on giving something (work, security) that can be returned to him only through submission.

77. "Spanish rule in America," as Ramiro de Maeztu wrote, "turned out to be a Roman empire without the legions, because the defense of the country was principally in the hands of the encomenderos and the military only appear, in small numbers, in the years of the conquest and, in larger numbers, when the New World splits off from the Metropolis."

78. In this case the Mexican exception can also be attributed both to the tradition of its popular "Revolution" and to U.S. support for liberal "Reform" (1861 and 1867) and its vindication against General Huertas of the U. S. role as the only gendarme of the zone (1914).

79. Beyond certain thresholds, the very power or speed of the processes makes them become "irresponsible": their ability to transform the environment *(alloplasticity)* does not allow them to attend to it, understand it, and respond effectively to it. Once all *autoplasticity* is lost, their growth becomes as fast as it is impermeable, as linear as it is vulnerable.

80. Greek virtue is valued for the form of its execution rather than its (subjective) intention or the (objective) consequences that derive from it. Hence the Greeks' idea of virtue has a bit of what we would call "virtuosity." The evolution from this idea to the one we are describing has its own history. I am dividing it here into the four steps we will be tracing:

1. In Greek the ideal type of *Kalós Kagathós (kalós* = beautiful, *agathós* = good) supposes an equilibrium or "syntony" (Isocrates) between the intimate and the physical, the personal and the social, the expressive and the conventional. The Beauty of the body is a virtue in itself (In the *Cratylus* Cratybulus confesses that he would not trade his beauty for the throne of Persia), but it demands composure ("do not allow your face to shame your heart," says Hesiod), containment ("in speaking, your arms must never leave the sphere of your body," counsels Theofrastos), and even the shyness or reserve shown by Plato's cousin, the beautiful Carmides. But because this inner life must also not appear in rigid contradiction with the environment and its requirements, the *kaloi kagathoi* are, for Pericles, only those "capable of adopting the

most diverse attitudes,... adapting to different circumstances with grace and versatility."

2. Roman *decorum* adds to all of this a tinge of official dignity and solemnity, as well as a deliberately patrician attempt to distinguish itself from all that is vulgar or *amorphos*. But only with the coming of Christianity does this equilibrium undergo a definitive breakdown when, on the one hand, beauty becomes associated with concupiscence (hence Tertullian's claim that Christ could not be handsome) and convention with hypocrisy. Celsus's *Against the Christians* is nothing more than a civilized call to Christians to accept the "rules of the game" – to throw incense at the foot of Caesar's statue and go on doing, thinking, or believing whatever they wish. A call to compromise that comes a cropper in light of the obstinate and sublime *non serviam* of the new "Christian subjectivity."

3. Chivalric *Wanderlust* brings us to the opening out of this new subjectivity onto the world. The "spirit of service" is now the shallow, warrior's translation of Roman *decorum* or Greek *kalokagathia*. Service to the Church above all ("in order that God be loved, known, honored, served and feared," says Raymond Lully's *Book of the chivalric order)*, whence derives also the protection of "widows, orphans and powerless men." But it is surely the "service of love" – love at *lonh*, distant and sublimated – that best allows the new Augustinian principle of love to be synthesized with the classic imperative of the external *geste*. The distance placed between the two worlds by Christianity forces the appeal to a sophisticated game of liturgies, allegories, and symbols to connect the world of faith and sentiment with that of the jousts (in which, as Martí de Riquer explains, sword = cross, to destroy the enemies of Christianity; spear = truth, for it is straight and unbending; spurs = diligence, and so on). Though mediated and softened by symbol, this contiguity between two so disparate dimensions encourages in turn the immense fragility or vulnerability of the subject, whose face, honor, dignity or name can be stained on any corner, by any gesture.

4. From this point on, I think, we can begin to acknowledge the specificity of Hispanic honor. With Alberti, Castiglione, and above all, Erasmus, a simplification and social reconversion of that first Christian and later chivalric subjectivity begins: the bourgeois identity is anticipated by the *honnête homme*. In opposition to chivalric arrogance and exuberance, Castiglione speaks of the *"austera strada della virtú"* and of the spontaneity *("sprezzatura")* that must preside over relationships. In his *De Civilitate,* Erasmus reminds us that virtue needs no ostentation; that instead human, honest, kind, clean, and simple bearing ought to define itself in its presence. A Dutchman and

two Italians thus speak to us of a new "urban" life. In Castile, however, unity is sought and achieved higher above, in national unification, leading, as M. Zambrano says, "to an absolutism of the individual existence (Don Juan), which is a response to the absolutism of the State." What elsewhere was a synthesis here becomes an exacerbation of the extremes. The political ideal to be served continues to be absolute, and even more abstract than the Church or the Beloved. The individual who would serve it does not feel obligated to purge his temperament of the liturgies of the "spirit of service" but, quite the contrary, to refine, sublimate and broaden them. His "surface contact" with the world is greater than ever. His vulnerability is now infinite. Honor is the only guarantor of his integrity. And his good name is his shield.

81. This still external or social character of the tribunal of Honor as opposed to that of Conscience has been underscored in Spain by J. L. Aranguren, J. A. Maravall, and recently, by R. Sánchez Ferlosio: "Only a spurious, individualistic, and in some sense 'Protestant' conception of honor, can have come to consider not dishonorable a solution in which the subject himself is erected, as if in response to the dictates of his 'personal interpretation,' as the arbiter of his own honor."

82. The lack of this sense of form and cultural or historical mediation is emblematically manifest in North American poetry and philosophy, which, from the time of Emerson, Whitman, or James to the counterculture of Roszak or Castaneda, rejects theoretical or stylistic conventions, and attempts to connect directly, with no mediation, with nature, progress, spirit, the cosmos.

83. According to J. A. Maravall, "many noble lineages, even aristocratic ones, linked up with rich *converso* families, and the lower classes never forgot this, using it to strengthen their position by throwing up to the powerful the frequent black marks on their genealogies." "To have a clean bloodline," Domingo Ortiz similarly points out,"was the pride of the lower classes, above all because they thought that often the members of the upper classes did not." J. H. Elliott has also pointed out these popular roots of the vindication of "pure blood" undertaken by Juan Martínez Silíceo, the archbishop of Toledo, from 1547 on.

84. This is the way Alcina Franch explains the genesis of the phenomenon: "The special situation and development of medieval Castilian history, sharing borders with and struggling against the Moors, gave access to the lower ranges of the nobility to any villin who could ride a horse and wield arms in

his lord's aid.... From the tenth century on, the counts of Castile bestow the lowest titles of nobility on many hundreds of farmers whom they call upon to serve as knights in the war."

85. Not even Nebrija's then-recent conception of the Castilian language as a factor of unification and control has much effect upon this temperament that permits, and indeed reinforces, the use of the vernacular languages even in the courts of justice. As we have seen, the original peace treaty between the Spanish on the one side and the Indians and Jesuits of Paraguay on the other is written in Guaraní, and only later are two copies made in Castilian and Portuguese. In Mexico, legal documents affecting the Indians continue to be written in Nahuatl, and even the "passive resistance" of many Indians to the use of Castilian is respected. "Witnesses who were known with certainty to speak Spanish," writes J. H. Parry, "denied having this knowledge and insisted on making their declarations through the interpreter."

86. "A Protestant civilization," writes R. M. Morse in *The Legacy of Latin America*," can develop its energies infinitely in uncultured regions, as it did in the United States. A Catholic civilization becomes stagnant when it is not in vital contact with the tribes and cultures of humanity."

87. "This symbolic articulation is what unites the law of attraction of bodies, the 'celestial mechanics,' to a 'mechanics of grace' that opens hearts to God. This is the same articulation that for Leibniz connects physical laws with the 'real presence' of Christ in the Eucharist" (A. Regalado). The emerging image of a world as *Machine* always postulates a transcendent Watchmaker and expels from its bosom (towards Heaven or towards the Soul) any not strictly rational dimension of the world. The baroque image, on the contrary, is that of an autonomous and flexible *Syntax* in which intuitive and irrational elements also find their place in the very heart of immanence. This image of the world was described by Eugeni d'Ors, without explicit reference to the Baroque, in the following fashion: "The universe is not a machine, but a syntax. If one sole piece is not rational, the machine no longer functions. But syntax only lives when the oil of irrationality comes along to lubricate it.... The very hunch attributed to Pascal was ruined by the famous *raisons du coeur*. 'Heart,' is sentiment, intuition, belief, pure life.... And this is not what we are talking about. We are talking about something as clearly organizable as reason, but less rigid. We are talking about Intelligence." Or perhaps it would be more exact to say baroque Ingeniousness, just as different from romantic Genius as it is from enlightened Reason.

88. In *De la Modernidad* I have countered the traditional idealism that sought

to *proscribe* experience with modern idealism, which, on the basis of ideas like the State, Reason or History has attempted to *prescribe* experience.

89. What I mean is this: but not with a transcendental projection, or aspiration to the infinite. From the speech in chapter 11 of the *Odyssey* till, at very least, the fourth century B. C., an almost allergic reaction to familiarity with the infinite – to anything outsized and boundless – can be traced. The Greeks do not associate it with perfection but much to the contrary: with the imprecise, amorphous, extravagant, or deliquescent. From Parmenides to Aristotle, being is complete and perfect to the extent it is finite. Just as this world, "not created by god or by man, which turns on and off in moderation" (Heraclitus), is also finite.

90. For Hegel, what allows for the blossoming of "absolute subjectivity" and the effective realization of "Christian freedom" (i.e., external reification that fosters the radical spiritualization of the subject) is the *Enzweigung* or split produced between the modern "anonymous society" he discovers on his visit to Paris and the isolated individual. What purified the "larva" of this subject in the Greek world, where it was doubtless latent, was its sublimation in tragedy or in the Orphic rites.

91. "The more we live on information," says Gracián, "the less we see.... Things are shadows of reality." This inscrutable world must now be read or interpreted by "depth probes" into the hidden designs and intentions of others: "One must be a very good reader in order not to read everything backwards, keeping the key close to the codebook to see if he who does you great courtesy is not in fact deceiving you, or if he who kisses your hand wishes to bite it, or if he who speaks the best prose is speaking worst of you, if he who promises much will comply least, if he who offers aid intends only neglect in order to get his way *"Oráculo manual..."*.

92. "In Calderón's *La Protestación de la Fe,* the allegorical figure of Avarice (which represents Nordic Protestantism associated with 'freedom of conscience' and the defense of the autonomy of reason) literally states: 'I cover the abyss with my syllogisms.' In contrast with this figure, the artistic and literary Baroque digs... resolutely into the center where the passions, the imagination, desire, perception and understanding come together in the abyss of human consciousness, in the *res cogitans* as the totality of a lived experience which tends more to include than to exclude all of its ambiguities and contradictions" (A. Regalado).

93. Regarding this point, see my *Self-Defeated Man*, pp. 125-131.

94. On his second sortie, attributed by Cervantes to the "Arabic manuscript," Don Quixote is confronting not only the world but the trail of his own legend as well. On the one hand, he is being received as the "hero" of his previous feats, and on the other, he must confront and refute the feats of the "false" Quixote written by Avellaneda that has preceded him on his journey to Saragossa. His determination to maintain the fantasy in the real world forced Cervantes – as it did Mateo Alemán in the second half of his picaresque novel, *Guzmán de Alfarache* – to "give an edge" to his own apocrypha. J. M. Valverde sums up this complex process in the following way:

> The labyrinthine multiplication of reflections and reflections of reflections in which we are lost when we look at Velázquez' *Las meninas*, in the *Quixote* becomes even more gnarled in its planes: the original novel; its transformation into a supposedly original Arabic version; the metamorphosis of all of the above into a book – now in fact published and well known to almost all the characters of the second part – which makes Don Quixote now appear within the book as the protagonist of a previous book; the surprise caused by another author's book that follows the plan being developed in the second part by Cervantes; the reaction, within the authentic second part, to his knowledge of the existence of the false version; and finally, his admission that the legitimate and the spurious books are both equally real or unreal, but that the authentic don Quixote and Sancho Panza are the ones in the book by Cervantes and not the ones in the other.

95. To take on this role required a strong democratic will exercised with a measured and delicate sense of balance between personal and institutional priorities – a balance that the king of Spain could and did find in his own dynastic tradition. Harold Nicolson, the British diplomat, wrote the following in this regard more than fifty years ago:

> I have observed this conventional attitude of royal impassivity or hierophantic inattention in the ceremonies of the Spanish court. Alphonse XIII was young and naturally exuberant; Queen Victoria was beautiful and urbane. And yet, in an official reception, each of them atop a dais, with golden lions flanking each step, they both wore an expression of not realizing there were people around them, watching the clouds out the window with vacant eyes, as diplomats, ministers and, finally, deputies passed before the throne in slow processional. Their salutations were never acknowledged. The eyes of both Alphonse and Victoria Eugenia continued looking on in languid distraction.... And then, when the last deputy had gone by, when the guards had struck the floor with their halberds, the royal effigies suddenly came to life and mixed among the crowd, lively and informal, moving hand in hand from one salon to the next....

96. "Public power is the right to make laws with the death penalty... for the purpose of regulating and preserving property"; "the great objective of men on

entering into society is the enjoyment of their property in peace and security" *(Two Essays on Civil Government,* II, 1 and II, 11).

97. The Kantian imperative urges us to act in such a way that we might wish our very act to become a principle of general legislation. "What for the (Kantian) moral man was an imperative of duty," replies Fichte, "must become the internal progress of life..., as a result of which not only external law disappears, but even internal law. The legislator of our heart is silenced, for now will, pleasure, love, and happiness have taken the law up in theirs."

98. For Bergson, only religion can give man back the global vision and the spirit of solidarity that entered into crisis along with the loss of the instincts and the appearance of an intelligence as analytical as it was puzzled, as instrumental as it was unsociable. He sees the *mythos,* then, as a consequence, not as an antecedent, of the *logos,* i.e., as the "cultural recuperation" of the collective instinct after its "logical crisis"; "as the other-worldly sanction upon the necessary sacrifice of individuals for the conservation of the species" (Maeztu). For Habermas, this solid foundation must be sought in an "ideal linguistic situation" that would make possible "the cooperative formation of the truth on the basis of shared information" – an aspiration that Eugenio Trías appropriately associates with that of the Hegelian "belle âme." I also believe, with Bergson or Habermas, that this agreement must be based on a *convention* rather than on a *conviction,* but I have in mind a symbolic and traditional convention that need not necessarily find religious ratification (Bergson) or be reduced to the strict arena of dialogue or express communication (Habermas). My objections to this last theory are diverse in nature: (1) The convention on which a politico-social agreement can be founded is always on another "logical level" than the agreement itself; the convention can function and be "used," but never "mentioned" as Habermas pretends, following the visionary tradition of Helvetius... *cet homme qui a dit le sécret à tout le monde.* (2) We are all born already "inhabiting" a particular language – Castilian, French – that *identifies* us and maps out the territory of our emotional identity long before it serves as the instrument of our rational accord. (3) Even within one same linguistic territory, the Hegelian will to "be right at all costs" dominates handily over the free and formal character of the process – the Platonic "dialogue" or the Simmelian "chat" being more an exception (a difficult and precarious construction) than an ordinary procedure. (4) In its very origins, therefore, language appears more closely tied to the emotions than to reason: "Necessity," said Rousseau, "dictated the first gestures; only the passions dragged out the first voices." (5) Born of the passions, language in turn favors their conflictive consolidation over all other considerations: self-righteous indignation, the hypnosis of slogans, the

identification with an abstract affront or with a nomenclature... This is most likely the reason that "naming" *(mentar)* is associated in Castilian with insulting (particularly regarding one's mother) and why the New Testament recommends, "Let your language be: yes, yes; no, no – for anything that goes beyond that comes from the Evil One."

99. These conventions always build up around crucial moments in life – birth, adolescence, initiation, marriage, death – when individuals confront a new territory both unknown and disquieting: another age, another sex, another life. Ceremonial forms bestow on such moments an impersonal and communal tinge that serves both to alleviate the fear of the individual and to socialize his sadness or joy; to protect him in these critical moments from both hard-core personal experience and mere abstract legal codification. That is why those borderline situations that, by their very borderline nature, cannot be named – which must remain at once manifest and tacit or, as Heidegger said, "showing and yet underlying" – come to be socialized. Everything that is simultaneously important and disturbing belongs to this category, which, like the God of the Jews, cannot be looked in the face or named in vain. The Spanish political transition has had its share of moments or borderline situations like these for which symbolic mediation turned out to be fundamental.

100. See note 65.

101. For D. Riesman, "the glory of democratic society is having developed social inventions like the market and the negotiation skills which allow us to invest only a part of ourselves in a situation." "Men who compete principally for wealth," Riesman goes on, "are relatively less dangerous than those who compete primarily for power – though it is evident that there are also violent and even totalitarian implications in the treatment of the workforce, in both the metropolis and the colonies, as pure merchandise." Some analogies between the North American empire and its Late Roman counterpart have been set out in my *Europa y otros ensayos* (pp. 65-71).

102. In *De la Modernidad* I have spent some time on the description of this process:

> Once the world has been disinfected, and the spirits inhabiting it have been demythified, they begin to constitute a separate and ideal reality. The enigma of the world is solved through its unfolding into two coherent and complementary worlds: the physical world of earthly deeds and the spiritual world of ideals or values. But this ideal world is no longer that of traditional Religion. Nowadays it is rather that of Art or Culture, of Love or Mysticism: a

separate reality, objective and ideal, which brings together all the qualities expurgated from a physical and social world conceived of as *res extensa*. In some cases an intermediate solution will be sought: instead of locating these qualities in an ideal world, an exotic country or ethnic group will be found to connect directly with this 'Separate Reality.' In such countries and ethnic groups a peculiar kind of cultural imperialism discovers the ability to think 'globally and systematically.' Either yogis or Transcendental Meditation are consulted in search of a technique for control of the subjective that will serve to counter and palliate technical control of the outer world. Now, with this second reality – the authentic superstructure of the first: both its negative and its complement – the type of relationship established with the original is literally reproduced; that is, it is treated as something to be had, like a reality to be controlled or possessed. And this is how the American "radical psychologists" propose to begin *replacing the production of objects with the production of relationships: replacing technological hardware with social software*. Such a design and production of relationships is meant to give birth to a new, intense, communal culture, felt and lived to the fullest; a new sociability made up of interactions, contacts and vibrations. In the California "relationship factories," emotions themselves are elaborated and promoted: spontaneity and intimacy, relaxation and informality. In these new supermarkets of "significant" experiences and relationships, instantaneous motivations, roots or deconditionings can be acquired according to one's liking: encounter groups, communication games, feeling therapy, human potential development, consciousness of one's own body, bio-energetic feedback, psychic massage, contact pedagogy... But it is clear that this systematic production of relationships or sensations does not suppose or obtain a return to the state of contact and immediacy that existed prior to the puritanical, productionist syndrome. It rather seems to be the interiorization of the very same process by which anything contingent or aleatory was abolished by institutionally-planned modes of behavior. But let there be no doubt: the systematic industrial production of anything – be they objects or relationships, utensils or feelings – always and inevitably transforms the thing being produced into something universal and impersonal: the only difference is that we now move on from the fetishism of merchandise to the fetishism of communication – from the Marxist *Verdinglichung* to the American *Vergeistlichung*.

103. In *Self-Defeated Man*, I suggested that if Europeans find it all too easy to be ironic about American recipes that seem to want to synthesize *Popular Mechanics* with the Tao, it is because our problems – and above all our awareness of our problems – are much more limited and domestic than their North American counterparts. In North America, experience and responsibility, much like that of primitive man, is more "cosmic." For this reason, I went on, the reasonable ideologies and the humanistic religions of our tradition give way in the United States to magic or exorcism, to the shaman or the guru. Even so, I ended up trying to argue my instinctive rejection of this sensibility in the following terms:

Personally, I must confess that I do not like the new American cult to the

Cosmic Spirit, for the same reason that American cooking usually doesn't appeal to me. Let me explain myself. I believe it was Claude Lévi-Strauss who pointed out that, while the taste of European cuisine is the product of the combination of several mild flavors, of the mixture of *delicate* flavors, American cooking tends to offer a fundamental foodstuff as a *neutral*, almost insipid, base (hamburgers, hot dogs and the like), to which it adds a *strong* condiment, ordinarily bottled, such as ketchup or mustard. Well, new American cults and fundamentalisms seem to me to be the spiritual "ketchup," so to speak, of a graceless, pragmatic and competitive world. In the Latin sphere, the basic substance of our lives, like that of our food, has never been so insipid as to call for such strong and specialized complements. We have never been so goal-minded as suddenly to need a good session of Transcendental Meditation or of consciousness of the Here-and-Now; never so terribly rational as to long for or even manufacture an *ad hoc* expeditious pedagogy of the irrational, never so individualistic as to have generated the need for a compensatory union with the One.

104. R. H. Tawney long ago described the "deep structure" of this mythology – "to get something out of nothing at the expense of whomever it may concern" – later developed and exemplified by D. Boorstin: "We expect anything and everything. We expect the contradictory and the impossible. We expect compact cars which are spacious; luxury cars which are economical. We expect to be rich and charitable, powerful and merciful, active and reflective, kind and competitive. We expect to be inspired by mediocre appeals for 'excellence,' to be made literate by illiterate appeals for literacy. We expect to eat and stay thin, to be constantly on the move and ever more neighborly, to go to a 'church of our choice' and yet feel its guiding power over us."

105. This is why the words spoken in 1934 by Ramiro de Maeztu still stand today: "It cannot be denied that a platoon of North American infantry cannot land in Nicaragua without wounding the patriotism of Argentina and Peru, Mexico and Spain, and even Brazil and Portugal." But it is a very different thing to maintain the extravagant notion that the contrast between the two colonizations owes to the fact that "the English abandoned the colonized peoples to their own natural propensities and salaciousness." "All of India," he concludes in his *Defensa de la Hispanidad,* "is aged and debilitated by sexual abuse. Many children marry at the age of five, six or eight, and this is why 20,000 Englishmen can dominate 350,000 Indians. They are impoverished by their salaciousness and because they have not been told – as we told the Filipinos, who have to a great extent managed to overcome the temptations of their enervating climate – emphatically and firmly, that they can mend their ways and be saved."

Appendix I

Tuesday, November 27

9:30 a.m.

VISITOR PROGRAM SERVICE of
Meridian House International
1776 Massachusetts Avenue, N.W.
Washington, D.C. 20036
Telephone: (202) 822-8688

Ms. Barbara Vasko, Program Officer
Ms. Patricia Kowall, Program Assistant

At this meeting, we will review the program we have
arranged for you.

11:30 a.m.

You have an appointment with:

Dr. James Billington
Director
Woodrow Wilson International Center for Scholars
1000 Jefferson Drive, S.W. – Castle Building
Room 340
Telephone: 357-2763

You will have lunch at the Center and meetings with
individuals involved in European Security issues.

Wednesday, November 28

10:00 a.m.

Please arrive at the Diplomatic Entrance, C Street
between 21st and 23rd Streets, N.W. of the State
Department. Please tell the receptionist that you
have an appointment with:

Mr. Richard Erdman
Desk Officer for Spain
Bureau of European Affairs
Room 5230
Telephone: 632-2633

10:30 a.m.

Mr. Erdman will accompany you to your appointment
with:

Mr. James Dobbins
Deputy Assistant Secretary of State for European
Affairs

2:20 p.m.	Please arrive at the River Entrance of the Pentagon. You will be met by a representative from Ms. Ruth Kirby's office, Directorate for Community Relations, and escorted to your appointments (697-7385).

Department of Defense
You have an appointment with:

2:30 p.m.	Mr. George Bader Principal Director for European Policy
3:30 p.m.	You have an appointment with:

Mr. Jim Morrison
Director, Regional Policy

Thursday, November 29

10:00 a.m.   *U.S. House of Representatives*
Subcommittee on Europe and the Middle East
Room B–359, Rayburn House Office Building
Telephone: 225-3345

You have an appointment with:

Dr. Michael Van Dusen
Staff Director

11:00 a.m.   *U.S. Senate*
Committee on Foreign Relations
Senate Dirksen Office Building – Room 446
Telephone: 224-5481

You have an appointment with:

Mr. Kenneth Myers
Professional Staff Member

3:00 p.m.   *U.S. Arms Control and Disarmament Agency*
320 21st Street, N.W.
Telephone: 632-8715

Please ask the guard to call Mr. Alvin Streeter at the number listed above. He will clear you into the building.

You have an appointment with:

Mr. Lucas Fischer
Bureau of Strategic Programs

Appendix II

SPAIN IN THE 1980s
The Domestic Transition and a Changing International Role

West European Program
The Woodrow Wilson International Center for Scholars
Washington, DC
and
Instituto de Cooperación Iberoamericana
Madrid

September 25–27, 1985

CONFERENCE PROGRAM

Wednesday, September 25, 1985

7:00 p.m.	Evening program – The Library, Smithsonian "Castle"

Welcoming remarks: James Billington, Director, Wilson Center
Luis Yañez, President, Instituto de Cooperación Iberoamericana

Opening address: José María Maravall, Minister of Education and Science of Spain, "Education for Democracy."

Response: William Bennett, U.S. Secretary of Education

Moderator: John Brademas, President, New York University

8:30 p.m.	Cocktails – The Lounge, Smithsonian "Castle"
8:45 p.m.	Dinner – The Great Hall, Smithsonian "Castle"

Thursday, September 26, 1985

9:30 a.m.	Coffee and pastries – The Rotunda, third floor, Smithsonian "Castle"
10:00 a.m.	Session One: "The Spanish Transition in Historical Perspective"

José Pedro Pérez Llorca, Former Minister of Foreign Affairs of Spain

183

Jordi Solé Tura, Professor of Political Science,
University of Barcelona

Response: Richard Gunther, Professor of Political
Science, Ohio State University

Moderator: John Brademas, President, New York
University

12:00 p.m.   Lunch

2:00 p.m.   Session Two: "The New Role of the Armed Forces,
the Autonomous States, and the Business
Community"

Lt. Gen. Gautier Larraínzar, Captain General of
Seville

Miquel Roca Junyent, Member of the Spanish
Congress of Deputies and Spokesman for the
Minoría Catalana

Gregorio Marañón, Spanish business leader

Response: Stanley Payne, Hilldale Professor of
History, University of Wisconsin

Moderator: John Hebert, Director, Hispanic
Division, Library of Congress

5:30 p.m.   Special private tour of National Air and Space
Museum

7:00 p.m.   Charter buses leave from National Air and Space
Museum for residence of Spanish Ambassador Gabriel
Mañueco
2801 16th Street, N.W.

10:00 p.m.   Charter buses return to the Wilson Center

Friday, September 27, 1985

8:30 a.m.   Coffee and pastries – The Rotunda, third floor,
Smithsonian "Castle"

9:00 a.m.   Session Three: "Economic and political Challenges of Spain's New International Role"

Carlos Westendorp, Spanish Deputy Secretary of
State for Relations with the European
Community

Luis Solana, President, Spanish State Telephone
Company

Miguel Herrero de Miñón, Member of the Spanish
Congress of Deputies and Spokesman for the
Popular Alliance Party

Response: Joseph Foweraker, Lecturer, University of
Essex and Fellow, the Wilson Center

Moderator: Raymond Carr, Warden, St. Antony's
College, Oxford University

11:30 a. m.	Sherry – The Great Hall, Smithsonian "Castle"
12:00 p.m.	Luncheon – The Commons, Smithsonian "Castle"

Address: Felipe González, President of the
Government of Spain

Responses: Richard Lugar, Chairman, U. S. Senate
Committee on Foreign Relations

Raymond Carr, Warden, St. Antony's College,
Oxford University

Moderator: William S. Baroody, Jr., Chairman,
Board of Trustees, The Wilson Center

Question and Answer session with President
González

3:00 p.m.   Session Four: "The Meaning for Latin America of the
Spanish Transition"

The Most Reverend Arturo Rivera y Damas,
Archbishop of San Salvador, El Salvador
(Archbishop Rivera y Damas will be
introduced by the Most Reverend James

Hickey, Archbishop of Washington, DC)

Moderator: Juan Linz, Professor of Sociology, Yale University

Responses: Carlos Andrés Pérez, former President of Venezuela

Francisco Fernández Ordóñez, Spanish Minister of Foreign Relations

Xavier Rubert de Ventós, Member, Commission for Foreign Affairs, Spanish Congress of Deputies

6:00 – 8:00   Reception – Smithsonian "Castle"

Conference Coordinators: Michael Haltzel, Secretary, West European Program, The Wilson Center

Xavier Rubert de Ventós, Member, Commission for Foreign Affairs, Spanish Congress of Deputies

Appendix III

The Domestic Transition and a Changing International Role

September 25 – 27, 1985

List of Participants

Carlos Abella, Minister for Cultural Affairs, Embassy of Spain
Robert Adams, Secretary, The Smithsonian Institution
Felipe Aguero, Professor of Political Science, Duke University
D.J. Alberts, The Pentagon, European Program
Dean Anderson, Assistant Secretary, The Smithsonian Institution

Juan Jose Arboli, Minister–Counselor, Embassy of Spain
Joaquin Arango, Ministry of Education of Spain
Inocencio Arias, Ministry of Foreign Affairs of Spain
Eric Baklanoff, Professor of Economics, University of Alabama
Samuel Barnes, Professor of Political Science, University of Michigan

William Baroody, Chairman of the Board, The Wilson Center
Sheridan Bell, Country Affairs Officer, Spain, United States Information Agency
William Bennett, U.S. Secretary of Education
James Billington, Director, The Wilson Center
Marjorie Billington, Washington, D.C.

Albert Bowker, Executive Vice President, University of Maryland
Carolyn Boyd, Professor of History, University of Texas
John Brademas, President, New York University
Raymond Caldwell, European Affairs, U.S. Department of State
Carlos Carderera, Counselor, Embassy of Spain

Raymond Carr, Warden, St. Antony's College, Oxford University
David Challinor, Assistant Secretary for Science, The Smithsonian Institution
Robert Clark, Professor of Political Science, George Mason University
Alvaro Corrada del Rio, Auxillary Bishop of Washington D.C.
John Coverdale, Lawyer: Fried, Frank, Harris, Shriver and Kampelman

Catherine Curtis, Special Trade Representative
Elías Díaz, Spanish Attorney at Law
Gabriel Elorriaga, Congress of Deputies of Spain
Thomas Enders, U. S. Ambassador to Spain
Julio Feo, Secretary General of the Presidency of Spain

Douglas Foard, National Endowment for the Humanities
Joseph Foweraker, Lecturer, University of Essex and Fellow, The Wilson Center

Richard Fox, United States Information Agency
Max Friedersdorf, Assistant to the President and Legislative Strategy
    Coordinator, White House
Jaime Fuster, U.S. Resident Commissioner of Puerto Rico

Enrique García, Information Officer, Embassy of Spain
Robert García, U.S. Representative from New York
Karen Garon, Staff, U.S. Representative Benjamin Gilman
Prosser Gifford, Deputy Director, The Wilson Center
Felipe González, Prime Minister, The Government of Spain

Gabriel Guerra-Mondragón, National Democratic Institute for International
    Affairs
Richard Gunther, Professor of Political Science, Ohio State University
Inmaculada de Habsburgo, Director, The Spanish Institute
Michael Haltzel, Secretary, West European Program, The Wilson Center
Miguel Herrero de Miñón, Congress of Deputies of Spain

Claudio Hidalgo-Núñez, Carnegie Endowment for International Peace
James Higgins, Mellon Bank, Member of the Wilson Center Council
David Hunn, Budget Examiner, Office of Management and Budget
Jocelyn Hunn, Staff Assistant, Committee on Appropriations, U.S. House of
    Representatives
Manuel Johnson, U.S. Undersecretary of Treasury

Bryan Jones, Research Assistant, West European Program, The Wilson Center
Richard Kagan, Professor of History, Johns Hopkins University
Charles Karelis, Special Assistant to U.S. Secretary of Education
Michael Kenney, Professor of Anthropology, The Catholic University
Gautier Larraínzar, Captain General of Seville

Michael Lekson, Spanish Affairs Officer, U.S. Department of State
Marjorie Lemb, U.S. Department of State
Juan Linz, Professor of Sociology, Yale University
Ernest Lluch, Minister of Health of Spain
Laureano López Rodó, former Minister of Economics of Spain

Richard Lugar, U.S. Senator (R– Indiana)
James McClure, U.S. Senator (R–Idaho)
Peter McDonough, Professor of Sociology, University of Michigan
Francis McNeil, U.S. Deputy Assistant Secretary of State for Intelligence and
    Research
Edward Malefakis, Professor of History, Columbia University

Gabriel Mañueco, Ambassador of Spain to U.S.
Gregorio Marañón, Attorney at Law of Spain
José María Maravall, Minister of Education and Science of Spain
Benjamin Martin, Author and Retired Foreign Service Officer
Kenneth Maxwell, Program Director, The Tinker Foundation

Jaime Mayor Oreja, Basque Parliament of Spain
Eudaldo Mirapeix, Director General of North America, Spanish Ministry of
    Foreign Affairs

Raimon Moino, Military Attache, Embassy of Spain
Richard Morse, Secretary, Latin American Program, The Wilson Center
Charles Murphy, President, Murphy Oil Corporation

Martha Muse, Chairman and President, The Tinker Foundation
Jeff Needell, The Wilson Center, Latin American Program
Raimon Obiols, Socialist Party of Catalonia of Spain
Debbie O'Dell, Program Assistant, West European Program, The Wilson Center
James Olson, Vice Chairman, AT&T

Francisco Fernández Ordóñez, Spanish Minister of Foreign Relations
Rafael Ordóñez, Chief of Cabinet of the Presidency of Aragon
Stanley Payne, Professor of History, University of Wisconsin
Howard Penniman, American Enterprise Institute
Carlos Andrés Pérez, Former President of Venezuela

Leonardo Pérez Rodrigo, Spanish Ambassador to the Organization of American
     States
Baltasar Porcel, Spanish writer and journalist
Charles Powell, St. Antony's College of Oxford University
Larry Pressler, U.S. Senator (R–SD)
Oriol Pi-Sunyer, Professor of Anthropology, University of Massachusetts

José Pedro Pérez Llorca, former Minister of Foreign Affairs of Spain
Gary Prevost, Professor of Government, St. John's University
Ralph Regula, U.S. Representative (R–Ohio)
John Reinhardt, Director of International Activities, The Smithsonian Institution
James Rial, Analyst, Spain, Central Intelligence Agency

Keith Richburg, Journalist, *The Washington Post*
Edward Rindler, United States Information Agency
Arturo Rivera y Damas, Archbishop of San Salvador
Joaquin Romero Maura, Vice President Capital Markets, Citicorp International
     Bank
Hewson Ryan, Professor of Law, Tufts University

Santiago Salas, Chief of Cabinet, Spanish Minister of Foreign Affairs
George Seay, Assistant Director, Development Office, The Wilson Center
Frank Shakespeare, U.S. Ambassador to Portugal
Joyce Shub, Special Advisor, Political Affairs, U. S. Department of State
Jed Snyder, The Hudson Institute

Javier Solana, Spanish Minister of Culture
Luis Solana, Spanish State Telephone Company
Jordi Solé Tura, Professor of Political Science, University of Barcelona
Peter Sommer, Staff, U.S. National Security Council
Charles Thomas, Deputy Assistant Secretary for Political Affairs, U.S.
     Department of State

Charlotte Thompson, Research Associate, West European Program, The Wilson
     Center
David Suárez Torres, Professor of Spanish, Georgetown University
Richard Thurman, Analyst, Spain, U.S. Department of State

Fernando Valenzuela, Chief of Cabinet, Secretary of State for International
     Cooperation
Marten Van Heuven, Director of the Office of Western European Affairs, U. S.
     Department of State

Xavier Rubert de Ventós, Spanish Congress of Deputies
Samuel Wells, Assistant Director, European Institute, The Wilson Center
Carlos Westendorp, Spanish Deputy Secretary of State for E.E.C. Relations
Robert Whealey, Professor of History, Ohio University
John Whitehead, U. S. Deputy Secretary of State

Howard Wiarda, American Enterprise Institute
Juan Antonio Yáñez, Chief of Cabinet of International Relations of the
     Presidency of Spain
Luis Yáñez, President, Instituto Cooperación Iberoamericana

Index